OData Programming Cookbook for .NET Developers

70 fast-track, example-driven recipes with clear instructions and details for OData programming with .NET Framework

Steven Cheng

BIRMINGHAM - MUMBAI

OData Programming Cookbook for .NET Developers

First published: July 2012

Production Reference: 1180712

Published by Packt Publishing Ltd.
Livery Place
35 Livery Street
Birmingham B3 2PB, UK.

ISBN 978-1-849685-92-4

www.packtpub.com

Cover Image by Sandeep Babu (sandyjb@gmail.com)

Credits

Author

Steven Cheng

Reviewers

Shayne Burgess

Ibrahim Sukru

Acquisition Editor

Dhwani Devater

Lead Technical Editor

Kedar Bhat

Technical Editors

Veronica Fernandes

Manasi Poonthottam

Zinal Shah

Copy Editors

Brandt D'Mello

Laxmi Subramanian

Project Coordinator

Joel Goveya

Proofreader

Ting Baker

Indexer

Tejal R. Soni

Graphics

Valentina D'silva

Manu Joseph

Production Coordinator

Arvindkumar Gupta

Cover Work

Arvindkumar Gupta

About the Author

Steven Cheng is a Senior Support Engineer at Microsoft CSS, China. He has been supporting Microsoft development products and technologies for more than seven years. He is also working actively in the Microsoft MSDN forum community.

His technical specialties have covered many popular Microsoft development technologies including .NET Framework, ASP.NET, XML WebService, Windows Communication Foundation, Silverlight, Windows Azure, and Windows Phone. His technical blog can be found at `http://blogs.msdn.com/stcheng`.

In 2010, he wrote the book *Microsoft Windows Communication Foundation 4.0 Cookbook for Developing SOA Applications, Packt Publishing*.

The publication of this book could not have been possible without the efforts put in by a large number of individuals. I would like to thank my colleagues Shayne Burgess, Yi-lun Luo, and Mog Liang who have given me lots of ideas and suggestions on the book recipes. And thanks goes to my friends Jasmine Gong and Le Fei who have helped me a lot during the entire book authoring lifecycle.

Most importantly, none of this would have been possible without the love and patience of my family. I would like to express my heartfelt gratitude to my family.

Lastly, I offer my regards and blessings to all of those who supported me in any respect during the completion of this book.

About the Reviewers

Shayne Burgess is a Program Manager on the SQL Server engineering team at Microsoft. He has worked on the OData team at Microsoft for the past four years, contributing to the definition of the OData protocol and building Microsoft implementations of OData.

Ibrahim Sukru is a Software Engineer from Istanbul. He is the founder of `xomila.com`. He developed several RESTful web services with ASP.NET MVC, OData, and WCF. He loves web standards and technologies, HTML, CSS, and Microformats and enjoys contributing to open source software and coffee.

www.PacktPub.com

Support files, eBooks, discount offers and more

You might want to visit www.PacktPub.com for support files and downloads related to your book.

Did you know that Packt offers eBook versions of every book published, with PDF and ePub files available? You can upgrade to the eBook version at www.PacktPub.com and as a print book customer, you are entitled to a discount on the eBook copy. Get in touch with us at service@ packtpub.com for more details.

At www.PacktPub.com, you can also read a collection of free technical articles, sign up for a range of free newsletters and receive exclusive discounts and offers on Packt books and eBooks.

http://PacktLib.PacktPub.com

Do you need instant solutions to your IT questions? PacktLib is Packt's online digital book library. Here, you can access, read and search across Packt's entire library of books.

Why Subscribe?

- Fully searchable across every book published by Packt
- Copy and paste, print and bookmark content
- On demand and accessible via web browser

Free Access for Packt account holders

If you have an account with Packt at www.PacktPub.com, you can use this to access PacktLib today and view nine entirely free books. Simply use your login credentials for immediate access.

Instant Updates on New Packt Books

Get notified! Find out when new books are published by following @PacktEnterprise on Twitter, or the *Packt Enterprise* Facebook page.

Table of Contents

Preface   **1**

Chapter 1: Building OData Services   **7**

Introduction   7

Building an OData service via WCF Data Service and
ADO.NET Entity Framework   8

Building an OData service with WCF Data Service and LINQ to SQL   13

Exposing OData endpoints from WCF RIA Service   16

Adding custom operations on OData service   20

Exposing database stored procedures in WCF Data Service   23

Using custom data objects as the data source of WCF Data Service   28

Using Interceptors to customize a WCF Data Service   32

Accessing ASP.NET context data in WCF Data Service   36

Creating a custom WCF Data Service provider   40

Chapter 2: Working with OData at Client Side   **51**

Introduction   52

Exploring an OData service through web browser   52

Using Visual Studio to generate strong-typed OData client proxy   57

Generating OData client proxy via DataSvcUtil.exe tool   63

Editing and deleting data through WCF Data Service client library   66

Accessing OData service via WebRequest class   70

Executing OData queries in an asynchronous manner   75

Filtering OData query results by using query options   80

Dealing with server-side paged entity sets from WCF Data Service   86

Performing WPF data binding with OData service data   89

Injecting custom HTTP headers in OData requests   94

Consuming HTTP compression enabled OData service   97

Using MSXML to consume OData service in unmanaged applications   99

Chapter 3: OData Service Hosting and Configuration   107

Introduction	107
Hosting a WCF Data Service in IIS server	108
Hosting a WCF Data Service in Console application	114
Deploying a WCF Data Service on Windows Azure host	117
Configuring WCF Data Service to return error details	124
Configuring WCF Data Service to return JSON-format response	127
Applying basic access rules on WCF Data Service	131
Getting rid of .svc extension by using ASP.NET URL Routing	134
Enabling dynamic compression for OData service hosted in IIS 7	137

Chapter 4: Using OData in Web Application   143

Introduction	143
Building data-driven ASP.NET Web Form pages with OData	144
Adopting OData in ASP.NET MVC web applications	148
Building ASP.NET Page UI with OData and XSLT	156
Building AJAX style data-driven web pages with jQuery	161
Consuming OData service with datajs script library	167
Using OData service in Silverlight data access application	171
Consuming WCF Data Service in PHP pages	179

Chapter 5: OData on Mobile Devices   187

Introduction	187
Accessing OData service with OData WP7 client library	188
Consuming JSON-format OData service without OData WP7 client library	196
Creating Panorama-style, data-driven Windows Phone applications with OData	201
Using HTML5 and OData to build native Windows Phone application	205
Accessing WCF Data Service in Android mobile application	213
Accessing WCF Data Service in iOS application	220

Chapter 6: Working with Public OData Producers   227

Introduction	227
Getting started with Netflix OData online catalog	228
Manipulating Sharepoint 2010 documents through OData endpoint	231
Using OData protocol for Windows Azure Table storage access	235
Query StackOverflow forums data with OData endpoint	240
Tracking information of NuGet packages through OData feeds	244
Exploring eBay online products catalog through OData service	248
Consuming SSRS 2008 R2 report through OData feed	252

Chapter 7: Working with Security   257
   Introduction   257
   Applying Windows authentication for OData service   258
   Using ASP.NET Forms authentication to secure OData service   261
   Securing OData service with HTTPS transport   266
   Implementing OData service authentication with custom HTTP Module   271
   Adding custom authorization with server-side processing pipeline   275
   Using Interceptors to control access for individual entity set   277
   Implementing role-based security for OData service   280

Chapter 8: Other OData Programming Tips   285
   Introduction   285
   Using LINQPad to compose OData query code   286
   Exploring OData service with ODataExplorer   289
   Using OData service in Windows PowerShell script   293
   Exploring OData service with Microsoft Excel PowerPivot component   296
   Inspecting OData HTTP traffic through Fiddler web debugger   299
   Using Open Data Protocol Visualizer to inspect the object model of
   OData service   303
   Consuming OData service in Windows 8 Metro style application   308

Chapter 9: New Features of WCF Data Service 5.0 (OData V3)   315
   Introduction   315
   Upgrading existing OData service to WCF Data Service 5.0   316
   Using geospatial types in OData service   319
   Using Any and All operators to filter OData entities   325
   Updating OData entities through HTTP PATCH requests   328
   Resolving base URI of OData entity sets dynamically   331
   Exposing binary data on OData entity with Named Resource Stream   334
   Extending OData service functionalities with Service Actions   342

Index   355

Preface

OData (Open Data Protocol) is a web protocol for querying and updating data, which can be freely incorporated in various kind of data access applications. OData makes it quite simple and flexible to use by applying and building upon existing well-defined technologies such as HTTP, XML, AtomPub, and JSON.

WCF Data Services (formerly known as ADO.NET Data Services) is a well-encapsulated component for creating OData services based on the Microsoft .NET Framework platform. It also provides a client library with which you can easily build client applications that consume OData services. In addition to WCF Data Services, there are many other components or libraries, which make OData completely available to the non-.NET or even non-Microsoft world.

This book provides a collection of recipes that help .NET developers to become familiar with OData programming in a quick and efficient way. The recipes have covered most OData features from the former ADO.NET Data Services to the current WCF Data Services platform. In addition, all the sample cases here are based on real-world scenarios and issues that .NET developers might come across when programming with OData in application development.

What this book covers

Chapter 1, Building OData Services, introduces how we can use WCF Data Services to create OData services based on various kind of data sources such as ADO.NET Entity Framework, LINQ to SQL, and custom data objects.

Chapter 2, Working with OData at Client Side, shows how to consume OData services in client applications. This will cover how we can use strong-typed client proxy, WebRequest class, and unmanaged code to access OData services. You will also learn how to use OData query options, asynchronous query methods, and other client-side OData programming features.

Chapter 3, OData Service Hosting and Configuration, discusses some typical OData service hosting scenarios including IIS hosting, custom .NET application hosting, and Windows Azure cloud hosting. This chapter also covers some service configuration scenarios such as applying basic access rules, exposing error details, and enabling HTTP compression.

Chapter 4, Using OData in Web Application, talks about how to take advantage of OData services for developing various data-driven web applications including ASP.NET Web Form application, ASP.NET MVC application, Silverlight web application, AJAX style web application, and PHP web application.

Chapter 5, OData on Mobile Devices, demonstrates how to use OData services in mobile application development. Recipes in this chapter will cover the most popular mobile device platforms including iOS, Android, and Windows Phone 7.

Chapter 6, Working with Public OData Producers, introduces some existing public products and services, which have adopted OData for exposing application data. The recipes in this chapter will demonstrate how to create client applications to consume data from these public OData producers.

Chapter 7, Working with Security, discusses some common and easy-to-use means for securing OData services. Topics covered in this chapter include applying Windows authentication, applying ASP.NET Forms authentication, using HTTPS transport, and implementing custom authentication/authorization code logic.

Chapter 8, Other OData Programming Tips, explores some trivial but useful OData programming topics. You will learn how to use some existing tools for testing and debugging OData services. This chapter also demonstrates how to consume OData services in Windows PowerShell scripts and Windows 8 Metro style applications.

Chapter 9, New Features of WCF Data Service 5.0 (OData V3), demonstrates some of the new features introduced in WCF Data Service 5.0 (OData V3). The new features covered in this chapter include geospatial types, "Any" and "All" query operators, Dynamic entity set URI resolving, Named Resource Stream, and custom Service Actions.

What you need for this book

All the recipes in this book are based on the .NET C# programming language. However, you don't have to be a very experienced C# Developer. In order to follow the recipes and run the corresponding sample code, you need a test environment with the following items:

- A development machine with Windows 7 or Windows Server 2008 OS
- Visual Studio 2010 Professional or Ultimate edition (with SP1)
- SQL Server 2005 (or 2008) Developer (or Expression) edition with Northwind sample database installed
- IIS 7.x (for Windows 7 or Windows 2008)
- IE 9 web browser
- Fiddler web debugger

For other software or components required by some specific recipes, they will be listed as prerequisites in the *Getting ready* section of the relevant recipe.

Who this book is for

If you are a .NET Developer and you want to learn how to use OData in real-world data access application development using a quick and efficient approach, then this book is for you. With this book you will be able to find quick and handy solutions for various kind of OData programming scenarios using Microsoft .NET Framework. To follow the recipes, you will need to be comfortable with .NET Framework, Visual Studio IDE, C# programming language, and the basics of web programming such as HTTP, XML, and JSON.

Conventions

In this book, you will find a number of styles of text that distinguish between different kinds of information. Here are some examples of these styles, and an explanation of their meaning.

Code words in text are shown as follows: "Finally, it comes to the `FileEntity` class."

A block of code is set as follows:

```
public partial class InitSession : System.Web.UI.Page
{
    protected void Page_Load(object sender, EventArgs e)
    {
        if (Session.Count == 0)
        {
            Session.Add("string item", "some text");
            Session.Add("int item", 120);
            Session.Add("boolean item", true);
            Session.Add("date item", DateTime.Now);
            Session.Add("array item", new int[]{1,2,3});
        }
    }
}
```

When we wish to draw your attention to a particular part of a code block, the relevant lines or items are set in bold:

```
namespace ODataEFService
{
    public class NWDataService : DataService<
        ODataEFService.NorthwindEntities >
    {
    public static void
        InitializeService(DataServiceConfiguration config)
        {
            config.DataServiceBehavior.MaxProtocolVersion =
                DataServiceProtocolVersion.V2;
```

```
          config.SetEntitySetAccessRule
               ("*", EntitySetRights.All);
        }
      }
   }
```

Any command-line input or output is written as follows:

DataSvcUtil.exe /in:Northwind.edmx /out:NWDataServiceProxy.cs

New terms and **important words** are shown in bold. Words that you see on the screen, in menus or dialog boxes for example, appear in the text like this: "Specify the necessary publish options in the **Publish Web** dialog."

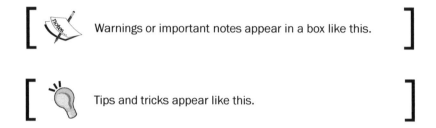

Warnings or important notes appear in a box like this.

Tips and tricks appear like this.

Reader feedback

Feedback from our readers is always welcome. Let us know what you think about this book—what you liked or may have disliked. Reader feedback is important for us to develop titles that you really get the most out of.

To send us general feedback, simply send an e-mail to feedback@packtpub.com, and mention the book title through the subject of your message.

If there is a topic that you have expertise in and you are interested in either writing or contributing to a book, see our author guide on www.packtpub.com/authors.

Customer support

Now that you are the proud owner of a Packt book, we have a number of things to help you to get the most from your purchase.

Downloading the example code

You can download the example code files for all Packt books you have purchased from your account at http://www.packtpub.com. If you purchased this book elsewhere, you can visit http://www.packtpub.com/support and register to have the files e-mailed directly to you.

Errata

Although we have taken every care to ensure the accuracy of our content, mistakes do happen. If you find a mistake in one of our books—maybe a mistake in the text or the code—we would be grateful if you would report this to us. By doing so, you can save other readers from frustration and help us improve subsequent versions of this book. If you find any errata, please report them by visiting http://www.packtpub.com/support, selecting your book, clicking on the **errata submission form** link, and entering the details of your errata. Once your errata are verified, your submission will be accepted and the errata will be uploaded to our website, or added to any list of existing errata, under the Errata section of that title.

Piracy

Piracy of copyright material on the Internet is an ongoing problem across all media. At Packt, we take the protection of our copyright and licenses very seriously. If you come across any illegal copies of our works, in any form, on the Internet, please provide us with the location address or website name immediately so that we can pursue a remedy.

Please contact us at copyright@packtpub.com with a link to the suspected pirated material.

We appreciate your help in protecting our authors, and our ability to bring you valuable content.

Questions

You can contact us at questions@packtpub.com if you are having a problem with any aspect of the book, and we will do our best to address it.

1
Building OData Services

In this chapter we will cover:

- ▶ Building an OData service via WCF Data Service and ADO.NET Entity Framework
- ▶ Building an OData service with WCF Data Service and LINQ to SQL
- ▶ Exposing OData endpoints from WCF RIA Service
- ▶ Adding custom operations on OData service
- ▶ Exposing database stored procedures in WCF Data Service
- ▶ Using custom data objects as the data source of WCF Data Service
- ▶ Using Interceptors to customize a WCF Data Service
- ▶ Accessing ASP.NET context data in WCF Data Service
- ▶ Creating a custom WCF Data Service provider

Introduction

Open Data Protocol (**OData**) is a web protocol for querying and updating data, which can be freely incorporated in various kinds of data access applications. OData makes itself quite simple and flexible to use by applying and building upon existing well-defined technologies, such as HTTP, XML, AtomPub, and JSON.

WCF Data Service is the main component for building OData service on .NET Framework platform. WCF Data Service supports exposing various data source models such as ADO.NET Entity Framework, LINQ to SQL, and CLR Objects through OData service endpoints. Also, we're not limited to these existing data models, we can build our own custom Data Service Provider or convert other services (such as WCF RIA service) to OData service. In this chapter, we will demonstrate several cases of using WCF Data Service to build OData services that can deal with different kinds of data source models.

Building an OData service via WCF Data Service and ADO.NET Entity Framework

There are various means to create an OData service on the .NET Framework platform. And by using different means, we might need to choose different kind of data sources to provide the actual data that will be published and exposed in the OData service. In this recipe, we will start from one of the most typical approaches—creating an OData service through WCF Data Service and ADO.NET Entity Framework data model.

Getting ready

As we will use ADO.NET Entity Framework as the data source of our OData service, make sure you have a sample database, such as Northwind, installed in a local SQL Server instance. You can use SQL Express instance (the free version of SQL Server) for convenience.

The source code for this recipe can be found in the `\ch01\ODataEFServiceSln\` directory.

How to do it...

To concentrate on the OData service generation and make the progress simple and clear, we will use an empty ASP.NET web application with a single OData service for demonstration. The detailed steps are as follows:

1. Launch Visual Studio 2010 IDE.
2. Fire the **New Project** menu and create an **ASP.NET Empty Web Application** through the **Add New Project** wizard (see the following screenshot).

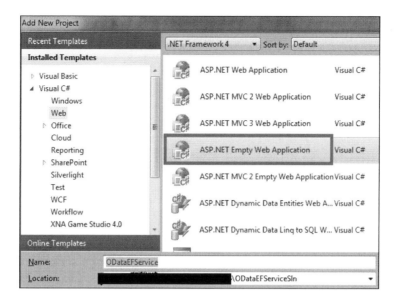

3. Use the **Project | Add New Item** context menu to add a new **ADO.NET Entity Data Model** (see the following screenshot).

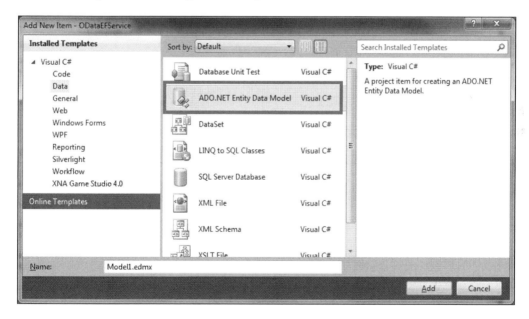

The wizard will guide you on selecting a source database (such as the Northwind database used in this case) .The following screenshot shows the entity classes generated through the Northwind sample database:

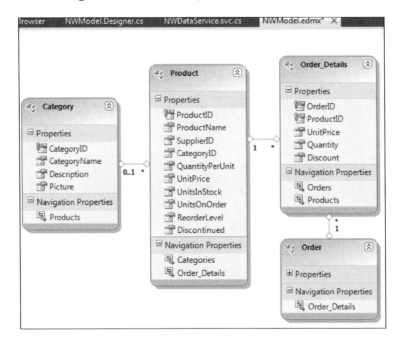

4. Create a new OData service via the **WCF Data Service** item template.

The **WCF Data Service** item template can be found in the Visual Studio 2010 built-in template list (see the following screenshot).

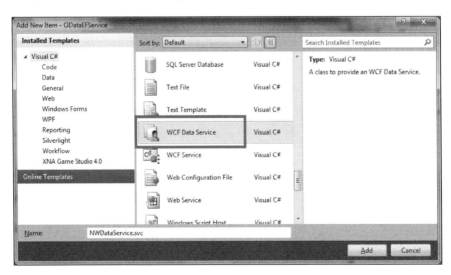

By clicking on the **Add** button, Visual Studio will automatically generate the `.svc` file and its associated code files for the WCF Data Service item.

5. Use **View Code** context menu to open the source file of the generated WCF Data Service and replace the default service type (the generic parameter) with the Entity Framework model class (generated in the previous step).

The following code snippet shows the WCF Data Service, which uses the Northwind data model class in this sample:

```
namespace ODataEFService
{
    public class NWDataService : DataService< ODataEFService.
        NorthwindEntities >
    {
        public static void
            InitializeService(DataServiceConfiguration config)
        {
            config.DataServiceBehavior.MaxProtocolVersion =
                DataServiceProtocolVersion.V2;
            config.SetEntitySetAccessRule
                ("*", EntitySetRights.All);
        }
    }
}
```

Downloading the example code

You can download the example code files for all Packt books you have purchased from your account at http://www.packtpub.com. If you purchased this book elsewhere, you can visit http://www. packtpub.com/support and register to have the files e-mailed directly to you.

6. Now, we can start running the service by selecting the `.svc` file in **Solution Explorer** and choose the **View in browser** context menu.

The default page of the WCF Data service will display all the OData entities that have been exposed in the service (see the following screenshot).

How it works...

In our sample web project, there are only two items. One is the ADO.NET Entity Framework data model and the other is the WCF Data Service item (as shown in the following project structure screenshot).

WCF Data Service has helped encapsulate all the underlying details of implementing an OData service. When using WCF Data Service to generate OData service, what we need to do is:

- ▶ Prepare the data source provider type (in our case, the ADO.NET Entity Framework model)
- ▶ Associate the data source provider with the WCF Data Service

Also, as the name indicates, WCF Data Service is a special implementation of WCF service. And more specifically, WCF Data Service is a specially implemented WCF service over the REST HTTP endpoint (by using the `WebHttpBinding` binding type). In most cases, we do not need to take care of those WCF service-specific configuration details (in `web.config` file). If we open the `web.config` file of our sample service, we can find that there is almost nothing defined within the `<system.serviceModel>` element for the WCF configuration (see the following screenshot).

```
<system.serviceModel>
  <serviceHostingEnvironment aspNetCompatibilityEnabled="true" />
</system.serviceModel>
</configuration>
```

See also

- ▶ *Exploring an OData service through web browser* recipe in *Chapter 2, Working with OData at Client Side*
- ▶ *Applying basic access rules on WCF Data Service* recipe in *Chapter 3, OData Service Hosting and Configuration*

Building an OData service with WCF Data Service and LINQ to SQL

In addition to ADO.NET Entity Framework, LINQ to SQL is another popular and powerful component we can use for mapping relational database objects to .NET CLR class objects. Many popular RDBMS (such as SQL Server and Oracle) have provided LINQ to SQL providers. And for WCF Data Service, it is quite reasonable to add support for exposing a LINQ to SQL based data source via OData service endpoints. In this recipe, we will introduce you to creating an OData service from a LINQ to SQL based data source model.

Getting ready

Make sure you have a sample database, such as Northwind, installed in a local SQL Server instance. You can use an SQL Express instance (the free version of SQL Server) for convenience.

The source code for this recipe can be found in the `\ch01\ODataLINQ2SQLServiceSln\` directory.

How to do it...

You can follow the steps given for creating an OData service from LINQ to SQL data entities:

1. Create a new ASP.NET Empty Web Application in Visual Studio 2010.

2. Create the LINQ to SQL data model types by using the **LINQ to SQL Classes** item template (see the following screenshot).

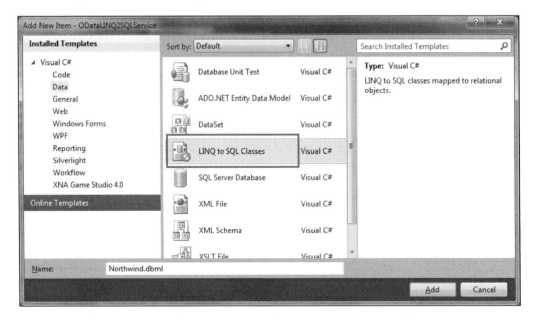

After the data model is created, we can use Visual Studio Server Explorer to drag certain tables (from the sample database) into the data model designer. This will make the Visual Studio IDE create the corresponding data entity types.

 Save all items in the project so as to make sure Visual Studio IDE has compiled the generated LINQ to SQL data model types.

3. Create a new WCF Data Service based on the generated LINQ to SQL data model.

   This time, we use the LINQ to SQL data model class as the generic parameter of the service class (see the following code snippet).

```
public class NWODataService : DataService< ODataLINQ2SQLService.
NorthwindDataContext >
{
    // This method is called only once to initialize service-wide
    // policies.
    public static void InitializeService(DataServiceConfiguration
        config)
    {
        config.DataServiceBehavior.MaxProtocolVersion =
            DataServiceProtocolVersion.V2;,
        config.SetEntitySetAccessRule("*", EntitySetRights.All);
    }
}
```

4. Select the `.svc` service file in Visual Studio and launch it through the **View in browser** context menu.

How it works...

Although we directly use the LINQ to SQL data model class as the data source, the WCF Data Service runtime actually treats the LINQ to SQL data model class like a custom data source type. Therefore, any public member (of the data model class) who implements the `IQueryable` interface will be exposed as an entity set in the generated service. We will talk more about using custom data source type for WCF Data Service within the *Using custom data objects as the data source of WCF Data Service* recipe of this chapter.

There's more...

By default, the WCF Data Service, which uses the LINQ to SQL data model class, does not support editing/updating operations. In order to make the LINQ to SQL based WCF Data Service support editing/updating, we need to implement the `IUpdatable` interface (under `System.Data.Services` namespace) on the LINQ to SQL data model class (see the following code snippet).

```
partial class NorthwindDataContext:    IUpdatable
{
    ......
}
```

For detailed information about implementing `IUpdatable` interface for LINQ to SQL data model class, you can refer to the following MSDN reference:

How to: Create a Data Service Using a LINQ to SQL Data Source (WCF Data Services) available at `http://msdn.microsoft.com/en-us/library/ee373841.aspx`

See also

▶ *Building an OData service via WCF Data Service and ADO.NET Entity Framework* recipe

▶ *Using custom data objects as the data source of WCF Data Service* recipe

Exposing OData endpoints from WCF RIA Service

WCF RIA Service is one of the great extension components based on the standard WCF service. WCF RIA Service is designed for building data access services (for *n*-tier solutions), which will not only expose data sets to clients but also encapsulate most of the business/application logics at service layer. With the latest WCF RIA Service version, we can make a WCF RIA Service expose data through various kinds of endpoints such as SOAP, OData, and JSON.

In this recipe, we will show you how to open an OData endpoint from an existing WCF RIA Service.

Getting ready

To play with WCF RIA Service, we need to install Visual Studio 2010 Service Pack 1, which includes the runtime and development tools for WCF RIA Service V1 SP1.

Visual Studio 2010 Service Pack 1 is available at `http://support.microsoft.com/kb/983509`.

The source code for this recipe can be found in the `\ch01\ODataRIAServiceSln\` directory.

How to do it...

1. Create a new ASP.NET Empty Web Application.
2. Create the ADO.NET Entity Framework data model from the sample database.

The following screenshot shows the class diagram of the data model created from the Northwind sample database (four tables are included):

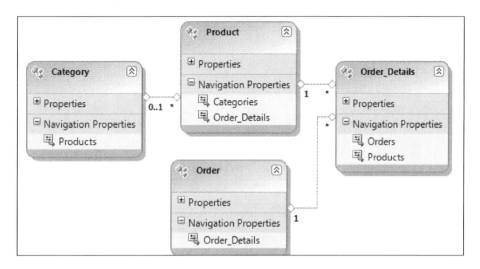

3. Create a new WCF RIA Service by using the **Domain Service Class** item template in Visual Studio (see the following screenshot).

4. Specify the service options (especially the one for enabling an OData endpoint) in the **Add New Domain Service Class** dialog (see the following screenshot).

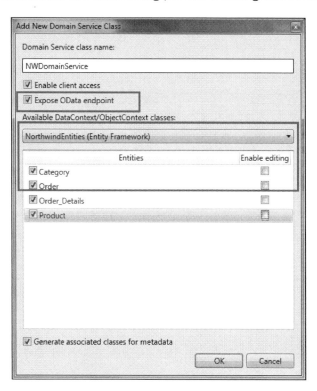

The following are all the options we need to set for a new WCF RIA Service:

- **Domain Service Class name**: This is the type name of our RIA service class.

- **Available DataContext/ObjectContext classes**: This is the data model class we will use for providing the underlying data objects. Make sure we have saved all items in the project so that the ADO.NET Entity Framework data model class will appear in the drop-down list.

- **Enable client access** and **Expose OData endpoint** options: As the name explains, these two options will enable the RIA service to be accessed from client applications and also add an additional endpoint on it so as to expose data entities in an OData compatible format.

5. Create a .svc file as the service access endpoint for the WCF RIA Service.

In the `.svc` file, we need to specify the `ServiceHostFactory` and `Service` types through the `@ServiceHost` directive (see the following code snippet).

```
<%@ ServiceHost Language="C#" Debug="true"
Service="ODataRIAService.NWDomainService" Factory="System.
ServiceModel.DomainServices.Hosting.DomainServiceHostFactory,
System.ServiceModel.DomainServices.Hosting, Version=4.0.0.0,
Culture=neutral, PublicKeyToken=31bf3856ad364e35" %>
```

As shown in the previous `@ServiceHost` directive, we need to supply the full name (including namespace and assembly name) of the `ServiceHostFactory` type in the `Factory` attribute.

> If you use the WCF service item template to create a new `.svc` file, Visual Studio will generate the `ServiceContract` and `Service` implementation code files automatically. To prevent this, you can create a Text or XML file instead and manually change the file extension to `.svc` (and adjust the file content correspondingly).

6. Launch the WCF RIA Service and access its OData endpoint by adding the **odata/** suffix to the URL.

    By adding the **odata/** suffix to the URL over the base service address, we can reach the OData endpoint exposed by the WCF RIA Service. The default output of the OData endpoint is just the same as a standard WCF Data Service (see the following screenshot).

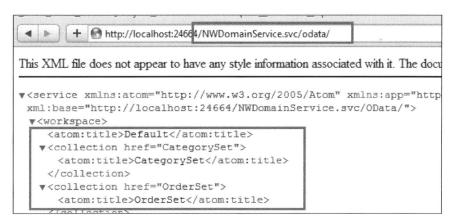

How it works...

When creating the sample WCF RIA Service, we enable the OData endpoint on it by selecting the **Expose OData endpoint** option in the **Add New Domain Service Class** dialog. Actually, we can find the magic behind the dialog within the `web.config` file (see the following configuration fragment).

```
    <domainServices>
      <endpoints>
        <add name="OData"
             type="System.ServiceModel.DomainServices.Hosting.ODataEndpointFactory,
      </endpoints>
    </domainServices>
    <serviceHostingEnvironment aspNetCompatibilityEnabled="true"
        multipleSiteBindingsEnabled="true" />
  </system.serviceModel>
</configuration>
```

The dialog adds a `domainServices/endpoints/add` element in the `<system.serviceModel>` section. This element tells the runtime to add a new endpoint for each WCF RIA Service and this endpoint will generate an OData format response (by using the `System.ServiceModel.DomainServices.Hosting.ODataEndpointFactory` type).

Likewise, if you have some existing WCF RIA Services, which were created without the OData endpoints enabled, we can simply make them OData enabled by adding the previous configuration settings manually in the `web.config` file.

See also

> ▸ *Building an OData service via WCF Data Service and ADO.NET Entity Framework* recipe

Adding custom operations on OData service

By default, WCF Data Service will expose all data object collections provided by the data source in the format of OData entity sets. In addition to this, we can also add custom methods/operations on a given WCF Data Service. By using such custom operations, we can further extend our OData services so as to expose additional data in arbitrary formats, such as XML, JSON, and Binary.

In this recipe, we will demonstrate how to add custom operations to a WCF Data Service.

Getting ready

This sample case still uses the same ADO.NET Entity Framework based WCF Data Service like what we've discussed in the previous recipes. We will add some custom operations to it so as to expose additional data to client.

The source code for this recipe can be found in the `\ch01\CustomOperationServiceSln\` directory.

How to do it...

1. Create a new ASP.NET Empty Web Application.

2. Create an ADO.NET Entity Framework based WCF Data Service through the Northwind sample database.

3. Add custom operations into the WCF Data Service class.

   We will add two operations here, one for retrieving the current time on service server (return `DateTime` value) and another for retrieving some test data entities of the `Category` entity type (see the following code snippet).

```
public class NWDataService : DataService<CustomOperationService.
NorthwindEntities>
{
    . . . . . .


    [WebGet]
    public DateTime GetServerTime()
    {
        return DateTime.Now;
    }


    [WebGet]
    public IQueryable<Category> GetDummyCategories()
    {
        var cates = new List<Category>();
        cates.Add(new Category() { CategoryID = 1, CategoryName =
            "Category 1", Description = "Desc of Category 1" });
        cates.Add(new Category() { CategoryID = 2, CategoryName =
            "Category 2", Description = "Desc of Category 2" });
        cates.Add(new Category() { CategoryID = 3, CategoryName =
            "Category 3", Description = "Desc of Category 3" });

        return cates.AsQueryable();
    }

}
```

As the shown in the previous code, both operation functions need to be public and non-static member methods of the service class.

> Don't forget the `WebGetAttribute` attribute on the declaration of each operation.

4. Enable the operation access rules in the service initialization code (see the following code snippet).

```
public static void InitializeService(DataServiceConfiguration
config)
{
    config.DataServiceBehavior.MaxProtocolVersion =
        DataServiceProtocolVersion.V2;
    config.SetEntitySetAccessRule("*", EntitySetRights.All);
    config.SetServiceOperationAccessRule("*",
        ServiceOperationRights.All);

}
```

5. Select the `.svc` file to launch the service and directly invoke the custom operations (by typing the operation address) in the web browser.

   The following screenshot shows the web browser window after invoking the `GetServerTime` operation:

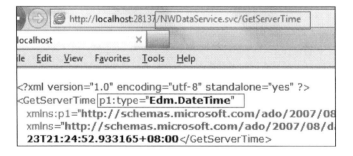

The following is the output obtained by invoking the `GetDummyCategories` operation:

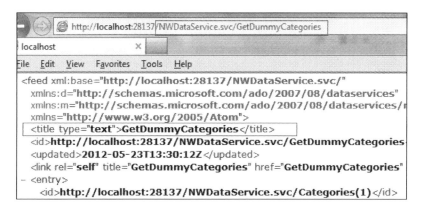

How it works...

As shown in the previous sample code, we can add custom operations to WCF Data Service in the same way as we add service operations to a standard WCF REST service. Also, the `WebGetAttribute` attribute over each sample operation indicates that the operation can be accessed through the HTTP GET method (the expected method for operations that return data). We can also apply the `WebInvokeAttribute` attribute so as to make the operation support other HTTP methods.

Also, in order to allow clients to invoke custom operations, we need to grant the access rules in the `InitializeService` function just like we do for entity sets exposed in WCF Data Service.

For more information about access rules and permission configuration on WCF Data Service, see *Chapter 7, Working with Security*.

See also

- *Building an OData service via WCF Data Service and ADO.NET Entity Framework* recipe

Exposing database stored procedures in WCF Data Service

When developing data access applications with relational databases, we will often use **stored procedures** to encapsulate some frequently used queries. We can also gain performance improvements by using stored procedures (compared to using raw SQL queries).

Then, can we also take advantages of database stored procedures in our WCF Data Services which expose data from relational database? Absolutely yes! In this recipe, we will discuss how to expose data entities from relational database via stored procedures.

Getting ready

The service here will expose two stored procedures from the Northwind database. They are the `CustOrdersOrders` procedure (return Order list of a given customer) and the `Ten Most Expensive Products` procedure. The following are the raw signatures of these two stored procedures:

```
ALTER PROCEDURE [dbo].[Ten Most Expensive Products] AS ...
ALTER PROCEDURE [dbo].[CustOrdersOrders] @CustomerID nchar(5)
AS ...
```

The source code for this recipe can be found in the `\ch01\ODataSPServiceSln\` directory.

How to do it...

1. Create a new ASP.NET Empty Web Application.

2. Create the ADO.NET Entity Framework data model and include the stored procedures together with the tables.

   We can select the database tables, views, and stored procedures we want in the **Choose Your Database Objects** dialog (see the following screenshot). In this case, we need to select all tables and two stored procedures.

3. Add **Function Import** for the stored procedures in the Data Model class.

4. Open the EF designer by double-clicking on the generated data model (.edmx file in Visual Studio Solution Explorer).

5. Right-click on the designer surface and fire the **Function Import...** context menu (see the following screenshot).

6. In the **Add Function Import** dialog, specify the detailed information of the target stored procedure we want to import.

    The following screenshot shows the import settings for the **CustOrdersOrders** procedure:

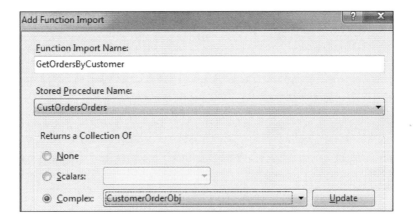

The return value of the previous stored procedure mapping function is a custom complex object. You can create this complex data type (based on the columns returned in the stored procedure) by using the **Create New Complex Type** button at the bottom of **Add Function Import** dialog (see the following screenshot).

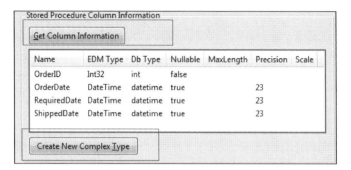

7. Add custom operations in the WCF Data Service class, which directly invokes the stored procedure mapping functions imported in the previous step.

    The following code snippet shows the custom operations definition in the sample WCF Data Service:

```
[WebGet]
public IQueryable<ExpProductObj> GetTop10ExpensiveProducts()
{
    return this.CurrentDataSource.
        GetTop10ExpensiveProducts().AsQueryable();
}


[WebGet]
public IQueryable<CustomerOrderObj> GetOrdersByCustomer(string
custID)
{
    return this.CurrentDataSource.
        GetOrdersByCustomer(custID).AsQueryable();
}
```

8. Launch the service and invoke the stored procedure based operations in the web browser.

The following screenshot shows the web browser output by invoking the GetOrdersByCustomer operation in the sample service:

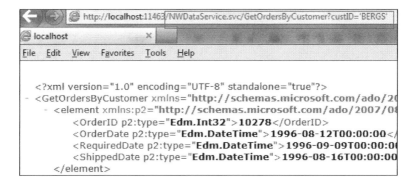

How it works...

To use stored procedures in WCF Data Service (using the ADO.NET Entity Framework data model as data source), we need to import stored procedures as functions in the generated EF data model class. In this sample, we create some custom data types for the return value of each stored procedure mapping function. This is because in most cases, the returned data columns from a given stored procedure don't exactly match a complete data entity type (corresponding to the target database table).

In addition to the imported functions on EF data model class, we also need to add custom operations within the WCF Data Service class. These operations simply delegate the operation call to the corresponding stored procedure mapping functions.

When calling a service operation mapping to a void stored procedure (which does not return any value), we can simply use the URL address of the operation (relative from the service base address). For stored procedures that take some input parameters, we can supply the parameters by using query strings in the operation URL (as shown in the previous GetOrdersByCustomer operation sample).

See also

▶ *Building an OData service via WCF Data Service and ADO.NET Entity Framework* recipe

▶ *Adding custom operations on OData service* recipe

Using custom data objects as the data source of WCF Data Service

So far we've explored several examples, which use relational database objects as the data provider (through Entity Framework, LINQ to SQL, or custom operations). However, we're definitely not limited to these data sources; WCF Data Service provides the flexibility for developers to use custom CLR objects as data sources.

In this recipe, we will see how to use custom data objects as a WCF Data Service data source and expose OData entitiy sets based on the data members of the custom data objects.

Getting ready

In this recipe, we will create a WCF Data Service for exposing some books and book categories information to clients. Instead of using ADO.NET Entity Framework or LINQ to SQL, we will define some custom CLR types to represent the data model of the sample service.

The source code for this recipe can be found in the `\ch01\CLRObjDataServiceSln\` directory.

How to do it...

1. Create a new ASP.NET Empty Web Application.

2. Create custom CLR types to represent the book and book category items.

   The following code snippet shows the definition of the sample CLR types:

   ```
   namespace CLRObjDataService
   {
       [DataServiceKey("ISBN")]
       [DataServiceEntity]
       public class BookInfo
       {
           public string ISBN { get; set; }
           public string Title { get; set; }
           public string Author { get; set; }
           public DateTime PubDate { get; set; }
           public BookCategory Category { get; set; }
       }

       [DataServiceKey("Name")]
       [DataServiceEntity]
       public class BookCategory
       {
   ```

```
        public string Name { get; set; }
        public List<BookInfo> Books { get; set; }
    }
}
```

3. Create a data context type that acts as a container for entity sets based on the custom CLR types (defined in the previous step).

   The following is the code of the sample data context type (see the following `BookServiceContext` class), which exposes two entity sets based on the `BookInfo` and `BookCategory` classes:

```
public class BookServiceContext
    {
        static IList<BookCategory> _categories = null;
        static IList<BookInfo> _books = null;

        public IQueryable<BookCategory> BookCategories
        {
            get
            {
                return _categories.AsQueryable();
            }
        }

        public IQueryable<BookInfo> Books
        {
            get
            {
                return _books.AsQueryable();
            }
        }

    }
```

   For demonstration, we have also defined a static constructor for generating some test data (see the following code snippet).

```
        static BookServiceContext()
        {
            _books = new List<BookInfo>();
            _categories = new List<BookCategory>();

            for(int i=1;i<=3;++ i)
            {
                var cate = new BookCategory() { Name = "Category_" +
                    i.ToString() };
```

```
                cate.Books = new List<BookInfo>();

                for (int j = 1; j <= 3; ++j)
                {
                    int bid = (i*10+j);
                    var book = new BookInfo()
                    {
                        ISBN = "ISBN" + bid.ToString(),
                        Title = "Book Title " + bid.ToString(),
                        Author = "Author",
                        PubDate = DateTime.Now,
                        Category = cate
                    };
                    _books.Add(book);
                    cate.Books.Add(book);
                }
                _categories.Add(cate);
            }
        }
```

4. Create a new WCF Data Service and use the custom data context type as its data source.

   The following code snippet shows the sample `BookDataService` class, which uses the `BookServiceContext` class (created in previous step) as the data source parameter:

```
public class BookDataService : DataService< BookServiceContext >
{
    public static void InitializeService
        (DataServiceConfiguration config)
    {
        config.DataServiceBehavior.MaxProtocolVersion =
            DataServiceProtocolVersion.V2;
        config.SetEntitySetAccessRule("*", EntitySetRights.All);
    }
}
```

   Like the ADO.NET Entity Framework-based WCF Data Service, we also need to set the proper entity set access rules in the initialization function.

5. Launch the service and view the custom data entity sets in the web browser.

For the sample service, we can access the exposed entity sets at the following locations:

- *Book category entity set* (`http://[server]:[port]/BookDataService.svc/BookCategories`)

- *Book entity set* (`http://[server]:[port]/BookDataService.svc/Books`)

We can also use the following URL to retrieve book entities that belong to a certain category entity:

```
http://[server]:[port]/BookDataService.svc/
BookCategories('Category_1')/Books
```

The following screenshot shows the book entities that belong to the first category entity:

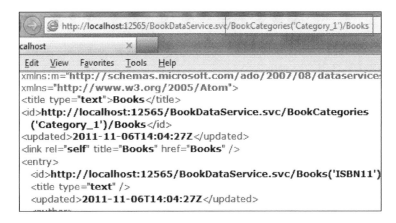

How it works...

Now, let's take a look at what makes these things work. As we can see, each entity set we expose in the sample service is coming from its corresponding member property defined in the data context type. Such member properties should be declared as `IQueryable<Entity Type>` type so that the WCF Data Service runtime can correctly locate them and expose them as entity sets in the service.

> For a given entity type `T`, we can only define one member property (on the data context class), which returns `IQueryable<T>`. In other words, we cannot expose multiple entity sets using the same entity type.

For each custom entity type, we must specify a key property by using the `DataServiceKeyAttribute` attribute. This key property is used for identifying entity instances in a given entity set (just like the **primary key** for the relational table).

The `BookCategory` entity type has a `Books` property of the `List<BookInfo>` type. Such kind of entity collection properties will be automatically treated as Navigation properties on the target entity type. For OData clients, they can use these Navigation properties (by using relative URI address) to retrieve the associated subentities from the primary entity instance (see the previous sample code).

There's more...

We have discussed LINQ to SQL based data sources in the previous recipe. Actually, LINQ to SQL is a special case of a custom data object based data source, since the LINQ to SQL data model has already done most of the work for us. If you are interested in finding out more about building WCF Data Service data source with a custom CLR type, you can refer to the following MSDN reference:

Reflection Provider (WCF Data Services) available at `http://msdn.microsoft.com/en-us/library/dd723653.aspx`

See also

▸ *Adding custom operations on OData service* recipe

▸ *Building an OData service with WCF Data Service and LINQ to SQL* recipe

Using Interceptors to customize a WCF Data Service

If you've been familiar with standard WCF service programming, you probably have been playing with the **Message Inspectors**, which are one of the WCF extension components for intercepting the request and response messages of service operation calls.

Well, for WCF Data Service, we also have the similar extension component called **Interceptors**, which can help intercepting the service requests issued from client callers.

By using WCF Data Service **Interceptors**, we can customize the code logic of certain operations against a given entity set. In this recipe, we will see how to do some customization on the data processing code logic in WCF Data Service by using custom Interceptors.

Getting ready

In this recipe we will build a WCF Data Service based on the Northwind EF data model. The service will expose two data entity sets, one is from the `Categories` table, and the other is from the `Products` table. For demonstration, we will add two custom Interceptors against these two entity sets so as to change their *query* and *delete* behavior.

The source code for this recipe can be found in the `\ch01\QIDataServiceSln\` directory.

How to do it...

1. Create a new ASP.NET Empty Web Application.

2. Create a WCF Data Service with ADO.NET Entity Framework data model (using the Northwind database).

   The service will only expose the `Categories` and `Products` entity sets from the data source (see the following screenshot).

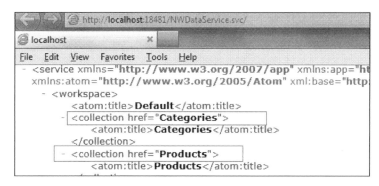

3. Add custom Interceptors in the WCF Data Service class and bind them with the target entity sets.

   There are two Interceptors to define here. The first one is a **QueryInterceptor** against the `Products` entity set. It will restrict the query result so as to expose Product entities that have `UnitsInStock > 0`. The second one is a **ChangeInterceptor** against the `Categories` entity set. By using it, no delete operation is allowed on the `Categories` entity set. The following code snippet shows the WCF Data Service class, which includes both Interceptors:

```
public class NWDataService : DataService< NorthwindEntities >
    {
        public static void
            InitializeService (DataServiceConfiguration config)
        {
        config.DataServiceBehavior.MaxProtocolVersion =
            DataServiceProtocolVersion.V2;
```

```
config.SetEntitySetAccessRule("*", EntitySetRights.All);
}

// Query Interceptor for Products entity set
[QueryInterceptor("Products")]
public Expression<Func<Product, bool>> onQueryProducts()
{
    // Only return products that have units in stock
    return p => p.UnitsInStock > 0;
}

// Change Interceptor for Categories entity set
[ChangeInterceptor("Categories")]
public void onChangeCategories
    (Category cate, UpdateOperations operations)
{
    if (operations == UpdateOperations.Delete)
        {
            throw new DataServiceException(400, "Delete
                operation is not supported on Categories
                entity set.");
        }
}
}
```

4. Launch the service and try accessing the entity sets, which have Interceptors applied.

    By accessing the Products entity set, we can find that all the entities returned by it have the UnitsInStock field greater than zero. Also, if we explicitly use query filter to look for Product entities that have UnitsInStock equal to zero, we will get empty results (see the following screenshot).

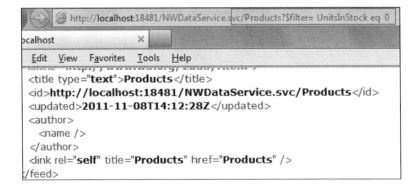

How it works...

In the sample service, we have applied a **QueryInterceptor** on the `Products` entity set. Actually, a `QueryInterceptor` is just a function, which returns a Lambda expression with the following signature:

```
Func<[Entity Type], bool>
```

Then, why does it use an expression instead of a delegate function directly? The reason is that by using an expression, it is more convenient for the underlying WCF Data Service runtime to forward such `QueryInterceptor` injected code logic to the actual query provider (such as the ADO.NET Entity Framework provider, which will generate T-SQL based on the query) that will fetch the data from the backend data source.

QueryInterceptor will be invoked when HTTP GET based query requests are received against the target entity set; while **ChangeInterceptor** will be invoked when update/modify operations are called. In this sample, our `onChangeCategories` Interceptor will check the incoming request to see if it is a delete operation against the `Categories` entity set. If the checking result is `true`, a `DataServiceException` will be thrown out. In a real-world case, we can apply more complicated code logic to change the default update/modify behavior against the target entity sets.

There's more...

For more information about using Interceptors in WCF Data Service, you can read the following MSDN reference:

Interceptors (WCF Data Services) available at `http://msdn.microsoft.com/en-us/library/dd744842.aspx`

See also

> ▸ *Building an OData service via WCF Data Service and ADO.NET Entity Framework* recipe

Accessing ASP.NET context data in WCF Data Service

OData protocol is naturally based on HTTP and other web standards. OData services built with WCF Data Service are often hosted in an ASP.NET web application. Therefore, it is quite possible that a WCF Data Service is deployed side-by-side with many other web resources, such as ASP.NET web pages, ASMX web services, and HTTP handlers. ASP.NET web pages can access many ASP.NET runtime specific context data such as session states, client user info, application states, cache, and HTTP request headers. Is this also possible for WCF Data Services (hosted in ASP.NET web applications)?

Well, this can be easily achieved with the current WCF Data Service programming model. In this recipe, we will introduce how to access ASP.NET context data in WCF Data Service code.

Getting ready

In this recipe, we will create a WCF Data Service, which will expose the session states and HTTP client user headers (of the ASP.NET host web application) as entity sets to the service callers. Also, to make the service code simple and clear, we will use custom CLR types instead of a ADO.NET Entity Framework data model as the service data source.

The source code for this recipe can be found in the \ch01\WebContextDataServiceSln\ directory.

How to do it...

1. Create a new ASP.NET Empty Web Application.

2. Define the custom classes, which will be used as entity types and data context type of the sample WCF Data Service.

    The following is the complete definition of the ClientInfoEntity and SessionItemEntity entity types in this sample:

```
[DataServiceEntity]
    [DataServiceKey("ID")]
    public class ClientInfoEntity
    {
        public int ID { get; set; }
        public string IPAddress { get; set; }
        public string UserAgent { get; set; }
        public bool Authenticated { get; set; }
    }

    [DataServiceEntity]
```

```
[DataServiceKey("KeyName")]
public class SessionItemEntity
{
    public string KeyName { get; set; }
    public string TypeName { get; set; }
}
```

The following `WebContextEntityContainer` class is used as the service data context (the container of the two sample entity sets):

```
public class WebContextEntityContainer
{
    public IQueryable<SessionItemEntity> SessionItems
    {
        get
        {
            var items = new List<SessionItemEntity>();
            foreach (string key in
                HttpContext.Current.Session.Keys)
            {
                var item = new SessionItemEntity()
                {
                    KeyName = key,
                    TypeName =
                        HttpContext.Current.Session[key].
                            GetType().FullName
                };
                items.Add(item);
            }
            return items.AsQueryable();
        }
    }

    public IQueryable<ClientInfoEntity> ClientInfos
    {
        get
        {
            var req = HttpContext.Current.Request;
            var clientInfo = new ClientInfoEntity()
            {
                ID = 1,
                Authenticated = req.IsAuthenticated,
                IPAddress = req.UserHostAddress,
                UserAgent = req.UserAgent
            };
```

```
                return new
                   ClientInfoEntity[]{clientInfo}.AsQueryable();
            }
        }
    }
```

3. Create a new WCF Data Service and use the `WebContextEntityContainer` class as a data source (see the following code snippet).

    ```
    public class ContextInfoDataService : DataService<
        WebContextEntityContainer >
    {
    ..
    }
    ```

4. Launch the service in the web browser and query the two entity sets, which return data specific to the current ASP.NET context.

    We can access the `SessionItems` and `ClientInfos` entity sets through the following URI addresses:

    □   `http://[server]:[port]/ContextInfoDataService.svc/SessionItems`

    □   `http://[server]:[port]/ContextInfoDataService.svc/ClientInfos`

    The following screenshot shows the query output of the first (also the only) entity instance from the `ClientInfos` entity set:

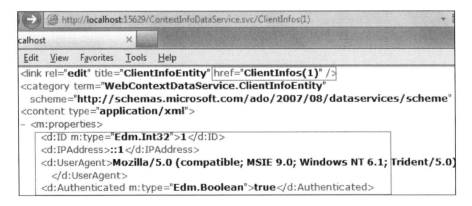

How it works...

The WCF Service programming model provides built-in support for service code to access ASP. NET context data in case the service is hosted in an ASP.NET web application. Since WCF Data Service is a special implementation of WCF Service, accessing ASP.NET context data in WCF Data Service code is naturally supported too. Actually, whenever a new WCF Data Service is created in Visual Studio (within an ASP.NET web project), the IDE will automatically enable the ASP.NET Compatibility mode (see the following screenshot) in the `web.config` file, which is necessary for WCF Service (also WCF Data Service) to access ASP.NET context data of the hosting web application.

```
<system.serviceModel>
  <serviceHostingEnvironment aspNetCompatibilityEnabled="true" />
</configuration>
```

For demonstration purposes, our sample ASP.NET web application also contains a simple ASP.NET web page, which will help in generating some test session states data (see the following `InitSession` page class).

```csharp
public partial class InitSession : System.Web.UI.Page
{
    protected void Page_Load(object sender, EventArgs e)
    {
        if (Session.Count == 0)
        {
            Session.Add("string item", "some text");
            Session.Add("int item", 120);
            Session.Add("boolean item", true);
            Session.Add("date item", DateTime.Now);
            Session.Add("array item", new int[]{1,2,3});
        }
    }
}
```

See also

▸   *Using custom data objects as the data source of WCF Data Service* recipe

Creating a custom WCF Data Service provider

So far we've explored various ways to build an OData service with .NET Framework platform including WCF Data Service with ADO.NET Entity Framework, LINQ to SQL, custom CLR objects, and WCF RIA service.

However, what if we want to expose some custom data through OData endpoints but none of the above means can help? Such conditions do exist, for example, we might have some data that is not of relational database structure, or the data object types are previously defined, which haven't applied those WCF Data Service specific attributes (necessary for using custom CLR objects based data source).

Don't worry, the WCF Data Service framework has already provided a powerful extension model, which can let you create a custom provider in order to expose arbitrary format custom data in a WCF Data Service. In this recipe, we will see how to create a custom WCF Data Service provider and use it to expose some custom data.

Getting ready

In this recipe, we will choose filesystem as an example and build a WCF Data Service, which exposes the information of all files within a given directory. Also, we will create several custom classes in order to implement the custom WCF Data Service provider. The following class diagram (generated via Visual Studio Architecture Modeling tools) can help you get an overview of these custom types and their dependency relationships:

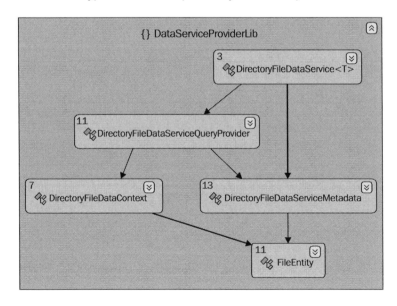

The source code for this recipe can be found in the \ch01\FileDataServiceSln\ directory.

How to do it...

1. Create a new ASP.NET Empty Web Application.

2. Create the custom class that represents individual file objects (see the following FileEntity class definition).

```
public class FileEntity
    {
        public int ID { get; set; }
        public string FileName { get; set; }
        public string Extension { get; set; }
        public DateTime Created { get; set; }
        public long Length { get; set; }
    }
```

3. Create the data context class that represents the data source and entity sets container of the sample service.

    The following code snippet shows the DirectoryFileDataContext class of the sample service:

```
public class DirectoryFileDataContext
    {
        public DirectoryInfo DirInfo { get; set; }
        public List<FileEntity> Files { get; set; }

        public DirectoryFileDataContext():
            this(Environment.CurrentDirectory)
        { }
        public DirectoryFileDataContext(string dirPath)
        {
            DirInfo = new DirectoryInfo(dirPath);

            int i=0;
            Files = (from fi in DirInfo.GetFiles()
            select new FileEntity
            {
                ID = ++i,
                FileName = fi.Name,
                Extension = fi.Extension,
                Created = fi.CreationTime,
                Length = fi.Length
            }).ToList();
        }
    }
```

4. Create a metadata provider class implementing the
IDataServiceMetadataProvider interface under System.Data.Services.
Providers namespace.

The following code snippet shows the overall definition of our metadata provider class
in this sample:

```
public class DirectoryFileDataServiceMetadata:
IDataServiceMetadataProvider
{
    private string _containerName = "";
    private string _namespace = "";
    private Dictionary<string, ResourceSet> _resSets = null;
    private Dictionary<string, ResourceType> _resTypes = null;


    ......


    #region IDataServiceMetadataProvider Members

    public string ContainerName
    {
        get { return _containerName; }
    }

    public string ContainerNamespace
    {
        get { return _namespace; }
    }

    ......


    public IEnumerable<ResourceSet> ResourceSets
    {
        get
        {
            return _resSets.Values;
        }
    }

    ......


    #endregion
}
```

In the constructor of the metadata provider, we need to add code to register the resource types and resource sets mapping to the data entities we want to expose in the WCF Data Service.

```
public DirectoryFileDataServiceMetadata(DirectoryFileDataContext
ctx)
{
    _containerName = "DirectoryFiles";
    _namespace = "http://odata.test.org/directoryfiles";
    _resSets = new Dictionary<string, ResourceSet>();
    _resTypes = new Dictionary<string, ResourceType>();

    // Init ResourceType set
    var fileEntityType = typeof(FileEntity);
    var fileResourceType = new ResourceType(
        fileEntityType,
        ResourceTypeKind.EntityType,
        null,
        fileEntityType.Namespace,
        fileEntityType.Name,
        false
    );

    AddPropertyToResourceType(fileResourceType, "ID", true);
    AddPropertyToResourceType(fileResourceType, "FileName",
        false);
    AddPropertyToResourceType(fileResourceType, "Extension",
        false);
    AddPropertyToResourceType(fileResourceType, "Created", false);
    AddPropertyToResourceType(fileResourceType, "Length", false);

    _resTypes.Add(fileResourceType.FullName, fileResourceType);

    // Init ResourceSet set
    var fileResourceSet = new ResourceSet
        ("Files", fileResourceType);
    _resSets.Add("Files", fileResourceSet);
}
```

5. Create a query provider class, which implements the
   IDataServiceQueryProvider interface under System.Data.Services.
   Providers namespace.

The following code snippet shows the main part of our sample
DirectoryFileDataServiceQueryProvider class:

```
public class DirectoryFileDataServiceQueryProvider:
IDataServiceQueryProvider
    {
        private DirectoryFileDataContext _ctx = null;
        private DirectoryFileDataServiceMetadata _metadata = null;

        public DirectoryFileDataServiceQueryProvider
            (DirectoryFileDataContext ctx,
            DirectoryFileDataServiceMetadata metadata)
        {
            _ctx = ctx;
            _metadata = metadata;
        }

        #region IDataServiceQueryProvider Members

        ......

        public IQueryable GetQueryRootForResourceSet
            (ResourceSet resourceSet)
        {
            // Our service provider only provides Files entity set
            return _ctx.Files.AsQueryable();
        }

        public ResourceType GetResourceType(object target)
        {
            return this._metadata.Types.Single
                (rt => rt.InstanceType == target.GetType());
        }
        ....

        #endregion
    }
```

In the previous code snippet, the GetQueryRootForResourceSet method is
the one in which we return the entity set data based on the requested entity set
type parameter.

6. Create the main service provider class, which derives from the `DataService<T>` base class (under `System.Data.Services` namespace) and implements the `IServiceProvider` interface.

The following is the definition of the main provider class (see the following `DirectoryFileDataService` class) in this sample. It takes a generic parameter which is derived from the data context class we defined earlier.

```csharp
public abstract class DirectoryFileDataService<T> :
    DataService<T>, IServiceProvider where T :
    DirectoryFileDataContext
{
    private DirectoryFileDataServiceMetadata _metaProvider = null;
    private DirectoryFileDataServiceQueryProvider _queryProvider =
        null;

    . . . . . .

    #region IServiceProvider Members

    public object GetService(Type serviceType)
    {
        if (serviceType == typeof(IDataServiceMetadataProvider))
        {
            if (_metaProvider == null)
            {
                InitServiceProviders();
            }
            return _metaProvider;
        }
        else if (serviceType == typeof(IDataServiceQueryProvider))
        {
            if (_queryProvider == null)
            {
                InitServiceProviders();
            }
            return _queryProvider;
        }
        else
        {
            return null;
        }
    }

    #endregion
}
```

To simplify the code logic, we will define a helper function to encapsulate the initialization code (see the following `InitServiceProviders` function).

```
private void InitServiceProviders()
{
    var dsObj = this.CreateDataSource();

    // Create metadata provider
    _metaProvider = new DirectoryFileDataServiceMetadata(dsObj);
    // Set the resource types and resource sets as readonly
    foreach (var type in _metaProvider.Types)
    {
        type.SetReadOnly();
    }
    foreach (var set in _metaProvider.ResourceSets)
    {
        set.SetReadOnly();
    }

    // Create query provider
    _queryProvider = new DirectoryFileDataServiceQueryProvider
        (dsObj, _metaProvider);
    _queryProvider.CurrentDataSource = dsObj;
}
```

7. Create a new WCF Data Service based on the main service provider and the data context classes created in the previous steps.

    The WCF Data Service class is derived from the `DirectoryFileDataService` class, which takes the `DirectoryFileDataContext` class as the generic parameter (see the following code snippet).

```
public class FileDataService :
    DirectoryFileDataService<DirectoryFileDataContext>
    {
        public static void InitializeService
            (DataServiceConfiguration config)
        {
            config.DataServiceBehavior.MaxProtocolVersion =
                DataServiceProtocolVersion.V2;
            config.DataServiceBehavior.AcceptProjectionRequests =
                true;
            config.SetEntitySetAccessRule
                ("*", EntitySetRights.AllRead);
        }

        protected override DirectoryFileDataContext
            CreateDataSource()
        {
```

```
var dc = new DirectoryFileDataContext
    (@"C:\Users\Public\Pictures\Sample Pictures");
return dc;
}
```

In addition, we need to override the `CreateDataSource` function of the service class and put the file directory initialization code there. You can specify any directory (avoid using Windows system directories for potential permission issues) on the local machine for testing purpose.

8. Launch the sample service in the web browser and query the `Files` entity set exposed in it.

   The following screenshot shows the default query result against the `Files` entity set:

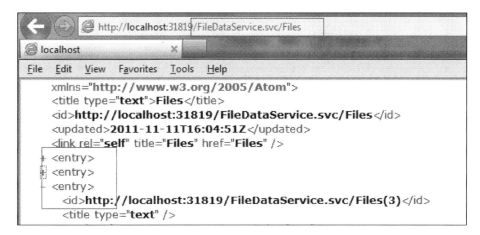

   We can also add additional query options to filter the query result based on the public properties defined in the `FileEntity` class (see the following screenshot).

How it works...

In the previous steps, we created all the custom provider classes from bottom to top according to the class structure diagram shown earlier. Now, let's have a look at how they work together in a top-to-bottom approach.

The `DirectoryFileDataService<T>` class is the top most type among all the custom provider classes. This class is derived from the `DataService<T>` base class so that it can be directly used by WCF Data Service as service class. The `DirectoryFileDataService<T>` class also implements the `IServiceProvider` interface because it will be asked to provide certain implementations of various kind of custom service providers. In this case, we have implemented the `metadata` provider (`IDataServiceMetadataProvider` interface) and the `query` provider (`IDataServiceMetadataProvider` interface), which are used for publishing service metadata and exposing entity sets. In addition, there are other providers used for implementing more advanced features, for example, the `IDataServiceUpdateProvider` interface for implementing update functions, the `IDataServicePagingProvider` interface for implementing paging functions, and the `IDataServiceStreamsProvider` interface for implementing data streaming functions. The following diagram shows the calling pipeline from WCF Data Service class to custom service providers and the backend data source objects:

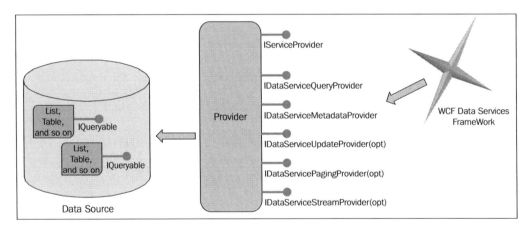

The `DirectoryFileDataService` type uses instances of the `DirectoryFileDataServiceQueryProvider` and `DirectoryFileDataServiceMetadata` types to serve the metadata and query service requests. These two provider instances also use the `DirectoryFileDataContext` type instance for retrieving the underlying data entity sets' type information and query root object.

Both the `DirectoryFileDataServiceQueryProvider` and `DirectoryFileDataServiceMetadata` classes have defined a parameter of the `DirectoryFileDataContext` class in their constructors. This is a common pattern when implementing custom service providers. Because most of the providers will need to get type information (for the entity or entity sets they will handle) from the data context object, the class constructor is a good place for them to hold such an object reference.

Finally, we come to the `FileEntity` class. You might think it is quite similar to the custom entity types we defined in the *Using custom data objects as the data source of WCF Data Service* recipe. The important difference is that we do not have to apply any additional attributes (such as the `DataServiceKey` and `DataServiceEntity` attributes) on the `FileEntity` class (compared to those entity types used by a custom CLR objects based data source). In other words, by using a custom WCF Data Service provider, we can make use of existing predefined custom data types (whether they have applied those special attributes under `System.Data.Services` namespace or not) as OData service entities.

There's more...

WCF Data Service providers have opened the door for developers to extend an OData service to their own data sources in a very flexible way. By using the provider-based model, we can control almost every aspect of WCF Data Service customization (such as the querying and updating processes). Whenever you want to customize a certain part of a WCF Data Service, just find the corresponding provider interface and implement it.

For more information about building custom WCF Data Service providers, you can refer to the following MSDN reference:

Custom Data Service Providers available at `http://msdn.microsoft.com/en-us/data/gg191846`

See also

► *Using custom data objects as the data source of WCF Data Service* recipe

2

Working with OData at Client Side

In this chapter we will cover:

- ▶ Exploring an OData service through web browser
- ▶ Using Visual Studio to generate strong-typed OData client proxy
- ▶ Generating OData client proxy via DataSvcUtil.exe tool
- ▶ Editing and deleting data through WCF Data Service client library
- ▶ Accessing OData service via WebRequest class
- ▶ Executing OData queries in an asynchronous manner
- ▶ Filtering OData query results by using query options
- ▶ Dealing with server-side paged entity sets from WCF Data Service
- ▶ Performing WPF data binding with OData service data
- ▶ Injecting custom HTTP headers in OData requests
- ▶ Consuming HTTP compression enabled OData service
- ▶ Using MSXML to consume OData service in unmanaged applications

Introduction

With OData services established, it is also quite important to find a simple and efficient means to consume the data from services. Since OData protocol is based on web standards such as HTTP, XML, and JSON, it is quite convenient for various programming platforms to build client applications that can consume OData services. For example, you can simply launch a web browser to explore an OData service, which will return data in the **AtomPub** format; you can also use the .NET **WebRequest** class to communicate with an OData service via a raw HTTP request/response. In more complicated situations, we can use the OData client SDK or GUI tools (such as the WCF Data Service client library and Visual Studio IDE) to generate a strong-typed client proxy to access OData service.

In this chapter, we will cover several cases of accessing OData services in client applications. We will start with some very basic OData client access approaches such as using a web browser, strong-typed client proxy classes, and raw WebRequest class. Then, we will dig into some more detailed OData client access scenarios such as editing and updating OData entity sets, asynchronous OData programming pattern, using built-in OData query options and server-side paged entity sets manipulation. In addition, some more complicated OData access cases such as consuming OData in Gzip compressed format, accessing an OData service in unmanaged clients are also covered at the end of this chapter.

Exploring an OData service through web browser

What is the simplest and most convenient means to access data entities exposed from an OData service or shall we always build a dedicated client proxy or use some OData client APIs to consume OData service? Of course not! Actually, what we need is just a web browser. By using a web browser, we can explore the metadata of an OData service and query any entity set exposed in the service in a quick and straightforward way. In this recipe, we will show you how to use a web browser to quickly explore the data exposed from an OData service.

Getting ready

The sample OData service we will use here is still based on WCF Data Service and ADO.NET Entity Framework. The Northwind database will be used as the backend data source.

The source code for this recipe can be found in the `\ch02\ NWDataServiceSln\` directory.

How to do it...

1. Create a new ASP.NET Empty Web Application.

2. Create a new WCF Data Service with the ADO.NET Entity Framework data model (using the Northwind database).

   The sample service needs to expose the following entity sets (from the corresponding Northwind database tables):

   - Categories
   - Products
   - Orders

3. Select the .svc service file in the web application and launch it using the **View in Browser** context menu (see the following screenshot).

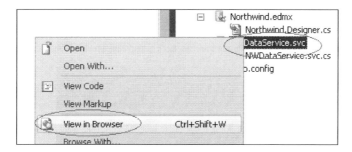

4. View the metadata of the sample service by using the **$metadata** URL suffix.

   We can directly append the **$metadata** suffix after the base URL of the sample service. The following screenshot shows the entity type definitions contained in the service metadata:

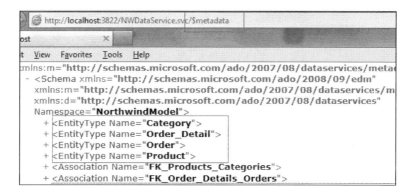

We can expand and collapse the elements in the metadata document to view data types and relations defined in the service.

The **$metadata** URL suffix is a WCF Data Service specific convention. Other OData service implementations might use different URL conventions for exposing service metadata.

Under the entity type definitions, we can also find the definitions of entity sets exposed in the service (see the following screenshot).

```
xmlns:d="http://schemas.microsoft.com/ado/2007/08/dataservices"
Namespace="NWDataService">
  <EntityContainer Name="NorthwindEntities"
  xmlns:p7="http://schemas.microsoft.com/ado/2009/02/edm/annotation"
  m:IsDefaultEntityContainer="true" p7:LazyLoadingEnabled="true">
    <EntitySet Name="Categories" EntityType="NorthwindModel.Category"/>
    <EntitySet Name="Order_Details" EntityType="NorthwindModel.Order_Detail"/>
    <EntitySet Name="Orders" EntityType="NorthwindModel.Order"/>
    <EntitySet Name="Products" EntityType="NorthwindModel.Product"/>
    <AssociationSet Name="FK_Products_Categories"
    Association="NorthwindModel.FK_Products_Categories">
```

5. View all entities within a given entity set by appending the entity set name after the base URL.

The following screenshot shows the web browser output by accessing the `Categories` entity set:

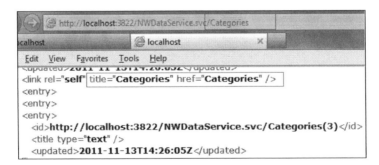

6. Access a specific entity instance by supplying the entity key value in the URL.

For example, we can use the following URL address to access the `Category` entity object whose key is 2 (see the following screenshot).

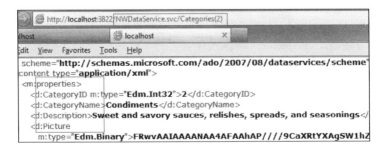

7. Navigate between entities or entity sets through reference or navigation properties.

    When exploring the OData service metadata, we can find that there are some `Association` and `AssociationSet` elements defined together with the entity and entity sets. By using such association information, we can navigate from one entity object to its associated entity or entity collection. We can use the following URL to access the `Product` entities associated with the given `Category` entity:

    `http://[server]:[port]/NWDataService.svc/Categories(2)/Products`

    The following screenshot shows the web browser output by executing the previous URL query:

8. Apply some OData query options in the URL.

    The following are two sample URLs, which have used the `$filter` and `$top` query options:

    - retrieve all order entities that have 'Brazil' as ShipCountry

      `http://[server]:[port]/NWDataService.svc/Orders?$filter=ShipCountry eq 'Brazil'`

    - retrieve the top 3 Order entities from service

      `http://[server]:[port]/NWDataService.svc/Orders?$top=3`

    The following is the web browser output by executing the second query given previously:

    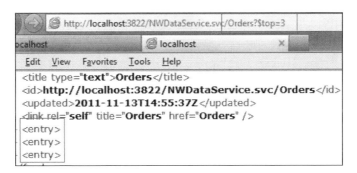

How it works...

Now, we know that we can use a web browser to view the entity sets exposed in OData services (with the corresponding URL addresses). It is because OData is based on HTTP protocol and enables data access via standard HTTP methods (such as GET, POST, and PUT). This also makes it quite convenient for any HTTP web-request-enabled client to access the data exposed by OData services.

Metadata is also very important to OData clients. By using the metadata document, we can get all the entity set and entity types' information of an OData service. And by using standard HTTP URL format addresses, we can access any kind of the following data resources exposed in OData services:

- ▸ An entity set
- ▸ An entity object
- ▸ Associated entity collection on a specific entity object
- ▸ Custom service operations
- ▸ An entity collection based on query filters

Even if you haven't got an overview of the entire service data structure (by using metadata), it is still quite straight and intuitive for you to discover the data exposed in an OData service. We can do it by accessing the default service document at the base service address. For example, we can view the default document of the sample Northwind OData service by typing the following URL in the web browser:

```
http://[server]:[port]/NWDataService.svc/
```

The default service document will show you all the exposed entity sets and their relative locations (through the href attribute). By appending the href relative address after the base service URL, we can drill into the specific entity set (such as the following Categories entity set URL).

```
http://[server]:[port]/NWDataService.svc/Categories
```

And if you add an entity key value in the entity set URL, you can view the data of a specific entity object only (see the following sample URL of a specific Category entity object).

```
http://[server]:[port]/NWDataService.svc/Categories(2)
```

Since each Category entity is associated with a collection of Product entities, you can further extend the query URL (by appending the Navigation property name) so as to view all the associated entity objects. The following URL is used to get all Product entities associated with a specific Category entity:

```
http://[server]:[port]/NWDataService.svc/Categories(2)/Products
```

By using this intuitive and self-explained data presentation style, it is quite handy for us to explore an OData service in a standard web browser and you will find it quite useful when you develop and test an OData service.

We have also shown some sample URLs, which use query options. We will discuss query options further within a dedicated recipe in this chapter.

There's more...

In case you want to know more about the OData metadata format and how we can query it, the following article is worth reading:

Queryable OData Metadata available at `http://www.odata.org/blog/2010/4/22/ queryable-odata-metadata`

See also

▸ *Filtering OData query results by using query options* recipe

Using Visual Studio to generate strong-typed OData client proxy

When we need to incorporate data from OData services in .NET Framework based applications, what would be the most straightforward and efficient means for consuming the services? The answer is using the strong-typed client proxy generated upon the WCF Data Service client library. And Visual Studio 2010 has provided GUI support on this through the **Add Service Reference** wizard.

Recipes in this book are using **Visual Studio 2010** as the main development tool. However, generating OData client proxy via the Add Service Reference wizard has already been supported since **Visual Studio 2008 SP1**.

In this recipe, we will demonstrate how to generate a strong-typed OData client proxy in Visual Studio 2010 and use the generated proxy to consume the target OData service.

Getting ready

The sample OData service here is still built with WCF Data Service and uses the ADO.NET Entity Framework data model (Northwind database). And we will create a strong-typed client proxy in Visual Studio to consume the service. This proxy generation approach will be used many times over the entire book.

The source code for this recipe can be found in the \ch02\VSODataClientSln\ directory.

How to do it...

1. Create a new ASP.NET web application, which contains the WCF Data Service based on the Northwind database (using ADO.NET Entity Framework data model).

2. Create a new Console application as an OData client.

3. Right-click on the project node in **Visual Studio Solution Explorer** and launch the proxy generation wizard by selecting the **Add Service Reference...** context menu (see the following screenshot).

4. Type the base address of the target OData service in the address bar of **Add Service Reference** dialog.

    In this sample, we will type the address of the local Northwind OData service (within the same solution) as follows:

    `http://localhost:14944/NWDataService.svc/`

    Optionally, you can click on the **Go** button to preview the entity sets exposed by the target OData service (see the following screenshot).

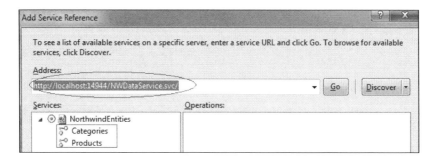

5. Click on the **OK** button (at the bottom of the dialog) to finish the proxy generation.

6. Inspect the auto-generated proxy code by double-clicking on the service reference item in **Visual Studio Class View** or **Object Browser**.

   The following is the declaration of the classes within the auto-generated proxy code:

```
public partial class NorthwindEntities : global::System.Data.
Services.Client.DataServiceContext
{
. . . . . .
}


[global::System.Data.Services.Common.EntitySetAttribute("Categori
es")] [global::System.Data.Services.Common.DataServiceKeyAttribute
("CategoryID")]
public partial class Category : global::System.ComponentModel.
INotifyPropertyChanged
{
. . . . . .
}


[global::System.Data.Services.Common.
EntitySetAttribute("Products")] [global::System.Data.Services.
Common.DataServiceKeyAttribute("ProductID")]
public partial class Product : global::System.ComponentModel.
INotifyPropertyChanged
{
. . . . . .
}
```

7. Use the generated proxy to query entity sets from the target service.

   The ListCategories function (see the following code snippet) creates an instance of the NorthwindEntities class and uses the Categories property to query all the Category entities.

```
static void ListCategories()
{
    var svcUri = new Uri("http://localhost:14944/NWDataService.
                         svc/");
    var svc = new NWDataSvc.NorthwindEntities(svcUri);
    foreach (var cate in svc.Categories)
    {
        Console.WriteLine(
            "CategoryID:{0}, CategoryName:{1}",
            cate.CategoryID,
            cate.CategoryName
            );
    }
}
```

And we can use a similar method to retrieve all the `Product` entities (see the following `ListProducts` function).

```
static void ListProducts()
{
        var svcUri = new Uri("http://localhost:14944/NWDataService.
                            svc/");
        var svc = new NWDataSvc.NorthwindEntities(svcUri);

        foreach (var prod in svc.Products)
        {
                // Load deferred property
                svc.LoadProperty(prod, "Category");
                Console.WriteLine(
                    "ID:{0}, Name:{1},Category:{2}, UnitPrice:{3},
                     UnitsInStock:{4}",
                    prod.ProductID,
                    prod.ProductName,
                    prod.Category.CategoryName,
                    prod.UnitPrice,
                    prod.UnitsInStock
                    );
        }
}
```

8. Use the generated proxy to invoke service operations against the target OData service (see the following code snippet).

```
static void ExecuteOperations()
{
        var svcUri = new Uri("http://localhost:14944/NWDataService.
                            svc/");
        var svc = new NWDataSvc.NorthwindEntities(svcUri);

        var operationUri =
            new Uri("GetProductCountByCategoryName?cateName=
                    'Beverages'", UriKind.Relative);

        var result = svc.Execute<int>(operationUri).First();

        Console.WriteLine("Result of 'GetProductCountByCategoryName'
                          operation: {0}", result);
}
```

How it works...

In this sample, the Visual Studio generated client proxy contains the following classes:

- The `NorthwindEntities` class
- The `Category` class
- The `Product` class

The `NorthwindEntities` class derives from the `DataServiceContext` class under the `System.Data.Services.Client` namespace. This class represents the service data context at the client side and holds one or more entity collection properties (such as the `Categories` and `Products` properties in this case) corresponding to the entity sets exposed in the target OData service.

At runtime, we first construct an instance of the data context class (by supplying the URL address of the target OData service) and then use **LINQ to Entity** methods to query or change the required entity objects. The data context type instance will track all the changes that have been made against the entity objects held by it until the client submits the changes to the server side. This is quite similar to how we use the ADO.NET Entity Framework data model to access a database directly.

One thing worth noticing is that for those entity types which have navigation properties (such as the `Products` property on `Category` entity type), we need to load the navigation properties before using them. This is because the WCF Data Service client library uses the **lazy loading** pattern for entity collections associated through navigation properties. To load such properties, we need to call the `LoadProperty` method of the data context class (the `NorthwindEntities` class in this case) so as to make sure the data in the navigation properties is ready for using.

As we've discussed in *Chapter 1, Building OData Services*, an OData service can expose not only data entities, but also service operations, which can return either entities or custom data objects. With a Visual Studio generated client proxy, we can also easily invoke service operations against the target OData service. In this recipe, we've demonstrated how we can use the `ExecuteOperations` function (of the OData proxy class) to invoke the `GetProductCountByCategoryName` operation against the sample Northwind OData service.

When constructing the data context object, we have to pass in the base address of the OData service. The WCF Data Service client library uses this address to locate the target OData service and perform all the network communication with the target service under the hood. By using Fiddler or other HTTP sniffer tools, we can find out the underlying HTTP requests (send by the WCF Data Service client library) for querying the entity sets (see the following screenshot).

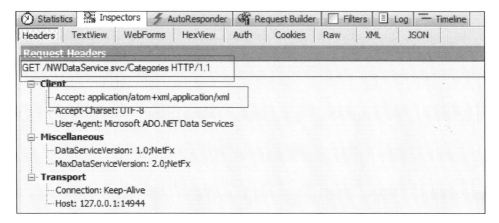

And after the service sends the response back in either XML or JSON format (see the following screenshot), the client library will also help deserialize the response content into the proper entity objects or custom data objects.

```
HTTP/1.1 200 OK
Server: ASP.NET Development Server/10.0.0.0
Date: Thu, 17 Nov 2011 14:42:35 GMT
X-AspNet-Version: 4.0.30319
DataServiceVersion: 1.0;
Content-Length: 122391
Cache-Control: no-cache
Content-Type: application/atom+xml;charset=utf-8
Connection: Close

<?xml version="1.0" encoding="utf-8" standalone="yes"?>
<feed xml:base="http://127.0.0.1:14944/NWDataService.svc/" xmlns:d="
  <title type="text">Categories</title>
  <id>http://127.0.0.1:14944/NWDataService.svc/Categories</id>
  <updated>2011-11-17T14:42:35Z</updated>
  <link rel="self" title="Categories" href="Categories" />
  <entry>
    <id>http://127.0.0.1:14944/NWDataService.svc/Categories(1)</id>
```

See also

▶ *Exploring an OData service through web browser* recipe

Generating OData client proxy via DataSvcUtil.exe tool

Although the Visual Studio Add Service Reference wizard is quite simple and convenient for generating a strong-typed OData client proxy, sometimes we still need to use command-line approaches for creating an OData client proxy. For example, when we need to integrate the OData proxy generation task into some automation jobs (such as the traditional batch execution files), using Visual Studio or other GUI-based tools will not work.

No problem! WCF Data Service has provided a built-in command-line tool (called `DataSvcUtil.exe`) for creating a OData client proxy. In this recipe, we will show you how to use the `DataSvcUtil.exe` tool to create a strong-typed client proxy for consuming OData services.

Getting ready

Make sure we have Microsoft .NET Framework 4.0 (or Visual Studio 2010) installed since the `DataSvcUtil.exe` tool is provided in Microsoft .NET framework 4.0 (which includes the WCF Data Service 4.0 runtime and tools). For an OData service, we will use the same Northwind sample service as we've used in the previous recipe (*Using Visual Studio to generate strong-typed OData client proxy*).

The source code for this recipe can be found in the `\ch02\ODataCmdClientSln\` directory.

How to do it...

1. Create a new ASP.NET web application which contains the WCF Data Service based on the Northwind database (using ADO.NET Entity Framework data model).

2. Create a new Console application as an OData client.

3. Locate the `DataSvcUtil.exe` tool and launch it in command-line prompt.

    The `DataSvcUtil.exe` tool can be found in the .NET Framework directory. For this sample case, it is located in `C:\Windows\Microsoft.NET\Framework\v4.0` (`C:\Windows\Microsoft.NET\Framework64\v4.0` for 64-bit version).

If you have Visual Studio 2010 installed, just start the Visual Studio Command Prompt through **Start | All Programs | Microsoft Visual Studio 2010 | Visual Studio Tools** menu and the `DataSvcUtil.exe` tool is available in the launched command-prompt (see the following screenshot).

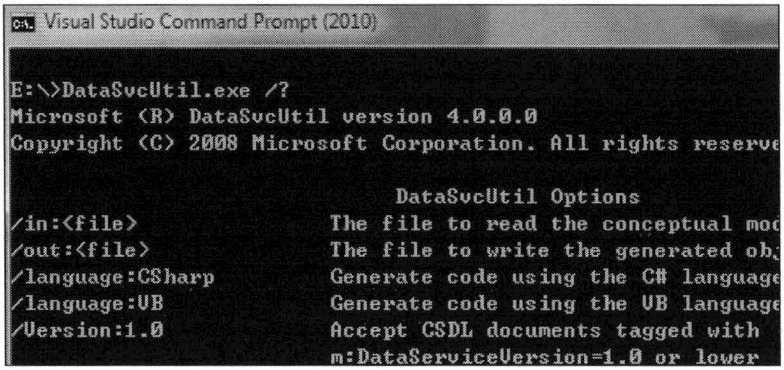

4. Use the **/?** option to view the command syntax and available options of the `DataSvcUtil.exe` tool (see the previous screenshot).

5. Execute `DataSvcUtil.exe` in the command prompt and supply the target service URL and output file path as arguments (see the following sample command).

```
DataSvcUtil.exe /out:"NWODataClient.cs" /uri:"http://
localhost:15035/NWDataService.svc/"
```

The following code snippet shows the main classes contained in the generated proxy code file:

```
namespace NorthwindModel
{
    public partial class NorthwindEntities : global::System.Data.
    Services.Client.DataServiceContext
    {......}

    [global::System.Data.Services.Common.DataServiceKeyAttribute
    ("CategoryID")]
    public partial class Category
    {......}

    [global::System.Data.Services.Common.DataServiceKeyAttribute
    ("ProductID")]
    public partial class Product
    {......}
```

6. Import the generated proxy code file into the client application.

7. Access the target OData service via the imported client proxy classes.

The following code snippet shows the sample function which queries the `Categories` entity set via the `DataSvcUtil.exe` generated client proxy classes:

```
static void QueryCategoriesEntitySet()
{
    var svcUri = new Uri("http://localhost:15035/NWDataService.
                          svc/");
    var ctx = new NorthwindModel.NorthwindEntities(svcUri);

    foreach (var category in ctx.Categories)
    {
        ctx.LoadProperty(category, "Products");
        Console.WriteLine("ID:{0}, Name:{1}, ProductCount:{2}",
            category.CategoryID,
            category.CategoryName,
            category.Products.Count
        );
    }
}
```

How it works...

When creating the OData client proxy in the command prompt, we supply the service base address and output code file path to the `DataSvcUtil.exe` command via the **/uri** and **/out** options. In fact, `DataSvcUtil.exe` also supports several other command line options. The following is the complete option list referenced from the MSDN document of the `DataSvcUtil.exe` tool.

Option	Description
`/dataservicecollection`	Specifies that the code required to bind objects to controls is also generated.
`/help` or `/?`	Displays command syntax and options for the tool.
`/in:<file>`	Specifies the .csdl or .edmx file or a directory where the file is located.
`/language:[VB|CSharp]`	Specifies the language for the generated source code files. The language defaults to C#.
`/nologo`	Suppresses the copyright message from displaying.
`/out:<file>`	Specifies the name of the source code file that contains the generated client data service classes.
`/uri:<string>`	The URI of the OData feed.
`/version:[1.0|2.0]`	Specifies the highest accepted version of OData. The version is determined based on the DataServiceVersion attribute of the DataService element in the returned data service metadata.

If we open the proxy code file generated by the `DataSvcUtil.exe` tool, we can find that it contains almost the same classes (the data context class and other related entity classes) such as those generated by the Visual Studio Add Service Reference wizard. Similarly, the code logic for accessing an OData service with the `DataSvcUtil.exe` generated proxy is equivalent to how we use the Visual Studio generated proxy.

There's more...

In addition to using OData service metadata (by supplying the service base address), `DataSvcUtil.exe` can also generate an OData client proxy via a given **conceptual schema definition language** (**CSDL**) or `.edmx` file. The latter is just the definition file used by the ADO. NET Entity Framework data model. The following command uses an `.edmx` file as input for generating an OData client proxy:

```
DataSvcUtil.exe /in:Northwind.edmx /out:NWDataServiceProxy.cs
```

This is very useful if the OData service uses ADO.NET Entity Framework as the data source and already has the `.edmx` data model file defined.

For more information about the `DataSvcUtil.exe` tool, you can refer to the following MSDN document:

WCF Data Service Client Utility (DataSvcUtil.exe) available at `http://msdn.microsoft.com/en-us/library/ee383989.aspx`

See also

▶   *Using Visual Studio to generate strong-typed OData client proxy* recipe

Editing and deleting data through WCF Data Service client library

We have learned how to query data and execute operations over an OData service via a strong-typed client proxy. But this is far from enough because in most data access applications, we need to deal with data editing and updating. With the help of the WCF Data Service client library (by using Visual Studio or `DataSvcUtil.exe` generated client proxy), it is quite convenient for us to manipulate (such as Create, Edit, Delete) OData service entities.

In this recipe, we will demonstrate how to perform common CRUD operations against OData service entities.

Getting ready

In this recipe, we will create an OData client, which uses a Visual Studio generated client proxy to access and update the Northwind OData service. The client application first creates a new `Product` entity and adds it into the `Products` entity set, then it makes some changes on the created entity, and finally it deletes the entity from the entity set.

The source code for this recipe can be found in the `\ch02\ODataEditUpdateSln\` directory.

How to do it...

1. Create a new ASP.NET web application which contains the WCF Data Service based on the Northwind database (using ADO.NET Entity Framework data model).

   Make sure we have enabled all access rights for all entities in the `InitializeService` function of the WCF Data Service class (see the following code snippet).

   ```
   public static void InitializeService(DataServiceConfiguration
   config)
   {
       . . . . . .
       config.SetEntitySetAccessRule("*", EntitySetRights.All);
   }
   ```

2. Create a new Console application as OData client.

3. Create the OData client proxy by using the Visual Studio Add Service Reference wizard in the Console application.

4. Add the function for creating a new entity object against the target OData entity set.

   The following `CreateNewProductEntity` function uses the strong-typed proxy to create a new `Product` entity object and add it into the `Products` entity set:

   ```
   static void CreateNewProductEntity()
   {
       var svcUri = new Uri("http://localhost:52150/NWDataService.
                              svc/");
       var ctx = new NWDataSvc.NorthwindEntities(svcUri);

       var id = DateTime.Now.Ticks;

       // Call factory method to create new entity instance
       var newProduct = NWDataSvc.Product.CreateProduct
           (0, "NewProduct_" + id, false);
       newProduct.CategoryID = 1;
       newProduct.QuantityPerUnit = "5 x 5";
   ```

```
newProduct.ReorderLevel = 3;
newProduct.SupplierID = 1;
newProduct.UnitPrice = 33;
newProduct.UnitsInStock = 22;
newProduct.UnitsOnOrder = 11;

// Insert the new entity and submit the changes
ctx.AddObject("Products", newProduct);
ctx.SaveChanges();
}
```

5. Add the function for modifying the entity object we have created in the previous step.

   The following `EditProductEntity` function first finds the `Product` entity we created earlier and updates the `UnitPrice` property of the obtained entity object:

```
static void EditProductEntity()
{
    var svcUri = new Uri("http://localhost:52150/NWDataService.
                             svc/");
    var ctx = new NWDataSvc.NorthwindEntities(svcUri);

    var product = ctx.Products.Where(p => p.ProductName.
        StartsWith("NewProduct")).FirstOrDefault();

    if (product != null)
    {
        product.UnitPrice = product.UnitPrice + 10;

        ctx.UpdateObject(product);
        ctx.SaveChanges();
    }
}
```

6. Add the function for deleting the entity object we have manipulated in the previous step.

   The following `DeleteProductEntity` function uses the `DeleteObject` method of the data context class to remove the `Product` entity object we have manipulated in previous steps:

```
static void DeleteProductEntity()
{
    var svcUri = new Uri("http://localhost:52150/NWDataService.
                             svc/");
    var ctx = new NWDataSvc.NorthwindEntities(svcUri);
```

```
var product = ctx.Products.Where(p => p.ProductName.
    StartsWith("NewProduct")).FirstOrDefault();

if (product != null)
{
    ctx.DeleteObject(product);
    ctx.SaveChanges();
}
}
```

How it works...

As the previous sample code demonstrates, when using the WCF Data Service client library based OData proxy to manipulate entity objects, we will use the following general process:

1. Create the data context object against the target service.

2. Locate the entity objects we want to manipulate.

3. Call the `AddObject`, `UpdateObject`, and `DeleteObject` methods (against the data context object) to perform **CUD** operations for the target entity objects.

4. Call the `SaveChanges` method against the data context object to submit all the changes we have made.

When we make changes to entity objects through the data context object, it will help track and record all the changes that have been made. When we call the `SaveChanges` method, the data context object will send all changes it has recorded (by translating the changes to the underlying HTTP requests) to the target OData service. By default, the data context object will send the request for each change one by one. However, if you want to submit all recorded changes in a single HTTP request (such as a batch update), you can call the override version of the `SaveChanges` method, which takes an additional parameter of `SaveChangesOptions` enum type. For example:

```
ctx.SaveChanges(SaveChangesOptions.Batch)
```

With this batch style change submission, we can save the HTTP communication round-trips between the service and client.

 Even if you submit changes in batch manner, the WCF Data Service client library will make sure the batch request keeps all the contained change operations in order that the server side will update the entity objects in the same order as the client side.

In the sample functions, we always obtain the entity object by querying the container entity collection on the data context object. Actually, this is not necessary. We can directly construct an entity instance (which does exist in the target OData service) and then use the `AttachTo` method to bind it with the data context object (see the following code snippet).

```
var svcUri = new Uri("http://localhost:52150/NWDataService.svc/");
var ctx = new NWDataSvc.NorthwindEntities(svcUri);

// Attach an existing entity object
var prod = NWDataSvc.Product.CreateProduct(78,
"NewProduct_634726951783606513", false);
    ctx.AttachTo("Products", prod);
// data context will start tracking the prod object now
```

Likewise, if we want to prevent an entity object from being tracked by the data context object, we can use the `Detach` method to dismiss the relationship between them (see the following code snippet).

```
// Detach an entity object from the data context object
    ctx.Detach(prod);
// data context will no longer strack the prod object now
```

See also

> ▶ *Using Visual Studio to generate strong-typed OData client proxy* recipe

Accessing OData service via WebRequest class

So far we have tried consuming an OData service through strong-typed proxy and web browser; the former is a pure programmatic approach relying on the WCF Data Service client library while the latter relies on the web browser to handle the underlying raw HTTP request/ response. However, sometimes we might need to combine the two approaches. For example, what if we want to consume an OData service in the .NET application but also want to directly handle the raw HTTP request/response messages (without using the strong-typed client proxy)? This would also give us maximum control over the underlying HTTP message exchange of the OData service communication.

In this recipe, we will take the .NET `WebRequest` class as an example and demonstrate how we can consume an OData service by manually handling the raw HTTP request/response messages.

Getting ready

In this sample, we will build a .NET Console application, which uses the `WebRequest` class to communicate with the Northwind OData service. demonstration purposes, the following two data access cases will be covered:

▶ Query all the entities in the `Products` entity set and display them

▶ Create a new `Product` entity and insert it into the `Products` entity set

The source code for this recipe can be found in the `\ch02\WebRequestClientSln\` directory.

How to do it...

1. Create a new ASP.NET web application which contains the WCF Data Service based on the Northwind database (using ADO.NET Entity Framework data model).

2. Create a new Console application as an OData client.

   Make sure the `System.Xml.Linq` assembly (which contains the necessary LINQ to XML classes) is referenced in the project.

3. Create a new function that queries all the `Product` entities from the `Products` entity set (see the following code snippet).

```
static void QueryProductsByWebRequest()
{
    // Generate the OData request Uri
    var svcUri = new Uri("http://localhost:47568/NWDataService.
                            svc/");
    var productsUri = new Uri(svcUri, "Products");

    // Create WebRequest object
    var req = WebRequest.Create(productsUri) as HttpWebRequest;
    req.Method = "GET";

    // Retrieve the query response and load it as Xml
    var rep = req.GetResponse() as HttpWebResponse;
    var doc = XDocument.Load(rep.GetResponseStream());
    rep.Close();

    // Parse the response XML with LINQ to XML
    var nsDefault = XNamespace.Get("http://www.w3.org/2005/Atom");
    var nsMetadata = XNamespace.Get("http://schemas.microsoft.com/
                            ado/2007/08/dataservices/
                            metadata");
```

```
            var nsData = XNamespace.Get("http://schemas.microsoft.com/
                                         ado/2007/08/dataservices");

            var elmsProducts = from p in doc.Descendants(nsDefault +
                                                         "entry")
                        select p.Descendants(nsMetadata +
                                             "properties").First();

        Console.WriteLine("There are {0} products.", elmsProducts.
                          Count());
        foreach (var elmProduct in elmsProducts)
        {
            var pID = elmProduct.Descendants(nsData + "ProductID").
                First().Value;
            var pName = elmProduct.Descendants(nsData +
                "ProductName").First().Value;
            var cateID = elmsProducts.Descendants(nsData +
                "CategoryID").First().Value;

            Console.WriteLine("ID:{0}, Name:{1}, CategoryID:{2}",
                pID,
                pName,
                cateID
                );
        }
    }
```

4. Create a new function that adds a new `Product` entity into the `Products` entity set
   (see the following code snippet).

```
static void CreateProductByWebRequest()
{
    // Compose OData request Uri(for creating entity)
    var svcUri = new Uri("http://localhost:47568/NWDataService.
        svc/");
    var productsUri = new Uri(svcUri, "Products");

    // Create WebRequest object(and initialize the proper headers)
    var req = WebRequest.Create(productsUri) as HttpWebRequest;
    req.Method = "POST";
    req.Headers.Add("DataServiceVersion", "1.0;NetFx");
    req.Headers.Add("MaxDataServiceVersion", "2.0;NetFx");
    req.Accept = "application/atom+xml,application/xml";
    req.ContentType = "application/atom+xml";

    // Construct the Xml element for the new entity
```

```
var elmNewProduct = CreateXElementForNewProduct();

// Write the Xml content into request stream of WebRequest
using (var reqWriter = XmlWriter.Create(req.
    GetRequestStream()))
{
    elmNewProduct.WriteTo(reqWriter);
}

// Retrieve and process the HTTP response
var rep = req.GetResponse() as HttpWebResponse;
if (rep.StatusCode == HttpStatusCode.Created )
{
    Console.WriteLine("New Product created at {0}", rep.
        Headers["Location"]);
}
else
{
    Console.WriteLine("New Product creation failed");
}
}
```

To make the code more readable, we have encapsulated the code for generating the new entity's XML fragment in a separate helper function (see the following code snippet).

```
static XElement CreateXElementForNewProduct()
{
    // Compose the HTTP request body via LINQ to XML
    var nsDefault = XNamespace.Get("http://www.w3.org/2005/Atom");
    var nsMetadata = XNamespace.Get("http://schemas.microsoft.com/
        ado/2007/08/dataservices/metadata");
    var nsData = XNamespace.Get("http://schemas.microsoft.com/
        ado/2007/08/dataservices");

    var id = DateTime.Now.Ticks;
    var elmProperties = new XElement(nsMetadata + "properties",
        new XElement(nsData + "ProductName", "NewProduct_" + id),
        new XElement(nsData + "CategoryID", "1"),
        new XElement(nsData + "Discontinued", "false"),
        new XElement(nsData + "QuantityPerUnit", "5 x 5"),
        new XElement(nsData + "ReorderLevel", "3"),
        new XElement(nsData + "SupplierID", "1"),
        new XElement(nsData + "UnitPrice", "33"),
        new XElement(nsData + "UnitsInStock", "22"),
        new XElement(nsData + "UnitsOnOrder", "11")
```

```
        );

    var elmCreateProduct = new XElement(nsDefault + "entry",
        new XElement(nsDefault + "title", "New Product Entity"),
        new XElement(nsDefault + "id"),
        new XElement(nsDefault + "updated", DateTime.Now),
        new XElement(nsDefault + "author"),
        new XElement(nsDefault + "content",
            new XAttribute("type", "application/xml"),
            elmProperties
        )
    );

    return elmCreateProduct;
}
```

How it works...

As shown in the previous sample functions, when using the `WebRequest` class to query an OData service, we can simply send an HTTP GET request to the target service by supplying the proper query URI address. By default, WCF Data Service will return response data in Atom XML format, and then we can choose our preferred XML processing components to parse it. Here we use the .NET LINQ to XML classes to parse the query response since it is quite simple and efficient for in-memory XML data manipulation.

When creating a new entity object (in the `CreateProductByWebRequest` function) via the WebRequest class, we need to send an HTTP POST request. And things get a bit more complicated here because we need to not only specify the request URI, but also supply the XML content which represents the entity object we want to create (in the HTTP request body). Like the query case, we use LINQ to XML to construct the XML content of the new `Product` entity instance.

Although LINQ to XML API is quite convenient for XML manipulation, it is still quite complex for us to construct an entire OData request message from scratch (especially for some more complicated data manipulation cases). In real-word scenarios that we need to manually construct OData request messages, we can first use Fiddler or other HTTP sniffer tools to capture the request/response messages generated by strong-typed OData client proxy (based on WCF Data Service client library). Then, we can manually compose the raw request messages based on the captured sample messages.

There's more...

The sample functions here handle the OData request/response in XML format, then how shall we handle JSON-format raw OData request/response messages in a .NET application?

Well, one simple way is to handle JSON-format data through the .NET data serialization/deserialization mechanism. The following are two JSON-specific data serializer classes we can leverage in .NET Framework 4.0:

- The `System.Runtime.Serialization.Json.DataContractJsonSerializer` class, which is included in the `System.Runtime.Serialization` assembly

- The `System.Web.Script.Serialization.JavaScriptSerializer` class, which is included in the `System.Web.Extensions` assembly

Like other .NET serialization engines (such as XML and binary), we need to define some classes, which can be mapped to the JSON-format response or request messages that we will handle. For more information about JSON serialization in .NET, you can refer to the following MSDN reference:

Stand-Alone JSON Serialization available at `http://msdn.microsoft.com/en-us/library/bb412170.aspx`

See also

- *Using Visual Studio to generate strong-typed OData client proxy* recipe

Executing OData queries in an asynchronous manner

After discussing several cases on consuming an OData service in client applications, we can find that the WCF Data Service client library based client proxy makes an OData service quite easy and straightforward to use. We simply construct the data context object and perform LINQ to Entity queries (or call the `Execute<T>` or other methods) against it so as to retrieve the entities from the target service. However, such kind of queries are executed by the WCF Data Service client library in a synchronous manner, which means the client application needs to wait for the current query request/response to complete before continuing with the execution of the next query (or other application code).

A synchronous service call might cause some performance and user experience issue (especially in GUI applications) since there will be response latency for data exchanged between the client and the server. Then, how can we improve the user interaction experience when presenting data from an OData service which might have a potential response latency issue? The answer is to use asynchronous operations for service queries.

In this recipe, we will show you how to make OData service queries in an asynchronous manner so as to keep the front application UI fully responsive.

Getting ready

In this recipe, we will build a .NET Windows Form application, which loads some `Product` entities from the Northwind OData service and uses a `DataGridView` control to present the entity objects. The following screenshot shows the main user interface of the sample application:

As the previous screenshot shows, there are three buttons on the main window, they are:

▶ **Load Products Sync** button: Load all `Product` entities synchronously and display them

▶ **Load Products Async** button: Load all `Product` entities asynchronously and display them

▶ **Load Specific Products Async** button: Load some specific `Product` entities asynchronously and display them

The source code for this recipe can be found in the `\ch02\AsyncODataClientSln\` directory.

How to do it...

1. Create a new ASP.NET web application which contains the WCF Data Service based on the Northwind database (using ADO.NET Entity Framework data model).

2. Create a new .NET **Windows Forms Application** (see the following screenshot) as the OData client.

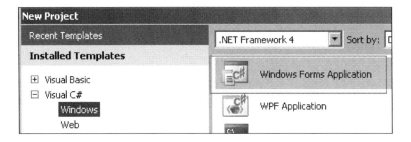

3. Add three `Button` controls and one `DataGridView` control on the main window surface and adjust the layout according to the screenshot in the *Getting ready* section.

4. Create the OData client proxy by using the Visual Studio Add Service Reference wizard in the Console application.

5. Add the `Click` event handler for the **Load Products Sync** button (see the following `btnLoadSync_Click` function).

```
private void btnLoadSync_Click(object sender, EventArgs e)
{
    var svcUri = new Uri("http://localhost:5558/NWDataService.
        svc/");
    var ctx = new NWDataSvc.NorthwindEntities(svcUri);

    gridProducts.DataSource = ctx.Products.ToList();
    gridProducts.Refresh();
}
```

6. Add the `Click` event handler for the **Load Products Async** button (see the following `btnLoadAsync_Click` function).

```
private void btnLoadAsync_Click(object sender, EventArgs e)
{
    gridProducts.DataSource = null;

    var svcUri = new Uri("http://localhost:5558/NWDataService.
        svc/");
    var ctx = new NWDataSvc.NorthwindEntities(svcUri);

    // Build the query against the entire Products entity set
    var query = ctx.Products;

    // Start async query execution (supply the query and callback
    // parameters)
    query.BeginExecute(
        LoadProductsAsyncComplete,
        query);
}
```

The `BeginExecute<T>` function used here requires a callback function parameter, which will be invoked when the asynchronous operation call finishes. The following code snippet shows the callback function (and its dependency functions):

```
private void LoadProductsAsyncComplete(IAsyncResult ar)
{
    var query = ar.AsyncState as DataServiceQuery<NWDataSvc.
        Product>;

    // Retrieve the query result
```

```
        var result = query.EndExecute(ar).ToList();

        // Update the DataGridView in main UI thread
        this.Invoke(
            new EventHandler(OnDataSourceLoaded),
            result,
            EventArgs.Empty
        );
    }

    private void OnDataSourceLoaded(object obj, EventArgs e)
    {
        gridProducts.DataSource = obj;
    }
```

7. Add the `Click` event handler for the **Load Specific Products Async** button (see the following `btnLoadSpecificAsync_Click` function).

```
    private void btnLoadSpecificAsync_Click(object sender, EventArgs
    e)
    {
        gridProducts.DataSource = null;

        var svcUri = new Uri("http://localhost:5558/NWDataService.
            svc/");
        var ctx = new NWDataSvc.NorthwindEntities(svcUri);

        // Compose the query via LINQ to Entity code
        var query = (from p in ctx.Products
                        where p.UnitPrice> 50
                        select p) as DataServiceQuery<NWDataSvc.
                            Product>;

        // Start async query execution
        query.BeginExecute(
            LoadProductsAsyncComplete,
            query);
    }
```

The `btnLoadSpecificAsync_Click` function uses the same callback function (`LoadProductsAsyncComplete`) used by the `btnLoadAsync_Click` function.

How it works...

In the sample OData client, we use three buttons to demonstrate different data loading approaches. By clicking on the **Load Products Sync** button, the application UI will get frozen since the OData service query call blocks the main UI thread. This behavior will not occur when we click on the other two buttons since both of them use asynchronous operations to query the OData service.

The WCF Data Service client library uses the `DataServiceQuery<T>` class for executing asynchronous OData query operations. The `DataServiceQuery<T>` class takes a generic parameter, which tells the runtime the kind of data we want to query (used in return value). In order to start and end the asynchronous operation call, we need to invoke the `BeginExecute` and `EndExecute` methods of the `DataServiceQuery<T>` class and this *Begin/End* method signature is aligned to the standard .NET Asynchronous Programming Model. Refer to the following MSDN reference for more information:

Asynchronous Programming Overview available at `http://msdn.microsoft.com/en-us/library/ms228963.aspx`

In the `LoadProductsAsyncComplete` function (the asynchronous callback function), we use the `Invoke` method of the `Form` class to populate the retrieved OData entities on the `DataGridView` control. This is necessary because the asynchronous callback function is called in a specific thread (instead of the main UI thread).

Therefore, we need to use the `Control.Invoke` method to marshal any UI-related code to the main UI thread.

There's more...

In this recipe, we build the query object (of the `DataServiceQuery<T>` class) by using LINQ to Entity code against the entity set properties of the data context object (of the client proxy). However, we're not limited to this approach. We can also manually construct a `DataServiceQuery<T>` object by supplying the query URI and callback function as parameters. The following code snippet shows how we can use this alternative approach to query the `Product` entities associated with a `Category` entity.

```
var svcUri = new Uri("http://localhost:5558/NWDataService.svc/");
var ctx = new NWDataSvc.NorthwindEntities(svcUri);

var productsUri = new Uri("http://localhost:5558/NWDataService.svc/
    Categories(1)/Products");

ctx.BeginExecute<NWDataSvc.Product>(
    productsUri,
    new AsyncCallback(LoadDataViaUriComplete),
    ctx);
```

See also

▸ *Using Visual Studio to generate strong-typed OData client proxy* recipe

Filtering OData query results by using query options

The OData protocol has defined many system query options, which can be used to control the format, number, order, and other characteristics of OData query responses. WCF Data Service has implemented most of the query options defined in the OData protocol. Applications which use a strong-typed OData proxy (based on the WCF Data Service client library) can use the built-in extension methods or LINQ operators to apply query options on OData service queries.

In this recipe, we will go through some commonly used OData query options and demonstrate how to use them in WCF Data Service client library based OData clients.

Getting ready

In this recipe, we will use the Northwind OData service as an example and demonstrate the following OData query options by performing some queries against the `Categories`, `Products`, and `Customers` entity sets:

▸ **Orderby** query option

▸ **Top** query option

▸ **Skip** query option

▸ **Filter** query option

▸ **Expand** query option

▸ **Select** query option

Also, in each step which demonstrates a query option, we will provide both the raw query URI syntax and the .NET code (based on the WCF Data Service client library) for using the query option.

The source code for this recipe can be found in the `\ch02\ODataQueryOptionsSln\` directory.

How to do it...

1. Create a new ASP.NET web application which contains the WCF Data Service based on the Northwind database (using ADO.NET Entity Framework data model).

2. Create a new Console application as an OData client.

3. Create the OData client proxy by using the Visual Studio Add Service Reference wizard in the Console application.

4. Use the `OrderBy` option to query all the `Category` entities and sort them by the `CategoryName` property.

   The following is the raw URI string for querying all the `Category` entities (sorted by the `CategoryName` property):

   ```
   NWDataService.svc/Categories()?$orderby=CategoryName desc
   ```

   The following code snippet shows the corresponding .NET code based on the WCF Data Service client library:

   ```
   static void QueryCategoriesViaOrderbyOption()
   {
       var ctx = GetDataContextInstance();

       var categories = from c in ctx.Categories
                        orderby c.CategoryName descending
                        select c;

       foreach (var c in categories)
       {
           . . . . . .
       }
   }
   ```

5. Use the `Top` option to query the first three entities from the `Categories` entity set.

   The following is the raw URI string of this query:

   ```
   NWDataService.svc/Categories()?$orderby=CategoryName desc&$top=3
   ```

   The following code snippet shows the corresponding .NET code based on the WCF Data Service client library:

   ```
   static void QueryCategoriesViaTopOption()
   {
       var ctx = GetDataContextInstance();

       var categories = (from c in ctx.Categories
                        orderby c.CategoryName descending
                        select c).Take(3);

       foreach (var c in categories)
       {
           . . . . . .
       }
   }
   ```

6. Use the `Skip` option to query all the `Category` entities and bypass the first three entities.

The following is the raw URI string of this query:

```
NWDataService.svc/Categories()?$orderby=CategoryName desc&$skip=3
```

The following code snippet shows the corresponding .NET code based on the WCF Data Service client library:

```
static void QueryCategoriesViaSkipOption()
{
    var ctx = GetDataContextInstance();

    var categories = (from c in ctx.Categories
                        orderby c.CategoryName descending
                        select c).Skip(3);

    foreach (var c in categories)
    {
        ......
    }
}
```

7. Use the `Filter` option to restrict the entities queried from the `Categories` entity set (by applying filter rules against the `CategoryName` and `CategoryID` properties).

The following is the raw URI string of this query:

```
NWDataService.svc/Categories()?$filter=startswith(CategoryName,
    'Con') and ((CategoryID mod 2) eq 0)
```

The following code snippet shows the corresponding .NET code based on the WCF Data Service client library:

```
static void QueryCategoriesViaFilterOption()
{
    var ctx = GetDataContextInstance();

    var categories = (from c in ctx.Categories
                        where c.CategoryName.StartsWith("Con") &&
                            c.CategoryID %2 == 0
                        select c);

    foreach (var c in categories)
    {
        ......
    }
}
```

8. Use the `Expand` option to preload the associated `Product` entities (via the `Products` navigation property) when querying the first two `Category` entities.

The following is the raw URI string of this query:

```
NWDataService.svc/Categories()?$top=2&$expand=Products
```

The following code snippet shows the corresponding .NET code based on the WCF Data Service client library:

```
static void QueryProductsFromCategoryViaExpandOption()
{
    var ctx = GetDataContextInstance();

    var query = ctx.Categories.Take(2) as
        DataServiceQuery<NWDataSvc.Category>;
    var categories = query.Expand("Products");

    foreach (var c in categories)
    {
        Console.WriteLine("Category ID:{0}, Name:{1}",
            c.CategoryID,
            c.CategoryName
            );
        foreach (var p in c.Products)
            Console.WriteLine("\tProduct Name:{0}",
                p.ProductName);
    }
}
```

9. Use the `Select` option to only return a subset of the `Customer` entity properties (include the `CustomerID`, `CompanyName`, `Country`, and `Phone` properties) when querying the `Customers` entity set.

The following is the raw URI string of this query:

```
NWDataService.svc/Customers()?$select=CustomerID,CompanyName,Country,Phone
```

The following code snippet shows the corresponding .NET code based on the WCF Data Service client library:

```
static void QueryCustomersViaSelectOption()
{
    var ctx = GetDataContextInstance();

    var customers = from c in ctx.Customers
                    select new
                    {
                        Name = c.CustomerID,
```

```
                            Company = c.CompanyName,
                            Country = c.Country,
                            Phone = c.Phone
                };


        foreach (var c in customers)
        {
            . . . . . .
        }
    }
```

How it works...

Now, let's have a look at the query options (demonstrated in the previous sample functions) one by one.

The `OrderBy` query option helps sort the entity objects (based on the specified properties) from the target entity set. The OData protocol uses the `$orderby` query string parameter to represent this option in the raw URI string. When using the WCF Data Service client library based proxy, we can use the `orderby` LINQ operator to apply this query option.

The `Top` query options help take the first N entity objects from the target entity set being queried. The OData protocol uses the `$top` query string parameter to represent this option in the raw URI string. When using the WCF Data Service client library based proxy, we can use the `Take` extension method in LINQ query to apply this query option.

The `Skip` query option helps bypass the first N entity objects and take the remaining ones from the target entity set being queried. The OData protocol uses the `$skip` query string parameter to represent this option in the raw URI string. When using the WCF Data Service client library based proxy, we can use the `Skip` extension method in LINQ query to apply this query option.

The `Filter` query option helps take the entity objects (from the target entity set), which satisfy the predicate expression (specified in the option value). The OData protocol uses the `$filter` query string parameter to represent this option in the raw URI string. The predicate expression supports logical or arithmetic operators in its own syntax. Refer to the following link for more information:

`http://www.odata.org/documentation/uri-conventions#FilterSystemQueryOption`

When using the WCF Data Service client library based proxy, we can use the `where` clause in the LINQ query to apply this query option.

The `Expand` query option helps indicate that the associated entity collection (via the `navigation` property) should be preloaded in the same query request against the main entity set being queried. The OData protocol uses the `$expand` query string parameter to represent this option in the raw URI string. When using the WCF Data Service client library based proxy, we can use the `Expand` extension method in LINQ query to apply this query option.

The `Select` query option helps project the properties of the entity objects from the target entity set being queried (so that only a subset of all entity properties will be returned in query response). The OData protocol uses the `$select` query string parameter to represent this option in the raw URI string, and all required properties are specified as the parameter value (separated by comma). When using the WCF Data Service client library based proxy, we can use the `select` clause in the LINQ query to apply this query option.

As we can see, when querying an OData service with the WCF Data Service client library based proxy, all the previous OData query options can be applied with their corresponding LINQ query operator/clause or extension methods. However, if you prefer specifying query options via their raw query string formats, you can use the `AddQueryOptions` method of the data context class instead (see the following code snippet).

```
var ctx = GetDataContextInstance();

var categories = from c in ctx.Categories
                    .AddQueryOption("$top", 6)
                    .AddQueryOption("$filter", "CategoryID gt 5")
                    .AddQueryOption("$orderby", "CategoryID desc")
                    select c;
```

There's more...

In addition to the six query options we mentioned here, the OData protocol has defined many other options. You can get the complete list from the following link:

System Query Options available at `http://www.odata.org/documentation/uri-conventions#SystemQueryOptions`

As for the WCF Data Service client library, although it can translate most LINQ query operators and extension methods to their corresponding format in the raw OData query URI, there are still quite a few LINQ specific query syntaxes that are not supported. For more information about how WCF Data Service runtime deals with LINQ query code, you can refer to the following MSDN article:

LINQ Considerations (WCF Data Services) available at `http://msdn.microsoft.com/en-us/library/ee622463`

See also

▸ *Exploring an OData service through web browser* recipe

▸ *Using Visual Studio to generate strong-typed OData client proxy* recipe

Dealing with server-side paged entity sets from WCF Data Service

In the previous recipe, we've gone through the built-in query options supported by OData for controlling the entity collection returned from OData service queries. By using the Skip and Top query options, we can easily implement data paging functionality in OData client applications and such kind of paging is completely controlled by the client-side query code. However, WCF Data Service also introduces a **server-side paging** feature, which can help control the maximum number of entity objects a single OData query can return.

In this recipe, we will introduce how to deal with entity sets, which have enabled server-side paging (exposed from WCF Data Service) in an OData client.

Getting ready

The sample case here will still use the Northwind OData service. For the service, it should at least expose the Orders entity set and enable the server-side paging restriction on it. This can be done by calling the SetEntitySetPageSize method (of the DataServiceConfiguration class) in the WCF Data Service's InitializeService function (see the following code snippet).

```
public static void InitializeService(DataServiceConfiguration config)
{
    ......
    config.SetEntitySetAccessRule("*", EntitySetRights.All);

    config.SetEntitySetPageSize("Orders", 3);
}
```

For demonstration purposes, we will first query the Orders entity set in the normal way (without considering the server-side paging restriction). Then, we will use both the DataServiceQuery<T> and DataServiceCollection<T> classes to perform the same query, but will retrieve all the entity objects page by page (according to the server-side paging restriction).

The source code for this recipe can be found in the \ch02\ODataPagingSln\ directory.

How to do it...

1. Create a new ASP.NET web application which contains the WCF Data Service based on the Northwind database (using ADO.NET Entity Framework data model).

2. Create a new Console application as the OData client.

3. Create the OData client proxy by using the Visual Studio Add Service Reference wizard in the Console application.

4. Add a function to query all `Order` entities belonging to a specific `Customer` entity without caring about server-side paging restriction (see the following code snippet).

```
static void LoadOrdersNormally()
{
    var ctx = GetDataServiceContext();

    var orders = from o in ctx.Orders
                 where o.CustomerID == "ANTON"
                 select o;

    foreach (var order in orders) PrintOrderObject(order);
}
```

5. Add a function that uses the `DataServiceQuery<T>` class to query all the `Order` entities that belong to a specific `Customer` entity and loads all paged results (see the following code snippet).

```
static void LoadOrdersPageByPage()
{
    var ctx = GetDataServiceContext();

    var query = (   from o in ctx.Orders
                    where o.CustomerID == "ANTON"
                    select o
                ) as DataServiceQuery<NWDataSvc.Order>;

    var response = query.Execute() as QueryOperationResponse<NWDat
        aSvc.Order>;

    DataServiceQueryContinuation<NWDataSvc.Order> pageCursor =
        null;
    do
    {
        if (pageCursor != null)
        {
            response = ctx.Execute<NWDataSvc.Order>(pageCursor);
        }

        // Print orders in current page
        foreach (var order in response) PrintOrderObject(order);
```

```
            pageCursor = response.GetContinuation();

        } while (pageCursor != null);
    }
```

6. Add a function that uses the `DataServiceCollection<T>` class to load all paged results of the same OData query used in the previous step (see the following code snippet).

```
static void LoadOrdersViaDataServiceCollection()
{
    var orders = new DataServiceCollection<NWDataSvc.Order>(
        _ctx.Orders.Where(o=>o.CustomerID == "ANTON")
        );

    while (true)
    {
        if(orders.Continuation == null) break;

        orders.Load(_ctx.Execute<NWDataSvc.Order>(orders.
            Continuation));
    }

    // Print all orders loaded in the collection
    foreach (var order in orders) PrintOrderObject(order);
}
```

How it works...

In the previous sample, the `LoadOrdersNormally` function doesn't contain any server-side paging related code logic. By using this function, we can only get at the most one page of `Order` entities (according to the page size configured at server side) from the entire query result. The `LoadOrdersPageByPage` function uses the `DataServiceQuery<T>` class to perform the query and it has included the code logic for handling entity collection (returned as query result), which has been paged at server side. The `LoadOrdersViaDataServiceCollection` function instead uses the `DataServiceCollection<T>` class for loading the server-side paged query result. Both the functions use a `while` loop to check for remaining pages (represented by the `DataServiceQueryContinuation<T>` class) of entity objects and load them one by one.

Actually, we can treat the `DataServiceQueryContinuation<T>` object like a *cursor* returned by the OData service. The OData client can use this cursor to retrieve all the entity objects in the query result page by page. If we use the web browser to execute the OData query used in the previous code, we can find that the `DataServiceQueryContinuation<T>` object is represented as an Atom `link` entry in the query response (see the following screenshot); and the link entry provides the complete URI address for fetching the next page of entities.

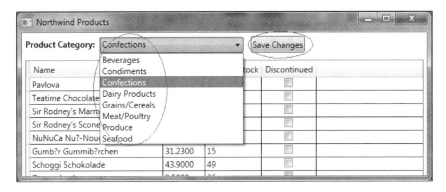

```
     http://localhost:38517/NWDataService.svc/Customers('ANTON')/Orders
localhost                    ×
File   Edit   View   Favorites   Tools   Help
     <id>http://localhost:38517/NWDataService.svc/Customers('ANTON')/Orders</id>
     <updated>2011-11-24T13:34:38Z</updated>
     <link rel="self" title="Orders" href="Orders" />
   + <entry>
   + <entry>
   + <entry>
     <link rel="next" href="http://localhost:38517/NWDataService.svc/Customers
       ('ANTON')/Orders?$skiptoken=10535" />
   </feed>
```

See also

> ▸ _Filtering OData query results by using query options_ recipe

Performing WPF data binding with OData service data

We have discussed several cases of how to consume an OData service by using various kind of client components and how to use built-in options to perform customized OData service queries. In this recipe, we will take the opportunity to introduce how we can use an OData service as a data source to perform data binding in WPF applications.

Getting ready

The sample WPF application here will present Categories and Products information retrieved from the Northwind OData service. Users can select a Category to view and edit the corresponding Products. The following screenshot shows the main UI of the WPF application:

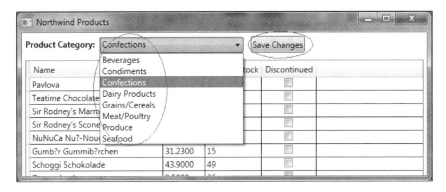

The source code for this recipe can be found in the `\ch02\WPFDataBindingSln\` directory.

How to do it...

1. Create a new ASP.NET web application which contains the WCF Data Service based on the Northwind database (using ADO.NET Entity Framework data model).

   The service should at least expose the `Categories` and `Products` entity sets.

2. Create a new **WPF Application** (see the following screenshot) as the OData client.

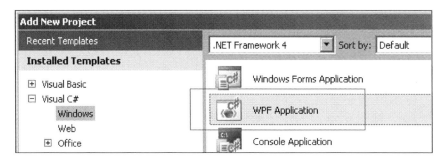

3. Create the OData client proxy by using the Visual Studio Add Service Reference wizard.

4. Compose the application UI by editing the XAML file of the main window.

   The main window contains the following WPF control elements:

   - A **Combobox** element for selecting the Category item

   - A **DataGrid** element for presenting Products that belong to the selected Category

   - A **Button** element for saving the changes

   The following is the complete XAML template of the main window:

```
<Window x:Class="WPFClientApp.MainWindow"
        xmlns="http://schemas.microsoft.com/winfx/2006/xaml/
           presentation"
        xmlns:x="http://schemas.microsoft.com/winfx/2006/xaml"
        Title="Northwind Products" Height="350" Width="525"
        Loaded="Window_Loaded">
    <Grid>
        <StackPanel Name="RootPanel" >
            <StackPanel Orientation="Horizontal" >
                <TextBlock Name="lblCategory"
                        Height="21" Margin="5,8,0,0"
                            Width="104" FontWeight="Bold"
                        Text="Product Category:"   />
                <ComboBox Name="lstCategories"
                        Height="23" Margin="5,5,5,0" Width="209"
```

```
                        ItemsSource="{Binding}" DisplayMemberPath
                            ="CategoryName"
                        SelectionChanged="lstCategories_
                            SelectionChanged" />
                <Button Name="btnSave" Margin="5,5,103,0"
                        Content="Save Changes"
                            Click="btnSave_Click" />
            </StackPanel>
            <DataGrid Name="gridProducts"
                AutoGenerateColumns="False"
                    Margin="5,10,5,5">
                <DataGrid.Columns>
                    <DataGridTextColumn Header="Name"
                                        Binding="{Binding
                                        Path=ProductName}" />
                    <DataGridTextColumn Header="Unit Price"
                                        Binding="{Binding
                                        Path=UnitPrice}" />
                    <DataGridTextColumn Header="Units In Stock"
                                        Binding="{Binding
                                        Path=UnitsInStock}" />
                    <DataGridCheckBoxColumn Header="Discontinued"
                                        Binding="{Binding
                                        Path=Discontinued}" />
                </DataGrid.Columns>
            </DataGrid>
        </StackPanel>
    </Grid>
</Window>
```

5. Define global variables to hold the data context object and `Category` entity collection (in the `MainWindow` class).

The following code snippet shows the declared member variables of the `MainWindow` class:

```
public partial class MainWindow : Window
{
    private Uri _svcUri = new Uri
    ("http://localhost:36512/NWDataService.svc/");

    // Reference to the data context object
    private NWDataSvc.NorthwindEntities _ctx = null;
    // Reference to the Category entity collection
    private DataServiceCollection<NWDataSvc.Category> _categories
        = null;
```

6. Use the `Load` event of the main window to initialize the `Category` items in the Combobox control.

   We will create a separate function that loads all `Category` entities from the OData service. This function is called in the main window's `Load` event handler (see the following code snippet).

```
private void Window_Loaded(object sender, RoutedEventArgs e)
{
    LoadCategories();
}


private void LoadCategories()
{
    _ctx = new NWDataSvc.NorthwindEntities(_svcUri);
    _categories = new
  DataServiceCollection<NWDataSvc.Category>
  (_ctx.Categories.Execute());

    RootPanel.DataContext = _categories;
    lstCategories.SelectedIndex = 0;
}
```

7. Hook the `SelectionChanged` event of `Combobox` and use the event handler to update the `DataGrid` with the `Product` entities associated to the newly selected Category item (see the following code snippet).

```
private void lstCategories_SelectionChanged
    (object sender, SelectionChangedEventArgs e)
{
    // Get the selected Category object
    var category = lstCategories.SelectedItem as
        NWDataSvc.Category;

    if (category != null)
    {
        // Load the associated Products (via navigation property)
        _ctx.LoadProperty(category, "Products");
        // Bind Products to the DataGrid
        // Products collection is of
        // DataServiceCollection<Product> type
        gridProducts.ItemsSource = category.Products;
    }
}
```

8. Add code to submit all changes against the `Product` entities (made in `DataGrid`) within the `Click` event of the **Save Changes** button (see the following ode snippet).

```
private void btnSave_Click(object sender, RoutedEventArgs e)
{
     _ctx.SaveChanges(SaveChangesOptions.Batch);
}
```

How it works...

In this sample, we use the `DataServiceCollection<T>` class to load both `Category` and `Product` entities (queried from the Northwind OData service). The `DataServiceCollection<T>` class derives from the `ObservableCollection<T>` class; therefore, we can directly use an instance of this class to perform data binding with WPF controls (such as the `Combobox` and `DataGrid` controls used in this sample).

The WPF data binding system supports two-way data binding, which automatically helps synchronize the data between the data source and WPF UI elements. Because the `DataServiceCollection<T>` class has implemented the `INotifyCollectionChanged` and `INotifyPropertyChanged` interfaces (necessary for two-way data binding), any changes (such as add, remove, and modify) on the data entity objects (through the WPF controls) will be synchronized to the `DataServiceCollection<T>` based data source object.

In addition, since the OData entities (contained in the `DataServiceCollection<T>` object) are retrieved by using the data context object (of WCF Data Service client library based proxy), all changes we have made against the entities are also tracked by the data context object. Thus, whenever we call the `SaveChanges` method on the data context object (in the `Click` event of the **Save Changes** button), all the changes made in the WPF client application are updated to the target OData service. For more information on WPF data binding, you can refer to the following MSDN reference:

Data Binding Overview available at `http://msdn.microsoft.com/en-us/library/ms752347.aspx`

See also

▶ *Using Visual Studio to generate strong-typed OData client proxy* recipe

▶ *Filtering OData query results by using query options* recipe

Injecting custom HTTP headers in OData requests

When invoking operations of standard WCF services or XML web services over HTTP, we can inject some custom HTTP headers into the underlying HTTP message of the corresponding operation call. By using such custom headers, we allow the service clients to supply additional context information without changing the original operation signature/contract. Then, how can we attach custom HTTP headers for OData service requests? Fortunately, the WCF Data Service client library has provided the built-in means for OData clients to inject custom HTTP headers. In this recipe, we will demonstrate how we can inject custom HTTP headers when using WCF Data Service client library based OData proxy to invoke custom service operations.

Getting ready

In this sample, we will use the Northwind OData service and add a custom service operation in it. The service operation demands a custom HTTP header (which should contain the MAC address of the client machine) from the client callers. The following code snippet shows how we implement the service operation in the sample OData service:

```
[WebGet]
public DateTime GetServerTime()
{
    var webCtx = WebOperationContext.Current;

    // Extract the HTTP header from the incoming request
    var clientMAC = webCtx.IncomingRequest.Headers["ODATA_CLIENT_
    MAC"];
    Trace.WriteLine(
        string.Format("GetServerTime executed by client:{0}",
            clientMAC)
        );

    return DateTime.Now;
}
```

Also, don't forget to add a text trace listener in the `web.conifg` file so that we can log the custom HTTP header and check it later (see the following screenshot).

```
<configuration>
  <system.diagnostics>
    <trace autoflush="true" indentsize="4">
      <listeners>
        <add name="txtListener"
             type="System.Diagnostics.TextWriterTraceListener"
             initializeData="odata_trace.log" />
        <remove name="Default" />
      </listeners>
```

In the next section, we will focus on the steps about how to create the OData client application, which will invoke the service operation exposed in the sample OData service and attach the custom HTTP header.

The source code for this recipe can be found in the `\ch02\CustomHeaderSln\` directory.

How to do it...

1. Create a new Console application as an OData client.

2. Create the OData client proxy by using the Visual Studio Add Service Reference wizard.

3. Add a function to invoke the `GetServerTime` service operation and supply the MAC address in a custom HTTP header (see the following `InvokeODataServiceOperation` function).

```
static void InvokeODataServiceOperation()
{
    var svcUri = new Uri("http://localhost:61881/NWDataService.
        svc");
    var ctx = new NWDataSvc.NorthwindEntities(svcUri);

    ctx.SendingRequest += (sender, args) =>
    {
        var defaultNI = NetworkInterface.GetAllNetworkInterfaces()
            [0];
        var macAddress = defaultNI.GetPhysicalAddress().
            ToString();
        args.RequestHeaders.Add("ODATA_CLIENT_MAC", macAddress);
    };

    var operationUri = new Uri("GetServerTime", UriKind.Relative);
    var result = ctx.Execute<DateTime>(operationUri).First();

    Console.WriteLine("Server Time: {0}", result);
}
```

4. Run the OData client application and check the logged HTTP header in the service trace file.

The following screenshot shows the text trace file generated by the sample OData service (which contains the client MAC addresses recorded by the service code):

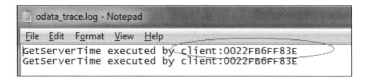

How it works...

As the previous `InvokeODataServiceOperation` function indicates, when using the WCF Data Service client library based proxy to invoke an OData service operation, we can use the `SendRequest` event (of the data context object) to inject custom headers into the underlying HTTP request. Actually, this works not only for service operation calls, but also for normal OData entity set specific queries.

By using Fiddler, we can capture the OData HTTP request sent by the sample client and verify the custom HTTP header injected in it (see the following screenshot).

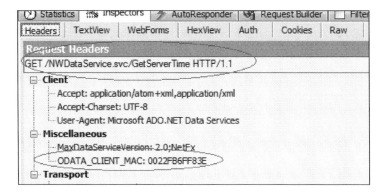

See also

▶ *Adding custom operations on OData Service* recipe in *Chapter 1, Building OData Services*

▶ *Using Visual Studio to generate strong-typed OData client proxy* recipe

Consuming HTTP compression enabled OData service

Nowadays, most web servers have supported data compression for the content or resource published by them. Such a data compression function is based on the standard HTTP protocol, which has included the compression scheme and negotiation methods. This is very useful for decreasing the network payload, which will then reduce transmission time between the client and the server. Since OData protocol relies on HTTP and uses text formats (such as XML and JSON) for data transmission, it is quite reasonable that web servers will prefer compressing the OData service responses if the client consumers are HTTP compression enabled.

By default, the WCF Data Service client library based OData proxy will not be able to handle HTTP compressed OData service responses. In this recipe, we will show you how to consume an OData service, which has enabled HTTP compression by using the WCF Data Service client library based proxy.

Getting ready

In the next section, we will provide the steps for creating an OData client application, which performs queries against the Northwind OData service. This time, the Northwind OData service needs to be HTTP compression enabled (by being hosted in an IIS server). For how to enable HTTP compression for an OData service hosted in an IIS server, you can refer to the *Enabling dynamic compression for OData service hosted in IIS 7* recipe in *Chapter 3, OData service Hosting and Configuration*.

The source code for this recipe can be found in the `\ch02\GZipCompressionSln\` directory.

How to do it...

1. Create a new Console application as an OData client.

2. Create the OData client proxy by using the Visual Studio Add Service Reference wizard.

3. Use the OData proxy to query the Northwind sample service and apply the HTTP compression and decompression settings in the `SendingRequest` event (of the data context object).

    In the `SendingRequest` event handler, we need to accomplish the following two things:

    ❑ Specify the supported compression methods via the `AcceptEncoding` HTTP header

    ❑ Enable automatic decompression (of the client proxy) via the `AutomaticDecompression` property

The following is the complete code of the sample OData client:

```
static void ConsumeGZipODataService()
{
    var svcUri = new Uri("http://localhost:8080/ODataServiceSite/
        NWDataService.svc");
    var ctx = new GZipDataSvc.NorthwindEntities(svcUri);

    ctx.SendingRequest += (sender, args) =>
    {
        var req = args.Request as HttpWebRequest;
        // Add header for supported compression types
        req.Headers.Add(HttpRequestHeader.AcceptEncoding,
            "gzip, deflate");
        // Enable auto decompression option
        req.AutomaticDecompression = DecompressionMethods.GZip |
            DecompressionMethods.Deflate;
    };

    foreach (var category in ctx.Categories)
    {
        Console.WriteLine("Name:{0}", category.CategoryName);
    }

}
```

How it works...

As shown in the previous sample code, for an OData client (based on the WCF Data Service client library) to consume HTTP compressed OData query responses, there are two important things to do. The first is to specify the Accept-Encoding HTTP header in the OData requests (by using the SendingRequest event of the data context object). This header tells the service (web server) which kind of compression methods the client supports. The following screenshot shows the Accept-Encoding header in the raw OData request sent by the sample client application (captured by Fiddler):

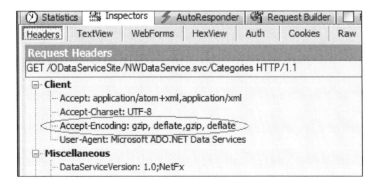

The second thing is to set the `AutoDecompression` property on the `WebRequest` instance used by the client proxy. This is also done in the `SendingRequest` event of the data context object. Thus, whenever a compressed OData response arrives at client, it will be decompressed by the underlying `WebRequest` object before the WCF Data Service client library handles it (such as performing data deserialization). The following screenshot shows the raw OData response (received by the sample client) before being decompressed:

```
HTTP/1.1 200 OK
Cache-Control: no-cache
Transfer-Encoding: chunked
Content-Type: application/atom+xml;charset=utf-8
Content-Encoding: gzip
Vary: Accept-Encoding
Server: Microsoft-IIS/7.5
DataServiceVersion: 1.0;
X-AspNet-Version: 4.0.30319
X-Powered-By: ASP.NET
Date: Wed, 23 Nov 2011 13:03:28 GMT

10890
□□□□□□□□□□□`I□%&/m□{□J□J□□t□□□`□$@□□□□□□□□iG#)□*□□eVe]f□@□침♦♦{♦♦♦{♦♦♦;♦N'♦♦♦?W

*** FIDDLER: RawDisplay truncated at 128 characters. Right-click to disable truncation. ***
```

Because we apply the HTTP compression/decompression settings through the underlying `WebRequest` class instance (used by the WCF Data Service client library), the same method will also work if you consume OData services via the .NET `WebRequest` class directly.

See also

▶ *Injecting custom HTTP headers in OData requests* recipe

▶ *Enabling dynamic compression for OData service hosted in IIS 7* recipe in *Chapter 3, OData Service Hosting and Configuration*

Using MSXML to consume OData service in unmanaged applications

We have discussed quite a few examples of consuming an OData service in .NET managed applications (including Console, Windows Form, and WPF). Though this book is targeting .NET developers, I would still like to take a chance to introduce OData service accessing in unmanaged client applications (at least, the server side is still implemented through .NET WCF Data Service).

In this recipe, we will show you how to play with an OData service in an Microsoft Excel client through VBA code.

Getting ready

For demonstration purposes, we will create an Excel 2010 workbook, which uses VBA code to retrieve and display the entity objects from the `Categories` and `Products` entity sets (of the Northwind OData service). The following is how the main UI of the sample Excel workbook appears:

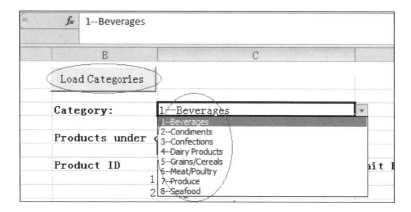

The source code for this recipe can be found in the `\ch02\ODataNativeClientSln\` directory.

How to do it...

The following are the steps for creating the sample Excel workbook:

1. Create a new empty Excel 2010 workbook.

2. Save the workbook as **Excel Macro-Enabled Workbook** (see the following screenshot).

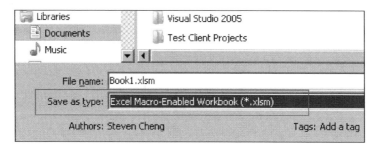

3. On the **File** tab, select the **Options** menu and enable the **Developer** ribbon option within the launched **Excel Options** dialog (see the following screenshot).

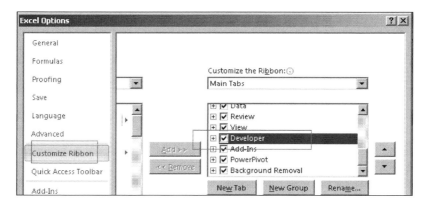

4. Add a `Button` control onto the workbook and adjust the document surface to look like the one shown in the *Getting ready* section.

   The following screenshot shows the drop-down menu for picking up the Button control:

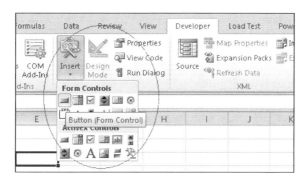

5. Use the **Visual Basic** tool button (on the **Developer** ribbon) or press **Alt + F11** to launch the VBA editor (see the following screenshot).

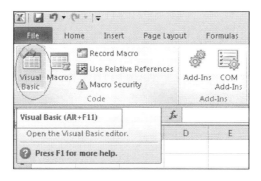

6. Add code for populating the `Category` drop-down list in the button's `Click` event handler (see the following `btnLoadCategories_Click` function).

```
Sub btnLoadCategories_Click()


    ' Declare variables
    Dim doc As MSXML2.DOMDocument
    Dim nodeList As MSXML2.IXMLDOMNodeList
    Dim bResult As Boolean
    Dim i As Integer
    Dim strName As String    ' CategoryName
    Dim strID As String      ' CategoryID
    Dim strCategoryList() As String ' Category list



    ' Create the XML document object
    Set doc = New MSXML2.DOMDocument
    doc.async = False

    ' Load the OData query result into XML document object
    bResult = doc.Load("http://localhost:30945/NWDataService.svc/
        Categories?$select=CategoryID,CategoryName")

    If bResult = True Then
        ' Select all the entity elements in the response document
        Set nodeList = doc.SelectNodes("//entry/content/
            m:properties")

        ' Construct the Category list (as a char separated string)
        ReDim strCategoryList(nodeList.Length)
        For i = 0 To nodeList.Length - 1
            strID = nodeList(i).SelectSingleNode("d:CategoryID").
                Text
            strName = nodeList(i).SelectSingleNode("d:CategoryName
                ").Text

            strCategoryList(i) = strID & "--" & strName
                Next i

        ' Assign the Category list to a cell as dropdown source
        With Range("$C$4").Validation
            .Delete
            .Add Type:=xlValidateList, _
            AlertStyle:=xlValidAlertStop, _
            Operator:=xlBetween, _
```

```
        Formula1:=Join(strCategoryList, ",")
    End With

    Range("$C$4").Value = strCategoryList(0)
Else
    MsgBox ("Failed to load Category list.")
End If
```

 At the bottom of the `btnLoadCategories_Click` function, we have assigned an initial value for the Category list drop-down cell so that the Product items associated with the default Category item will be loaded first.

7. Add the code for populating the `Product` list whenever a new `Category` item is selected.

The following `LoadProductsByCategory` function contains code for loading all `Product` entities of a specific `Category` item (by supplying the `CategoryID` property):

```
Sub LoadProductsByCategory()

    Dim doc As MSXML2.DOMDocument
    Dim nodeList As MSXML2.IXMLDOMNodeList
    Dim bResult As Boolean
    Dim i As Integer
    Dim strUrl As String
    Dim strCategoryID As String

    ' Get selected CategoryID
    strCategoryID = Split(Range("$C$4").Value, "--")(0)

    Set doc = New MSXML2.DOMDocument
    doc.async = False

    ' Build the URL for querying Products
    strUrl = "http://localhost:30945/NWDataService.svc/Products?" &  _
    "$select=ProductID,ProductName,  UnitPrice&" & _
    "$filter=CategoryID eq " & strCategoryID

    bResult = doc.Load(strUrl)
```

```
       If bResult = True Then

           ' Load the product elements from the response document
           Set nodeList = doc.SelectNodes("//entry/content/
               m:properties")

           Dim strProductID As String
           Dim strProductName As String
           Dim strUnitPrice As String

           ' Populate each product's properties into the proper cell
           For i = 0 To nodeList.Length - 1
               strProductID = nodeList(i).
                   SelectSingleNode("d:ProductID").Text
               strProductName = nodeList(i).SelectSingleNode
                   ("d:ProductName").Text
               strUnitPrice = nodeList(i).
                   SelectSingleNode("d:UnitPrice").Text

               Cells(9 + i, 2) = strProductID
               Cells(9 + i, 3) = strProductName
               Cells(9 + i, 4) = strUnitPrice
           Next i
       Else
           MsgBox ("Failed to load Product list.")
       End If
End Sub
```

Also, we need to add a function for handling the `change` event (of the drop-down cell containing the Category list), which is triggered whenever a new Category is selected. This could be done by defining a `Worksheet_Change` function (see the following code snippet) within the main worksheet's code.

```
Private Sub Worksheet_Change(ByVal Target As Range)
    If Target.Cells.Count > 1 Or IsEmpty(Target) Then Exit Sub

    If Target.Address = "$C$4" Then
        ' Load the products based selected category
        ODataModule.LoadProductsByCategory
    End If
End Sub
```

8. Save the workbook and run the VBA code we've defined in the previous steps.

   By clicking on the **Load Categories** button, all the `Category` entities will be loaded and used as a drop-down source for the **Category:** cell. If we select a new Category item from the drop-down list, the Product list under the **Products under category:** cell will be updated correspondingly (see the following screenshot).

How it works...

As shown in the **btnLoadCategories_Click** and **LoadProductsByCategory** VBA functions, the main code logic of the sample Excel workbook relies on the `DOMDocument` component of the **MSXML** library. This component can help in sending HTTP requests to the target OData service (by using the raw query URI string) and loading the response XML data into memory. After the response data is loaded into memory, we can then use XPath to extract the OData entity objects (and their properties) from the in-memory `DOMDocument` object.

Actually, this is quite similar to how we use the `WebRequest` class to access OData services in .NET clients. However, since MSXML is a COM based library, we can use it for OData consumption in unmanaged applications such as native C++, Delphi, and Visual Basic (used in this recipe).

One thing worth noticing is that we need to save the Excel workbook as an **Excel Macro Enabled Workbook**, which uses `.xlsm` as its file extension. This is because the default Excel document format (with `.xlsx` or `.xls` file extension) cannot contain any Macro code.

For more information about VBA programming with Microsoft Office Excel 2010, the following MSDN article is a good reference:

Getting Started with VBA in Excel 2010 available at `http://msdn.microsoft.com/en-us/library/ee814737.aspx`

See also

- ▸ *Accessing OData service via WebRequest class* recipe
- ▸ *Filtering OData query results by using query options* recipe

3
OData Service Hosting and Configuration

In this chapter we will cover:

- ▶ Hosting a WCF Data Service in IIS server
- ▶ Hosting a WCF Data Service in Console application
- ▶ Deploying a WCF Data Service on Windows Azure host
- ▶ Configuring WCF Data Service to return error details
- ▶ Configuring WCF Data Service to return JSON-format response
- ▶ Applying basic access rules on WCF Data Service
- ▶ Getting rid of .svc extension by using ASP.NET URL Routing
- ▶ Enabling dynamic compression for OData service hosted in IIS 7

Introduction

For server-side service applications, during the development or deployment stage, we need to find a proper environment to host them. When deploying a service in the production environment, we not only make the service officially accessible to client consumers, but also allow the service to fully leverage various hosting features (such as logging, performance, security, and reliability) of the target environment. In addition, developers or administrators might need to apply various kind of configuration settings to OData services (at development or deployment stage) so as to enable some particular behavior or functionalities.

When developing OData services through WCF Data Service, it is possible for us to take advantage of the existing hosting and configuration support of a standard WCF service. Currently, we can use almost all kinds of .NET managed applications to host WCF Data Service including, ASP.NET web application (via IIS server), Windows service application, Windows Forms application, WPF application, Console application, or even Windows Azure based cloud applications. And when the WCF Data Service is hosted in IIS or Windows Azure hosts, it can leverage the built-in hosting and configuration options provided by the underlying IIS or Windows Azure server infrastructure.

In this chapter, we will discuss some typical OData service (built via WCF Data Service) hosting scenarios including using an IIS server host, using a .NET managed Console host and Windows Azure cloud host. In addition, we will introduce some OData service configuration scenarios supported by WCF Data Service and certain hosting environments such as applying basic access rules to OData entity sets, using dynamic HTTP compression for IIS hosted OData services, and configuring WCF Data Service to return a JSON-format response.

Hosting a WCF Data Service in IIS server

There is no doubt that IIS will always be the first choice for hosting web applications on a Windows server platform. You might already be familiar with the IIS server if you've originally developed applications based on the CGI/ISAPI extensions, classic ASP, ASP.NET WebForms, ASP.NET Web Services, or WCF Services.

Well, we will start the first recipe in this chapter by exploring how to host a WCF Data Service in IIS 7.

Getting ready

Since we are going to use IIS 7 as the service host, we need to make sure the operating system (either the Windows client or server version) of our development machine has IIS 7 installed. For IIS 7 installation and configuration, you can refer to the following website:

`http://go.microsoft.com/fwlink/?LinkID=132128`

The source code for this recipe can be found in the `\ch03\ODataIISHostSln\` directory.

How to do it...

1. Create a new ASP.NET web application that contains the sample OData service.

   The sample service here is built through WCF Data Service and ADO.NET Entity Framework (with Northwind database).

    For detailed information on creating the sample Northwind OData service, you can refer to the *Building an OData service via WCF Data Service and ADO.NET Entity Framework* recipe in *Chapter 1, Building OData Services*.

   The following screenshot shows the web application project structure in Visual Studio:

2. Right-click on the web application project in Visual Studio and select the **Publish...** context menu to launch the **Publish Web** wizard (see the following screenshot).

   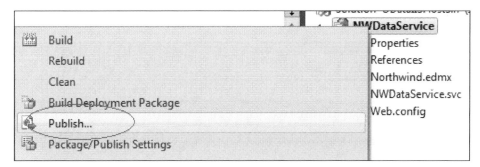

3. Specify the necessary publish options in the **Publish Web** dialog.

The following screenshot shows the publish options, which are used to deploy the sample web application to the local IIS server:

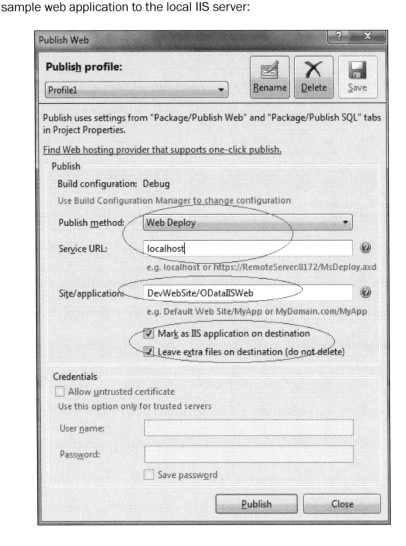

Here we have chosen **Web Deploy** as the **Publish method** and specified localhost as the **Service URL**. The **Site/application:** field contains the target website and web application names in the local IIS server.

Whenever you've specified a new set of publish options, you can use the **Save** button (at the top right of the **Publish Web** dialog) to save the settings as a profile which can be reused the next time you use the wizard to publish web applications in Visual Studio.

4. Click on the **Publish** button to start the publishing process.

   The following screenshot shows the output in Visual Studio after the web application has been successfully published:

```
------ Publish started: Project: NWDataService, Configuration: Debug Any CPU ------
Transformed Web.config using Web.Debug.config into obj\Debug\TransformWebConfig\tran
Auto ConnectionString Transformed obj\Debug\TransformWebConfig\transformed\Web.confi
Copying all files to temporary location below for package/publish:
obj\Debug\Package\PackageTmp.
Updating setAcl (DevWebSite/ODataIISWeb).
Updating setAcl (DevWebSite/ODataIISWeb).
Publish is successfully deployed.
========== Build: 1 succeeded or up-to-date, 0 failed, 0 skipped ==========
========== Publish: 1 succeeded, 0 failed, 0 skipped ==========
```

5. Launch the **Internet Information Services (IIS) Manager**.

   You can find the IIS Manager within **Control Panel | System and Security | Administrative Tools** (see the following screenshot) or you can directly launch it by executing `inetmgr.exe` in the command-line prompt.

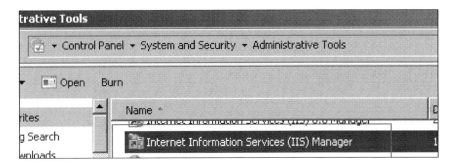

6. Locate the published web application and adjust the configuration settings based on deployment requirements.

When selecting an application node in the left panel of IIS manager, you can find all the configuration settings available (including both ASP.NET and IIS specific ones) in the right panel (see the following screenshot).

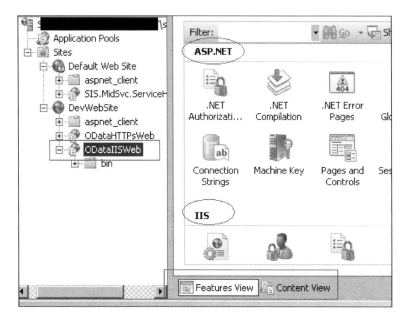

7. Switch to the **Content View** and right-click on the `.svc` service file to launch the OData service (see the following screenshot).

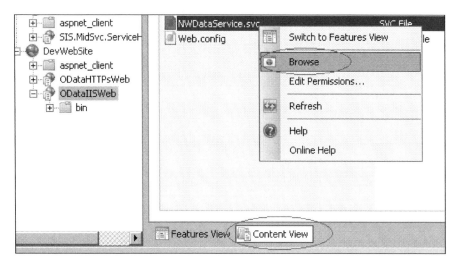

How it works...

As shown in the previous steps, the Visual Studio **Publish Web** wizard provides a simple and straightforward means for deploying WCF Data Service (contained in ASP.NET web application) into an IIS server. In this case, we choose the **Web Deploy** method in the publishing settings. If we use this method for a remote IIS server, it requires that the target IIS server should have a Web Deploy component installed (see `http://www.iis.net/download/webdeploy` for more information).

In addition to the **Web Deploy** method, we can also use **File System** as the publishing method, which will deploy the web application to the target IIS server through the filesystem path (see the following screenshot).

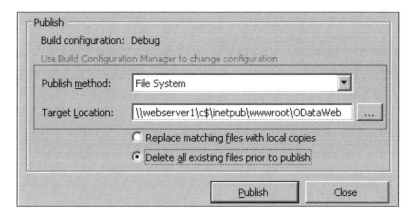

As shown in the previous screenshot, since Windows OS by default creates hidden administrative shares for *Root* drives by using the drive letter name appended with the $ sign (such as C$ for C drive and D$ for D drive), we can use this means to get the filesystem path of the remote IIS website or web application.

If you want to manually create the application virtual directory in the IIS server, you can follow the instructions in the following MSDN reference:

How to: Create and Configure Virtual Directories in IIS 7.0 available at
`http://msdn.microsoft.com/en-us/library/bb763173(v=vs.100).aspx`

See also

▶ *Building an OData service via WCF Data Service and ADO.NET Entity Framework* recipe in *Chapter 1, Building OData Services*

Hosting a WCF Data Service in Console application

In most cases, we will host WCF Data Service in an IIS server, which is also the common host for other web applications and services on the Windows platform. Though the IIS server is quite powerful for hosting web applications, sometimes we might still need to host WCF Data Service in some other applications such as Console, Windows Service, or WPF applications. No problem! Like a standard WCF service, WCF Data Service also supports a **Self-hosting** scenario. In this recipe, we will introduce how to create a WCF Data Service and host it in a .NET Console application.

Getting ready

The source code for this recipe can be found in the `\ch03\ODataSelfHostSln\` directory.

How to do it...

1. Create a new **Console Application** (see the following screenshot) as the OData service application.

2. Add the following assembly references in the Console project:
    - ❑ `System.ServiceModel.dll`
    - ❑ `System.ServiceModel.Web.dll`
    - ❑ `System.Data.Services.dll`

3. Create the ADO.NET Entity Framework data model from the Northwind database.

   The data model should at least include the **Category** and **Product** entity types (see the following screenshot).

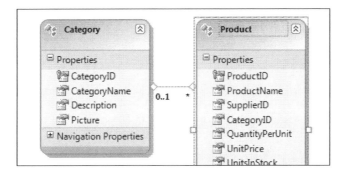

4. Create the WCF Data Service class, which derives from the `DataService<T>` class and uses the Entity Framework data model as the data source (see the following code snippet).

```
class NorthwindDataService: DataService<NorthwindEntities>
{
    public static void InitializeService
        (IDataServiceConfiguration config)
    {
        config.SetEntitySetAccessRule("*", EntitySetRights.All);
    }

}
```

5. Add the service hosting function by using the `DataServiceHost` class (see the following code snippet).

```
static void Main(string[] args)
{
    RunDataService();
}

static void RunDataService()
{
    var svcUri = new Uri("http://localhost:8177/NorthwindData/");

    DataServiceHost host = new DataServiceHost(
        typeof(NorthwindDataService),
        new Uri[]{svcUri}
        );
```

```
        host.Open();
        Console.WriteLine("Service started at: {0}",
            host.BaseAddresses[0]);
        Console.WriteLine("Press any key to exit...");
        Console.ReadLine();

        host.Close();
    }
```

6. Start up the Console application by pressing *Ctrl + F5* in Visual Studio.

    The following is the Console screen of the sample service application:

7. Use the web browser to access the service via its base URI address (see the following screenshot).

How it works...

When developing WCF Data Service hosted in the Console application (or other non-web applications), we need to manually create the service class, which derives from the `DataService<T>` class. The data source is still specified through the generic class parameter of the service class.

The service hosting code relies on the `DataServiceHost` class. We first create a new instance of a `DataServiceHost` class by supplying the service type and service address. Then, we simply call the `Open` method to bring the service to life.

▶ *Building an OData service via WCF Data Service and ADO.NET Entity Framework* recipe in *Chapter 1, Building OData Services*

Deploying a WCF Data Service on Windows Azure host

Windows Azure is the official Microsoft cloud computing platform that enables you to quickly build, deploy, and manage various kind of applications either based on Microsoft or non-Microsoft technologies. As .NET web developers, it is quite convenient for us to deploy an ASP.NET web application or WCF service application to the Windows Azure based hosting environment. In this recipe, we will demonstrate how to deploy a WCF Data Service web application to the Windows Azure host.

Getting ready

This recipe uses Windows Azure Web Role for OData service hosting and uses SQL Azure for hosting the Northwind database. Before you go ahead, make sure you have a Windows Azure and SQL Azure account ready.

For Windows Azure development in Visual Studio 2010, you need to have the proper Windows Azure Tools for Visual Studio installed. It is available at `http://go.microsoft.com/fwlink/?LinkID=129513`.

The SQL Azure Migration Wizard tool can help in migrating the local SQL Server database to SQL Azure instance and we can use it for setting up the Northwind database. For more information, refer to the following article:

SQL Azure Migration Wizard available at `http://sqlazuremw.codeplex.com/`

Alternatively, we can also use the *Adventure Works for SQL Azure* sample database, which is available at the following CodePlex workspace:

`http://msftdbprodsamples.codeplex.com/`

The source code for this recipe can be found in the `\ch03\WindowsAzureODataSln\` directory.

How to do it...

1. Create a new ASP.NET web application, which contains the Northwind OData service.

    The following is the web application project structure in **Visual Studio Solution Explorer**:

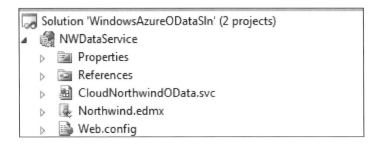

    Also, the Entity Framework data model should connect to the Northwind database on an SQL Azure instance (see the following connection string).

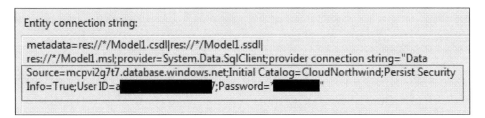

2. Create a new **Windows Azure Project** in the sample solution (see the following screenshot).

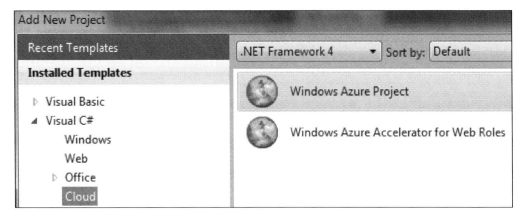

When creating the **Windows Azure Project**, *do not* add any new *Web Role* or *Worker Role* since we will use the existing ASP.NET web application created in the previous steps.

3. Add the ASP.NET web application (created earlier) as a **Web Role** of the **Windows Azure Project** (see the following screenshot).

Now, the sample solution structure should look like the following screenshot:

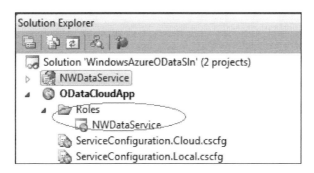

4. Select the **Windows Azure Project** and launch the package deployment wizard through the **Package...** context menu (see the following screenshot).

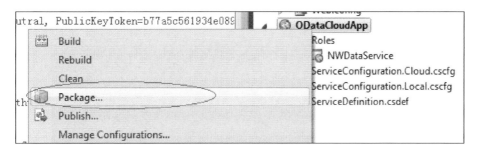

5. Select the proper deployment configurations in the **Package Windows Azure Application** dialog (see the following screenshot).

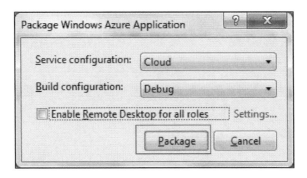

6. Click on the **Package** button to finish the package generation process.

A new explorer window will be prompted to show you the generated deployment package files (see the following screenshot).

7. Launch a web browser and navigate to the **Windows Azure Management Portal** at `http://windows.azure.com`.

8. Sign in the portal application with the **Windows Live ID** of your Windows Azure account (see the following screenshot).

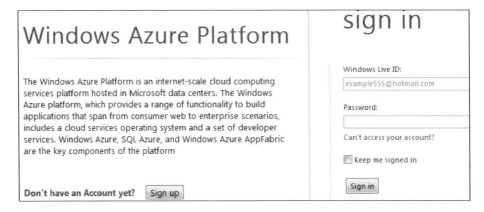

9. Open the **Hosted Services, Storage Accounts & CDN** view (by selecting the node in left panel) and select an existing **Hosted Services** instance or create a **New Hosted Service** (see the following screenshot).

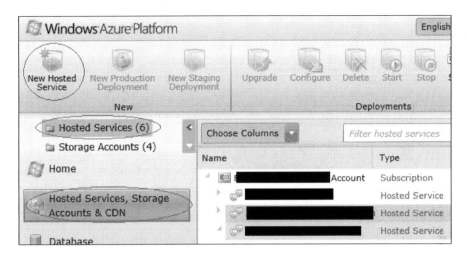

10. Launch the new deployment wizard by clicking on the **New Staging Deployment** button (see the following screenshot).

In addition to the **New Staging Deployment** button, there is another **New Production Deployment** button, which is also used for deploying application packages.

 Normally, we will use **Staging Deployment** for testing purposes and use **Production Deployment** for final release and publishing.

11. Supply the deployment information within the **Create a new Deployment** dialog.

    In the dialog, we can specify a display name for the deployment instance and select the deployment package files created in previous steps (see the following screenshot).

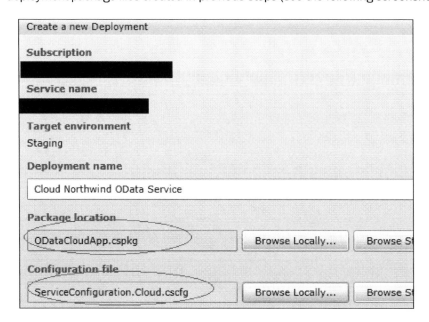

12. Click on the **OK** button to submit the deployment package.

    It will take a while for the portal to upload the package files and finish the deployment on the target Hosted Service instance.

13. Verify the deployment status under the **Hosted Service** instance node within the right panel of the portal application.

    The following screenshot shows the **NWDataService** Web Role instance deployed in the sample Hosted Service instance:

14. Access the cloud hosted WCF Data Service in the web browser (see the following screenshot).

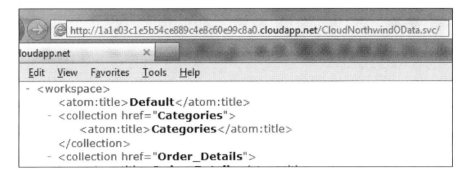

The base address of the deployed Web Role uses the `cloudapp.net` domain name. We can find the base address in the **Properties** panel (see the following screenshot).

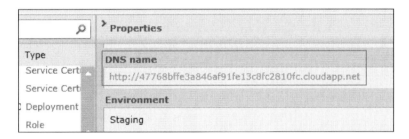

How it works...

After installing the **Windows Azure Tools for Visual Studio**, we will get the **Windows Azure Project** template, which simplifies the development and deployment of .NET Framework based Windows Azure applications. Each application hosted in Windows Azure is represented as a *Role* in the **Windows Azure Project**. The project template will autogenerate some configuration files, such as the `.cscfg` and `.csdef` files. We can use these files to configure some hosting features, such as an OS version, load-balance instance count, and data connection string. You can get more information about configuring Windows Azure application from the following article:

Configuring a Windows Azure Project available at `http://msdn.microsoft.com/en-us/library/windowsazure/ee405486.aspx`

When creating a new deployment task on the **Windows Azure Management Portal**, we can choose either **Production Deployment** or **Staging Deployment** type. For debugging and testing, we recommend the **Staging Deployment**; while the **Production Deployment** is preferred for release deployment. But, for a given Hosted Service instance, we can create at the most one Production Deployment and one Staging Deployment. For more information about the lifecycle management of Windows Azure application, you can refer to the following document:

Application Life Cycle Management for Windows Azure Applications available at `http://msdn.microsoft.com/en-us/library/ff803362.aspx`

There's more...

In this example, we deploy the Windows Azure Project (containing the sample WCF Data Service) by creating a deployment package and submitting it through the management portal. In addition to this, we can also use the Publish Windows Azure Application wizard to deploy Windows Azure Project in Visual Studio IDE. By using this wizard, we can deploy a Windows Azure application just like how we publish an ASP.NET web application into IIS server. For more information, refer to the following MSDN reference:

Publish Windows Azure Application Wizard available at `http://msdn.microsoft.com/en-us/library/windowsazure/hh535756.aspx`

See also

▶ Building an OData service via WCF Data Service and ADO.NET Entity Framework recipe in *Chapter 1, Building OData Services*

Configuring WCF Data Service to return error details

When developing WCF Data Service, we will probably encounter some unexpected errors; some might be caused by our service's code logic and some others might be caused by some issues from the WCF Data Service or .NET Framework infrastructure. By default, WCF Data Service will only return a general error message when any unhandled exception occurs in service. This is not quite convenient for us to troubleshoot the root cause of the problem. In this recipe, we will show you how to configure WCF Data Service to expose detailed error information.

Getting ready

The source code for this recipe can be found in the `\ch03\ODataErrorInfoSln\` directory.

How to do it...

1. Open the ASP.NET web application, which contains the WCF Data Service we want to configure.

2. Use the `web.config` file to enable the `includeExceptionDetailInFaults` option for the WCF Data Service.

   You can find the `includeExceptionDetailInFaults` option through the `<serviceDebug>` element, which is nested in the `<serviceBehaviors>` configuration section (see the following screenshot).

```
<behaviors>
  <serviceBehaviors>
    <behavior>
      <serviceDebug includeExceptionDetailInFaults="true"/>
    </behavior>
  </serviceBehaviors>
</behaviors>
</system.serviceModel>
configuration>
```

3. Turn on the `UseVerboseErrors` setting in the WCF Data Service initialization code (see the following code snippet).

```
public class NWDataService : DataService<NorthwindEntities>
{
    public static void
        InitializeService(DataServiceConfiguration config)
    {
        config.DataServiceBehavior.MaxProtocolVersion =
            DataServiceProtocolVersion.V2;



        config.UseVerboseErrors = true;
    }
}
```

How it works...

The first `includeExceptionDetailInFaults` option is a standard WCF setting. By enabling this option, the WCF Service runtime will propagate information about the server-side unhandled exception to the client. Since WCF Data Service is a special implementation of WCF, it is necessary to enable this option for debugging purposes.

The second `UseVerboseErrors` option is a WCF Data Service specific setting. By turning this option on, WCF Data Service will return more detailed error information in case any error occurs in the service code.

The following is the custom service operation (defined in our sample service) as an example:

```
[WebGet]
public int Divide(int lv, int rv)
{
    return lv / rv;
}
```

If we provide `0` as the `rv` parameter, the runtime will throw a `DivideByZero` exception. However, by default, a very general error message is returned, which doesn't help much for troubleshooting (see the following screenshot).

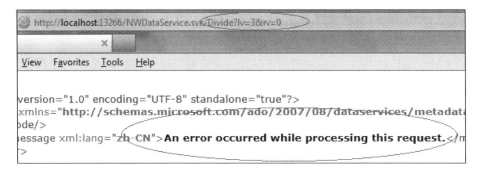

With the previous two options turned on, the service will instead return detailed exception information including exception type and call `stacktrace` (see the following screenshot).

```
<error xmlns="http://schemas.microsoft.com/ado/2007/08/dataservices/metadata">
  <code />
  <message xml:lang="en-US">An error occurred while processing this request.</message>
  <innererror>
    <message>Exception has been thrown by the target of an invocation.</message>
    <type>System.Reflection.TargetInvocationException</type>
    <stacktrace>at System.RuntimeMethodHandle._InvokeMethodFast(IRuntimeMethodI
      methodAttributes, RuntimeType typeOwner) at System.RuntimeMethodHandle.Inv
      MethodAttributes methodAttributes, RuntimeType typeOwner) at System.Reflectio
      parameters, CultureInfo culture, Boolean skipVisibilityChecks) at System.Reflectio
      parameters, CultureInfo culture) at System.Data.Services.Providers.BaseServiceP
      System.Data.Services.RequestUriProcessor.CreateFirstSegment(IDataService ser
      Boolean& crossReferencingUrl) at System.Data.Services.RequestUriProcessor.Crea
      System.Data.Services.RequestUriProcessor.ProcessRequestUri(Uri absoluteReques
      System.Data.Services.DataService`1.ProcessIncomingRequestUri() at System.Dat
    <internalexception>
      <message>Attempted to divide by zero.</message>
      <type>System.DivideByZeroException</type>
```

It is strongly recommended that we turn on the `includeExceptionDetailInFaults` and `UseVerboseErrors` options only at development or testing time. Using them for production deployment will raise security risks as we're exposing the vulnerability of our service to the client.

See also

▶ *Adding custom operations on OData Service* recipe in *Chapter 1, Building OData Services*

Configuring WCF Data Service to return JSON-format response

OData service supports both Atom XML format and JSON format for service data transfer. WCF Data Service by default returns the response data of OData queries and service operations in Atom XML format. If you need to get JSON-format response, you can explicitly set the `Accept` HTTP header to `application/json` so that the service will return response data in JSON format (see the following screenshot).

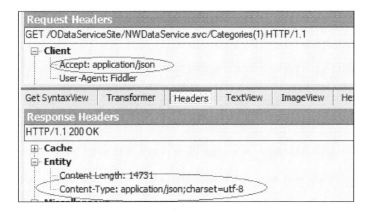

Then, is there any setting to control the WCF Data Service response format at the server side (without changing the client)? Unfortunately, so far WCF Data Service hasn't provided such a built-in configuration setting. However, there is always a way to work around it. In this recipe, we will demonstrate how we can force the WCF Data Service hosted in IIS 7 to return a JSON format response.

Getting ready

This recipe will require some ASP.NET HTTP Module development knowledge. In case you're not familiar with this, the following MSDN reference is a good one to get started:

HTTP Handlers and HTTP Modules Overview available at `http://msdn.microsoft.com/en-us/library/bb398986.aspx`

The source code for this recipe can be found in the `\ch03\ODataServiceWithJSONSln\` directory.

How to do it...

1. Create a new ASP.NET web application, which contains the sample WCF Data Service (based on the Northwind database).

2. Create a custom HTTP Module to intercept the OData requests and manipulate the `Accept` HTTP header (see the following `ODataHttpModule` type).

```
public class ODataHttpModule : IHttpModule
{
    public void Init(HttpApplication context)
    {
        context.BeginRequest += new
            EventHandler(context_BeginRequest);
    }

    void context_BeginRequest(object sender, EventArgs e)
    {
        HttpApplication app = sender as HttpApplication;
        HttpContext ctx = app.Context;

        string strUrl = ctx.Request.RawUrl;
        if (strUrl.Contains("NWDataService.svc") &&
            !ctx.Request.RawUrl.Contains("$metadata"))
        {

            ctx.Request.Headers.Add("Accept", "application/json");
        }
    }
}
```

3. Register the custom HTTP Module in the `web.config` file of the sample web application.

    We will use the `<system.webServer>` configuration section to register the HTTP Module (see the following screenshot).

```
<system.webServer>
    <modules>
        <add name="ODataModule"
             type="NWDataService.ODataHttpModule, NWDataService"/>
    </modules>
</system.webServer>
</configuration>
```

4. Deploy the sample ASP.NET web application to IIS 7.

    You can refer to the *Hosting a WCF Data Service in IIS server* recipe for more information on this.

5. Select the application pool (of the deployed web application) in IIS manager and make sure it is using the **Integrated** pipeline mode within the **Basic Settings...** dialog (see the following screenshot).

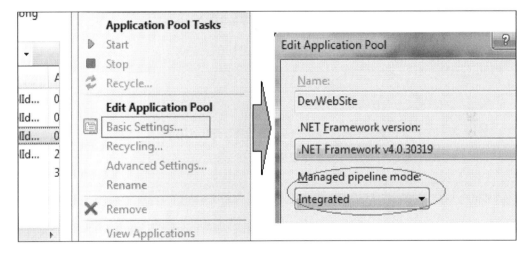

6. Access the WCF Data Service and verify that it is always returning a JSON-format response as expected.

    The following screenshot shows the HTTP request headers and response data of the sample service (captured by Fiddler):

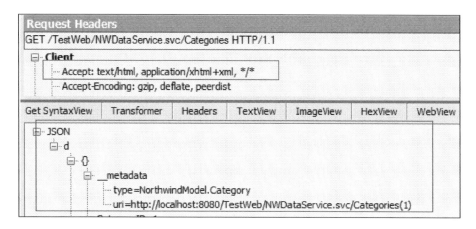

How it works...

The basic idea here is to use ASP.NET HTTP Module to intercept and modify the `Accept` HTTP header of each OData request (before the WCF Data Service runtime handles it). Thus, by specifying the `Accept` header value, we can control the data format of the WCF Data Service responses.

Also, when deploying the host web application to IIS 7, we have chosen the **Integrated** pipeline mode for the IIS application pool. This is a new feature of IIS 7, which helps to make sure that all requests coming to the web application (which use an **Integrated** mode application pool) will be handled by the registered HTTP Modules. For more information about the **Integrated** pipeline mode of IIS 7, you can refer to the following article:

How to Take Advantage of the IIS 7.0 Integrated Pipeline available at `http://learn. iis.net/page.aspx/244/how-to-take-advantage-of-the-iis-integrated- pipeline/`

See also

- ▶ *Injecting custom HTTP headers in OData requests* recipe in *Chapter 2, Working with OData at Client Side*

- ▶ *Hosting a WCF Data Service in IIS server* recipe

Applying basic access rules on WCF Data Service

When talking about rule-based access control in service development, we will often think about the security authentication and authorization concepts. WCF Data Service has provided a built-in setting for controlling the access rules over the entity sets and operations exposed in the service. In this recipe, we will demonstrate how we can use this feature to perform basic access control against entity sets exposed by WCF Data Service.

Getting ready

We will use the Northwind OData service (built with WCF Data Service and ADO.NET Entity Framework) as an example and apply some access rules to the entity sets exposed from it.

The source code for this recipe can be found in the `\ch03\ODataBasicRulesSln\` directory.

How to do it...

1. Create a new ASP.NET web application, which contains the Northwind OData service.

   For demonstration, we will expose four entity sets in the service, which contain the `Category`, `Order`, `Order_Detail`, and `Product` entity types (see the following screenshot).

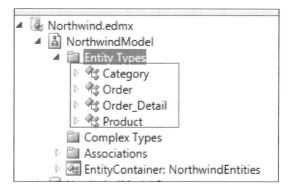

2. Apply access rules for entity sets in the WCF Data Service initialization function.

   The following is the list of access rules we will apply on the sample service's entity sets:

   - Client can perform all read access on `Categories` entity set
   - Client can perform read access to single entity only on `Products` entity set

- ❑ Client can perform read access to entity list only on `Orders` entity set
- ❑ Client cannot perform any access on `Order_Details` entity set

The following code snippet shows the complete initialization function:

```
public class NWDataService : DataService<NorthwindEntities>
{
    public static void InitializeService(DataServiceConfiguration
        config)
    {
        config.DataServiceBehavior.MaxProtocolVersion =
        DataServiceProtocolVersion.V2;

        // Grant read access on Categories entity set and single
        //Category entity
        config.SetEntitySetAccessRule("Categories",
            EntitySetRights.AllRead);
        // Grant read access on a single Category entity
        config.SetEntitySetAccessRule("Products",
            EntitySetRights.ReadSingle);
        // Grant read access on Orders entity set
        config.SetEntitySetAccessRule("Orders",
            EntitySetRights.ReadMultiple);
        // Do not allow any access on Order_Details entity set
        config.SetEntitySetAccessRule("Order_Details",
            EntitySetRights.None);

    }
}
```

How it works...

As shown in the previous code, by using the `SetEntitySetAccessRule` method of `DataServiceConfiguration` class, we can apply access rules against every entity set exposed in a WCF Data Service. In the sample service, we have applied some rules through the `AllRead`, `ReadSingle`, `ReadMultiple`, and `None` flags (of `EntitySetRights` enumeration type).

 None is the default access rule setting for every entity set in a WCF Data Service.

There are many other access rule flags such as `AllWrite`, `WriteAppend`, `WriteDelete`, `All`, and so on. We can use the **Bit Or** operator to apply a combination of such flags on a given entity set. For example, the following code snippet applies both `WriteAppend` and `WriteDelete` rules on the `Orders` entity set, so that service consumers can perform both create and delete operations:

```
config.SetEntitySetAccessRule("Orders", EntitySetRights.AllRead
                            | EntitySetRights.WriteAppend
                            | EntitySetRights.WriteDelete);
```

In addition to entity sets, we can also apply the same basic access rules on service operations defined in a WCF Data Service by using the `SetServiceOperationAccessRule` method of the `DataServiceConfiguration` class (see the following code snippet).

```
config.SetServiceOperationAccessRule("operation1",
ServiceOperationRights.All);
config.SetServiceOperationAccessRule("operation2",
ServiceOperationRights.ReadSingle);
```

For more information on the built-in access rules, please refer to the *Minimum Resource Access Requirements* section in the following MSDN document:

Configuring the Data Service (WCF Data Services) available at `http://msdn.microsoft.com/en-us/library/ee358710.aspx`

There's more...

Although the built-in access rules setting can help in controlling the **CRUD** permissions on entity sets exposed in WCF Data Service, it is just an ad-hoc like setting which is suitable for basic access control scenarios. For example, if we want to completely restrict the read or write access for a given entity set, then the built-in access rules will be quite sufficient for us. If what you need to do is implementing more complicated access control such as role-based service authorization (based on client user identity or other claims), then the built-in access rules setting is far from enough. We will discuss more on implementing custom authorization rules in *Chapter 7, Working with Security*.

See also

> ▶ *Building an OData service via WCF Data Service and ADO.NET Entity Framework* recipe in *Chapter 1, Building OData Services*

Getting rid of .svc extension by using ASP.NET URL Routing

When we create a WCF Data Service in a web application or website project, Visual Studio 2010 will add a `.svc` file and its associated code-behind file (see the following screenshot) in the project. This is the standard file extension for a WCF service item in Visual Studio.

When we access the WCF Data Service, the service address also includes the `.svc` file extension as shown in `http://localhost:8188/NWDataService.svc/$metadata`.

Then, the question comes of whether we can get rid of the `.svc` extension in the service address of the WCF Data Service hosted in a web application (just like what we can do for WCF Data Service hosted in a Console application). In this recipe, we will show you how to achieve this by using the ASP.NET **URL Routing** feature.

Getting ready

This sample case will use ASP.NET URL Routing to provide a customized base address for the Northwind OData service.

The source code for this recipe can be found in the `\ch03\UrlRoutingSln\` directory.

How to do it...

1. Create a new ASP.NET web application, which contains the Northwind OData service.

2. Add an assembly reference to `System.ServiceModel.Activation.dll` in the web application.

3. Create a **Global Application Class** (`Global.asax`) in the ASP.NET web application (see the following screenshot).

4. Register the routing rule (for the customized WCF Data Service address) in the `Application_Start` event of `Global.asax` class (see the following code snippet).

```
public class Global : System.Web.HttpApplication
{

    protected void Application_Start(object sender, EventArgs e)
    {
        // Register URL Routing rules
        RouteTable.Routes.Add(
            new ServiceRoute(
                "NorthwindOData",
                new DataServiceHostFactory(),
                typeof(NWDataService)
            )
        );
    }
}
```

5. Make sure `AspNetCompatibilityMode` is enabled (under the `<system.serviceMode>` section) in the `web.config` file (see the following screenshot).

```
<system.serviceModel>
  <serviceHostingEnvironment aspNetCompatibilityEnabled="true" />
```

6. Register the **UrlRoutingModule** and turn on the **runAllManagedModulesForAllRequests** option (under the `<system.webServer>` section) in the `web.config` file (see the following screenshot).

```
<system.webServer>

  <modules runAllManagedModulesForAllRequests="true">

    <remove name="UrlRoutingModule"/>
    <add name="UrlRoutingModule"
         type="System.Web.Routing.UrlRoutingModule, System.Web, Version

  </modules>
```

7. Launch the web application and access the WCF Data Service through the `.svc` less address (see the following screenshot).

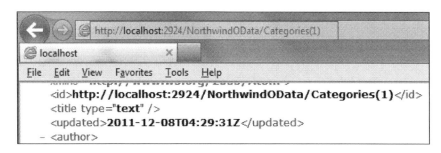

```
<id>http://localhost:2924/NorthwindOData/Categories(1)</id>
<title type="text" />
<updated>2011-12-08T04:29:31Z</updated>
- <author>
```

How it works...

The service address customization here is totally relying on the ASP.NET URL Routing feature. This feature is introduced in ASP.NET 4.0 and it can be used for various .NET web applications (such as WebForm, MVC, and WCF) hosted in an IIS server. Also, .NET Framework 4.0 provides the `ServiceRoute` class, which can help enable the URL Routing feature for WCF REST services (including WCF Data Service). What we need to do is simply add a route rule within the `Application_Start` event of `Global.asax` class.

In addition, to make URL Routing work in an IIS server, we need to make sure the `UrlRoutingModule` is registered in the `web.config` file so that the incoming requests (target the web application) can be routed based on the registered routing rules.

If you want to know more about ASP.NET URL Routing, the following blog entry is a good one to get started:

URL Routing with ASP.NET 4 Web Forms available at `http://weblogs.asp.net/scottgu/archive/2009/10/13/url-routing-with-asp-net-4-web-forms-vs-2010-and-net-4-0-series.aspx`

See also

*   ▶ *Building an OData service via WCF Data Service and ADO.NET Entity Framework* recipe in *Chapter 1, Building OData Services*

*   ▶ *Hosting a WCF Data Service in Console application* recipe

Enabling dynamic compression for OData service hosted in IIS 7

OData protocol relies on Atom XML and JSON formats for transferring data entities over HTTP between services and clients. Since both Atom XML and JSON are text-based data formats, it would cause potential performance issues (due to large data size or network latency) when we transfer large number of data entities in OData service queries. Surely, there are many methods we can use to prevent such kind of performance issues. For example, we can use query projection to restrict the entity properties returned in responses, we can use server-side paging to restrict the number of entities returned in responses, or we can better design our service data types. However, the HTTP transport protocol has already provided us a good solution on this, which is to apply standard HTTP compression for OData service responses. In this recipe, we will show you how to apply HTTP compression for OData services hosted in IIS 7.

Getting ready

The topics discussed in this recipe require the usage of the IIS 7 Dynamic Content Compression feature. So we need to make sure the Dynamic Content Compression component has been installed correctly on the server machine. You can use the **ServerManager | Roles | Web Server Role** (for Windows Server OS) or **Control Panel | Program Features | Windows Features | Internet Information Services** (for Windows Client OS) path to install the **Dynamic Content Compression** component (see the following screenshot).

How to do it...

1. Deploy the OData service web application to IIS 7 on the target server.

2. Open the IIS Manager on the target server.

3. Select the root server machine node in IIS Manager and launch the **Configuration Editor** (see the following screenshot).

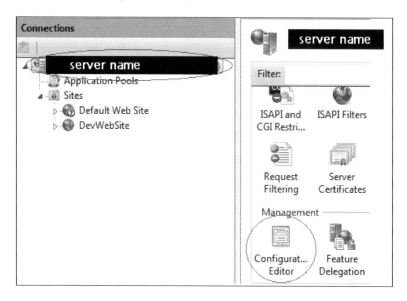

4. Select the **system.webServer/httpCompression** section in **Configuration Editor** and edit the **dynamicTypes** property (see the following screenshot).

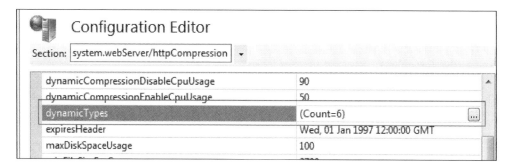

5. Add the following **mimeType** entries in the prompted **Collection Editor** dialog (see the following screenshot):

    ❑ **application/atom+xml;charset=utf-8**

    ❑ **application/atom+xml**

    ❑ **application/json;charset=utf-8**

    ❑ **application/json**

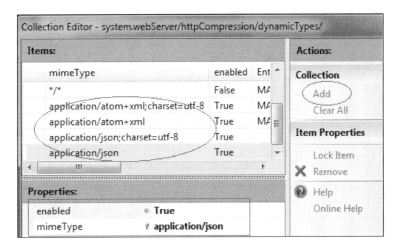

6. Select the deployed OData service web application in IIS Manager and open the **Compression** setting (see the following screenshot).

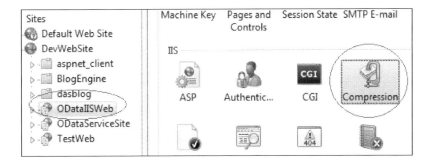

7. Make sure the **Enable dynamic content compression** and **Enable static content compression** options are checked in the **Compression** setting panel (see the following screenshot).

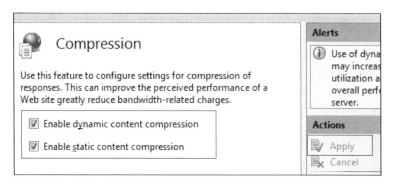

8. Restart the IIS server to ensure the changes have been applied.

9. Access the OData service and use Fiddler to verify that the service responses are compressed at the HTTP layer.

The following screenshot shows a sample OData response (captured in Fiddler), which has been compressed with the **gzip** method:

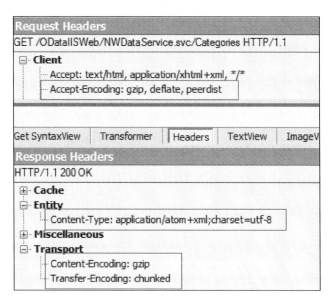

How it works...

The IIS 7 Dynamic Content Compression feature uses the compression methods of HTTP protocol to compress the response data generated by the dynamic server documents (such as ASP.NET web pages, and WCF services). Also, the IIS server uses the MIME type (content type) of the response data to determine if compression should be applied. For OData services, we only need to take care of the `application/atom+xml` (for Atom XML format) and `application/json` (for JSON format) MIME types.

 Enabling **Dynamic Content Compression** will cause the server machine to use significant CPU time and memory resources. Therefore, we should use it only if it is necessary and the server machine has sufficient spare CPU time.

In addition, the configuration steps we mentioned here are using the IIS Manager; but we can also use the `AppCmd.exe` tool to apply the same settings from the command-line prompt. Refer to the following Knowledge Base article for more information:

How to use the Appcmd.exe command-line tool to enable and configure HTTP logging and other features in Internet Information Services 7.0 available at `http://support.microsoft.com/kb/930909`

There's more...

By default, the WCF Data Service client library based OData proxy will not be able to handle HTTP compressed responses. For how to enable strong-typed OData proxy to support HTTP compressed responses, please refer to the *Consuming HTTP compression enabled OData service* recipe in Chapter 2, *Working with OData at Client Side*.

See also

- ▶ *Building an OData service via WCF Data Service and ADO.NET Entity Framework* recipe in *Chapter 1, Building OData Services*
- ▶ *Consuming HTTP compression enabled OData service* recipe in *Chapter 2, Working with OData at Client Side*
- ▶ *Hosting a WCF Data Service in IIS server* recipe

4

Using OData in Web Application

In this chapter we will cover:

- ▶ Building data-driven ASP.NET Web Form pages with OData
- ▶ Adopting OData in ASP.NET MVC web applications
- ▶ Building ASP.NET Page UI with OData and XSLT
- ▶ Building AJAX style data-driven web pages with jQuery
- ▶ Consuming OData service with datajs script library
- ▶ Using OData service in Silverlight data access application
- ▶ Consuming WCF Data Service in PHP pages

Introduction

Nowadays, web applications have become more and more popular as the choice for developing various kinds of applications; not only for traditional HTML web page based Internet websites, but also for intranet or business-specific applications. This is because web applications use HTML and script-based web pages as the main user interfaces, which can be adapted by different web browsers and require little or zero installation on the client side. In addition, the HTTP-based transport makes web applications quite easy to work across a complicated network environment.

With the support of new, rich client features in web browsers, it is quite convenient for us to develop rich and powerful web applications by using JavaScript or other technologies such as Flash, Silverlight, or HTML 5. Also, such kinds of applications often use asynchronous or background channels to exchange data with a server so as to avoid frequent refreshing on the web browser. The most common data exchanging approaches used are XML- or JSON-based web services, which can be implemented by many existing service development technologies, such as ASP.NET Web Service, and WCF service. Since OData is naturally HTTP + XML/JSON based, it is quite a good choice for implementing the services for data exchanging in rich interactive web applications. In this chapter, we will demonstrate how to take advantage of OData service (especially, the WCF Data Service implementation) in various kinds of web application development scenarios including ASP.NET Web Form application, ASP.NET MVC application, Plain HTML+ jQuery-based AJAX web application, Silverlight web application, and PHP web application.

Building data-driven ASP.NET Web Form pages with OData

Back to the earlier stage of Microsoft .NET Framework, ASP.NET has already been provided as the main web application development platform. And the Web Form programming model (which uses **Web Server Controls** and **PostBack** events to simulate desktop windows application like UI interactions) really simplifies the development of a rich, functional, and dynamic web page. And with the help of ASP.NET data binding and rich **DataBound Controls**, we can build various kinds of powerful data-driven web pages. In this recipe, we will introduce how to incorporate OData service as a data source for building data-driven web pages through the ASP.NET Web Form page framework.

Getting ready

In this sample, we will create an ASP.NET Web Form page, which uses some built-in controls to display the Categories and Products information from the Northwind OData service.

The source code for this recipe can be found in the \ch04\ODataDrivenWebAppSln directory.

How to do it...

1. Create a new ASP.NET web application as the Web Form page container.
2. Create the OData client proxy against the Northwind OData service (see the following screenshot).

3. Create a new **Web Form** page in the web application (see the following screenshot).

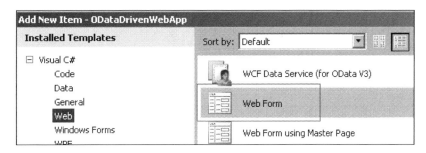

Now, the web application should look like the following structure in Visual Studio Solution Explorer:

4. Open the .aspx page file and add the DropDownList and GridView controls (for displaying the Categories and Products entities) in the HTML markup (see the following code snippet).

```
<body>
    <form id="form1" runat="server">
    <div>
        <div>
            Categories: <asp:DropDownList ID="lstCategories"
runat="server"
                AutoPostBack="true" DataTextField="CategoryName"
DataValueField="CategoryID"
                onselectedindexchanged="lstCategories_
SelectedIndexChanged">
            </asp:DropDownList>
```

```
        </div>
        <div>
            Products under selected Category:
            <asp:GridView ID="gridProducts" runat="server"
AutoGenerateColumns="true">

            </asp:GridView>
        </div>
    </div>
    </form>
</body>
```

 By switching to the **Design** view in the Visual Studio page editor, we can have a rough outlook of the **Web Form** page under editing (see the following screenshot).

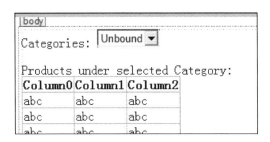

5. Add the code for populating the Categories and Products data in the **Web Form** page's code-behind file (see the following code snippet).

```
public partial class ProductsByCategoryPage : System.Web.UI.Page
{
    protected void Page_Load(object sender, EventArgs e)
    {
        if (!IsPostBack)
        {
            var ctx = CreateODataProxy();
            lstCategories.DataSource = ctx.Categories;
            lstCategories.DataBind();

            int id = int.Parse(lstCategories.SelectedValue);
            BindProductsByCategory(id);
        }
    }

    protected void lstCategories_SelectedIndexChanged(object
sender, EventArgs e)
```

```
    {
        int id = int.Parse(lstCategories.SelectedValue);
        BindProductsByCategory(id);
    }

    void BindProductsByCategory(int categoryID)
    {
        var ctx = CreateODataProxy();
        var products = ctx.Products.Where(p => p.CategoryID ==
categoryID);
        gridProducts.DataSource = products;
        gridProducts.DataBind();
    }

    . . . . . .

}
```

6. Launch the **Web Form** page and use the `DropDownList` control to filter the
    `Product` items based on selected `Category` (see the following screenshot).

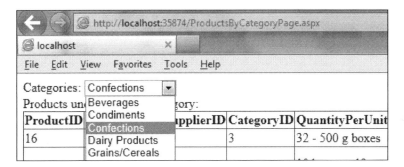

How it works...

The sample Web Form page uses the Visual Studio generated OData proxy for retrieving
the `Categories` and `Products` data from the Northwind OData service. Since the OData
query results generated by the strong-typed proxy are of `IQueryable` type, we can directly
bind them to those ASP.NET built-in WebForm DataBound controls, such as `DropDownList`,
`GridView`, `DataList`, `ListView`, and so on. What we need to do is simply assign the OData
entity collection (returned by the query) to the `DataSource` property of the target DataBound
Controls and call the `DataBind` method. In the sample page, we bind all the `Category`
entity objects to the `DropDownList` control, when the page is loaded at the first time. Then,
whenever a new `Category` item is selected, the code within the `SelectedIndexChanged`
event (of the `DropDownList` control) will retrieve the new `Product` entity objects from the
service and bind them to the `GridView` control.

See also

▶ *Building an OData service via WCF Data Service* recipe and *ADO.NET Entity Framework* in *Chapter 1, Building OData Services*

▶ *Using Visual Studio to generate strong-typed OData client proxy* recipe in *Chapter 2, Working with OData at Client Side*

Adopting OData in ASP.NET MVC web applications

Ever since ASP.NET 3.5, there has been a new ASP.NET web application programming model called **ASP.NET MVC**, which provides an alternative to the ASP.NET Web Form pattern for developing web applications. ASP.NET MVC is a lightweight, highly testable presentation framework, which follows the famous Model-View-Controller design pattern. By using ASP.NET MVC, it is quite convenient for us to separate the page UI presentation from the data processing code logic.

Since OData service provides a simple and straight means for data accessing and manipulation, it is quite reasonable to incorporate OData service into an ASP.NET MVC web application as part of the Model layer. In this recipe, we will demonstrate a sample case which uses ASP.NET MVC + OData service to build typical data-driven web pages.

Getting ready

We will create an ASP.NET MVC web application, which allows users to view and edit the Category entities exposed in the sample Northwind OData service. Make sure you have installed ASP.NET MVC 3.0 (or higher) and its related developer tools. For more information on ASP.NET MVC 3.0 have a look at *Getting Started with ASP.NET MVC 3* at http://www.asp.net/mvc.

The source code for this recipe can be found in the \ch04\ODataMVCWebSln directory.

How to do it...

1. Create a new ASP.NET web application which contains the Northwind OData service.

   For demonstration, we need to enable both AllRead and AllWrite access rules on the Categories entity set (see the following code snippet).

   ```
   public class NWDataService : DataService<NorthwindEntities>
   {
       public static void InitializeService(DataServiceConfiguration config)
       {
   ```

```
......          config.SetEntitySetAccessRule("Categories",
EntitySetRights.AllRead | EntitySetRights.AllWrite);
    }
}
```

2. Create new **ASP.NET MVC 3 Web Application** (see the following screenshot).

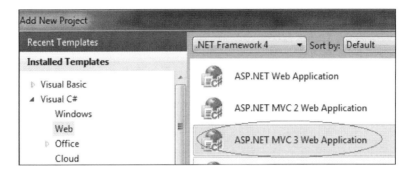

After creating **ASP.NET MVC 3 Web Application**, we can find the predefined project structure (in Visual Studio) as shown in the following screenshot:

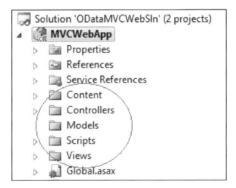

3. Create the OData client proxy (against the Northwind OData service) by using the Visual Studio Add Service Reference wizard (see the following screenshot).

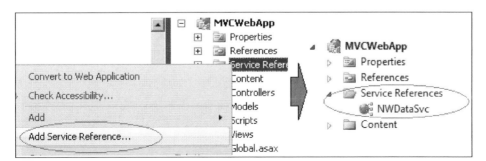

4. Create a helper class to encapsulate the entire code logic for performing an OData service query and update (see the following `ODataHelper` class).

```
public class ODataHelper
{
    static Uri _svcUri = new Uri("http://localhost:2766/
NWDataService.svc/");
    static NorthwindEntities _ctx = null;

    public static NorthwindEntities GetServiceContext(){
        if(_ctx == null) {
            _ctx = new NorthwindEntities(_svcUri);
        }
        return _ctx;
    }

    public static List<Category> GetCategoryList(){
        var ctx = GetServiceContext();
        var categories = ctx.Categories.ToList();
        return categories;
    }

    public static Category GetSingleCategory(int id)
    {
        var ctx = GetServiceContext();
        var category = ctx.Categories.Where(c => c.CategoryID ==
id).First();
        return category;
    }

    public static void UpdateCategory(Category category)
    {
        var ctx = GetServiceContext();

        var dataObj = ctx.Categories.Where(c => c.CategoryID ==
category.CategoryID).First();
        dataObj.CategoryName = category.CategoryName;
        dataObj.Description = category.Description;

        ctx.UpdateObject(dataObj);
        ctx.SaveChanges();
    }
}
```

5. Create a new **MVC 3 Controller Class** (see the following screenshot) and name it as NorthwindCategoryController.

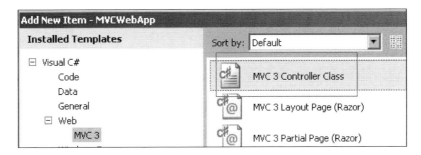

6. Add the Action methods (within the NorthwindCategoryController class) for displaying and editing Category data.

The following code snippet shows all the three Action methods defined in the sample controller class:

```
public class NorthwindCategoryController : Controller
{
    public ActionResult Index()
    {
        var categories = ODataHelper.GetCategoryList();

        return View(categories);
    }

    public ActionResult Edit(int id)
    {
        var category = ODataHelper.GetSingleCategory(id);
        return View(category);
    }

    [HttpPost]
    public ActionResult Edit(Category category)
    {
        try
        {
            ODataHelper.UpdateCategory(category);

            return RedirectToAction("Index");
        }
        catch(Exception ex)
        {
            return Content(ex.ToString());
        }
    }
}
```

7. Select the `Index` Action method (in the `NorthwindCategoryController` class) and right-click to launch the **Add View...** wizard (see the following screenshot).

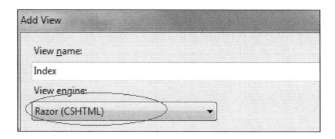

8. In the prompted **Add View** dialog, specify **View name** and select **Razor (CSHTML)** as the **View engine** (see the following screenshot).

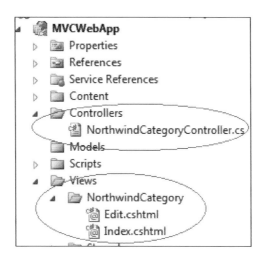

9. Repeat steps 7 and 8 to create the View for the `Edit` Action method.

Now, the ASP.NET MVC web application should look like the following structure in Visual Studio:

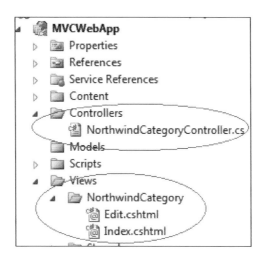

10. Define the HTML template (for each View) within the `.cshtml` file.

The following is the main HTML fragment of the `Index.cshtml` file (for the `Index` View):

```
<body>
    <div>
        <h1>Category List</h1>
        <table>
            <thead>
                <tr>
                    <th>ID</th>
                    <th>Name</th>
                    <th>Description</th>
                    <th>Edit</th>
                </tr>
            </thead>
            <tbody>
                @foreach (var c in Model)
                {
                <tr>
                    <td>@c.CategoryID</td>
                    <td>@c.CategoryName</td>
                    <td>@c.Description</td>
                    <td>@Html.ActionLink("Edit", "Edit", new
RouteValueDictionary {{"id", c.CategoryID} })</td>
                </tr>
                }
            </tbody>
        </table>
    </div>
</body>
```

And the main HTML fragment of the `Edit.cshtml` file (for the `Edit` View) is shown as follows:

```
<body>
    @using (Html.BeginForm()) {
        @Html.ValidationSummary(true)
        <fieldset>
            <legend><h1>Edit Category Fields</h1></legend>

            @Html.HiddenFor(model => model.CategoryID)

            <div class="editor-label">
                @Html.LabelFor(model => model.CategoryName)
            </div>
```

```
            <div class="editor-field">
                @Html.EditorFor(model => model.CategoryName)
                @Html.ValidationMessageFor(model => model.
    CategoryName)
            </div>

            <div class="editor-label">
                @Html.LabelFor(model => model.Description)
            </div>
            <div class="editor-field">
                @Html.EditorFor(model => model.Description)
                @Html.ValidationMessageFor(model => model.
    Description)
            </div>

            <p>
                <input type="submit" value="Save" />
            </p>
        </fieldset>
    }
    <div>
        <h2>@Html.ActionLink("Back to List", "Index")</h2>
    </div>
</body>
```

11. Launch the ASP.NET MVC web application and access
    `NorthwindCategoryController` in web browser.

    The following screenshot shows the output in the web browser by invoking the `Index`
    Action method:

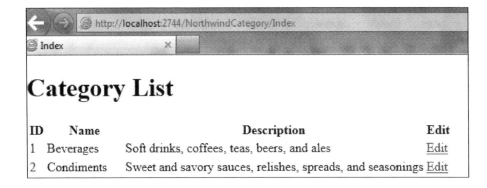

And the following is the web browser output by invoking the `Edit` Action method, which can be triggered through the **Edit** hyperlink on each category row:

How it works...

The ASP.NET MVC framework relies on three key components. They are Model, View, and Controller. Model takes care of the application data logic. View takes care of the UI presentation. Controller handles client requests, cooperates with Model to process data, and finally selects proper View to render output.

In this sample, the `NorthwindCategoryController` class acts as Controller, which contains two Action methods. The Action methods use the `ODataHelper` class to query and update the `Category` entities. The `Category` entity objects returned by helper class then act as Model. As for the `.cshtml` file based Views, they simply accept the `Category` entities passed from the Model and render the HTML content to the client. Such a loose-coupled programming model really makes the underlying code logic (such as data query and manipulation) clearly separated from the front-web UI.

The `.cshtml` View used in this sample is based on a new View engine called **Razor** introduced in ASP.NET MVC 3.0. The Razor engine uses simpler and cleaner syntax compared to the Web Form (`.aspx`) View engine, which makes it quite convenient to edit both in Visual Studio IDE and plain text editors. The following blog entry is a good one for you to get started on the Razor View engine.

```
http://weblogs.asp.net/scottgu/archive/2010/07/02/
introducing-razor.aspx
```

Another thing worth noticing is that ASP.NET MVC framework relies on the **ASP.NET URL Routing** feature. To make sure the *Controller* and *Action* name-based URL address patterns work, we need to register the proper URL Routing rules (modify the default values generated by the ASP.NET MVC project template) in the `Application_Start` event of the `Global.asax` class (see the following code snippet below).

```
public static void RegisterRoutes(RouteCollection routes)
{
    routes.IgnoreRoute("{resource}.axd/{*pathInfo}");

    routes.MapRoute(
        "Default", // Route name
        "{controller}/{action}/{id}", // URL with parameters
        new { controller = "NorthwindCategory", action = "Index", id =
UrlParameter.Optional } // Parameter defaults
    );
}

protected void Application_Start()
{
......
    RegisterRoutes(RouteTable.Routes);
}
```

For more information about ASP.NET MVC development, you can visit the ASP.NET MVC official site at `http://www.asp.net/mvc`.

See also

> ▶ *Using Visual Studio to generate strong-typed OData client proxy* recipe in *Chapter 2, Working with OData at Client Side*

> ▶ *Editing and deleting data through WCF Data Service client library* recipe in *Chapter 2, Working with OData at Client Side*

Building ASP.NET Page UI with OData and XSLT

Now, we have gone through two cases about building data-driven ASP.NET web applications with OData service. And both cases use a strong-typed OData client proxy for accessing the target OData service. Then, what if we do not want to use a strong-typed client proxy? There are surely other alternatives for us to build a web page UI without using the strong-typed client proxy. In this recipe, we will demonstrate a special case which uses raw OData response (of **Atom XML** format) and **XSLT** (Extensible Stylesheet Language Transformation) to construct the UI for ASP.NET data-driven web pages.

Getting ready

The source code for this recipe can be found in the \ch04\ODataXSLTWebSln directory.

How to do it...

1. Get the Northwind OData service ready and make sure the Categories and Products entity sets are exposed.

2. Create a new ASP.NET empty web application.

3. Add a new Web Form page in the web application.

4. Open the Web Form page (.aspx file) and add the following four controls into it:

   □ An XmlDataSource control for supplying the Category list

   □ An XmlDataSource control for supplying Products associated with the selected Category

   □ A DropDownList control for displaying the Category list

   □ A GridView control for displaying Products associated with the selected Category

   After adding the preceding Controls, the HTML markup of the page should look as follows:

```
<div>
        <asp:XmlDataSource ID="dsXmlCategories" runat="server"
            TransformFile="~/TransformCategory.xslt"
            XPath="//category" />
        <asp:XmlDataSource ID="dsXmlProducts" runat="server"
            TransformFile="~/TransformProduct.xslt"
            XPath="//product" />

        <b>Categories: </b><asp:DropDownList ID="lstCategories"
runat="server"
            DataSourceID="dsXmlCategories"
            DataTextField="name" DataValueField="id"
AutoPostBack="True"
            onselectedindexchanged="lstCategories_
SelectedIndexChanged" >
        </asp:DropDownList>
        <br /><br />
        Products under selected Category:
        <br />
        <asp:GridView ID="gridProducts" runat="server"
            AutoGenerateColumns="false"
            DataSourceID="dsXmlProducts" >
```

```
                    <Columns>
                        <asp:BoundField DataField="ID"
HeaderText="ID" />
                        <asp:BoundField DataField="Name"
HeaderText="Product Name" />
                        <asp:BoundField DataField="SupplierID"
HeaderText="Supplier ID" />
                        <asp:BoundField DataField="UnitPrice"
HeaderText="Unit Price" />
                        <asp:CheckBoxField DataField="Discontinued"
HeaderText="Discontinued" />
                    </Columns>
            </asp:GridView>
        </div>
```

5. Open the page's code-behind file and add code for populating the Categories and Products data from the OData service (see the following code snippet).

```
public partial class ProductsByCategoryWithXSLT : System.Web.
UI.Page
{
    const string SVC_BASE = "http://localhost:4297/NWDataService.
svc/";

    protected void Page_Load(object sender, EventArgs e)
    {
        if (!IsPostBack)
        {
            // Init the two XmlDataSource controls
            dsXmlCategories.DataFile = SVC_BASE + "Categories?$sel
ect=CategoryID,CategoryName";
            dsXmlProducts.DataFile = SVC_BASE + "Categories(1)/
Products";
        }
    }

    protected void lstCategories_SelectedIndexChanged(object
sender, EventArgs e)
    {
        var categoryID = lstCategories.SelectedValue;
        dsXmlProducts.DataFile =
            string.Format(
                SVC_BASE + "Categories({0})/Products",
                categoryID
            );

        gridProducts.DataBind();
    }
}
```

6. Create the XSLT files for transforming the Atom XML format OData query responses.

The following is the content of the `TransformCategory.xslt` file, which helps transform the `Category` list query response:

```
<xsl:stylesheet version="1.0"
     xmlns:xsl="http://www.w3.org/1999/XSL/Transform"
     xmlns:m="http://schemas.microsoft.com/ado/2007/08/
dataservices/metadata"
     xmlns:d="http://schemas.microsoft.com/ado/2007/08/
dataservices"
              >
<!-- root template -->
  <xsl:template match="/">
    <categories>
      <xsl:apply-templates/>
    </categories>
  </xsl:template>

<!-- individual category template -->
  <xsl:template match="m:properties">
    <category>
      <xsl:attribute name="id">
        <xsl:value-of select="./d:CategoryID" />
      </xsl:attribute>
      <xsl:attribute name="name">
        <xsl:value-of select="./d:CategoryName" />
      </xsl:attribute>
    </category>
  </xsl:template>
</xsl:stylesheet>
```

And the `TransformProduct.xslt` file (used for transforming the `Product` list query response) looks quite similar (see the following XSLT fragment).

```
<!-- root template -->
  <xsl:template match="/">
    <products>
      <xsl:apply-templates/>
    </products>
  </xsl:template>

<!-- individual product template -->
  <xsl:template match="m:properties">
    <product>
      <xsl:attribute name="ID">
        <xsl:value-of select="./d:ProductID" />
```

```
        </xsl:attribute>
        <xsl:attribute name="Name">
          <xsl:value-of select="./d:ProductName" />
        </xsl:attribute>
        <xsl:attribute name="SupplierID">
          <xsl:value-of select="./d:SupplierID" />
        </xsl:attribute>
        <xsl:attribute name="UnitPrice">
          <xsl:value-of select="./d:UnitPrice" />
        </xsl:attribute>
        <xsl:attribute name="Discontinued">
          <xsl:value-of select="./d:Discontinued " />
        </xsl:attribute>
      </product>
    </xsl:template>
```

7. Launch the Web Form page in the web browser. The following screenshot shows the web browser output when browsing the `ProductsByCategoryWithXSLT.aspx` page in the sample web application:

Categories: Grains/Cereals ▾

Products under selected Category:

ID	Product Name	Supplier ID	Unit Price	Discontinued
22	Gustaf's Kn?ckebr?d	9	21.0000	☐
23	Tunnbr?d	9	9.0000	☐
42	Singaporean Hokkien Fried Mee	20	14.0000	☑

How it works...

In the preceding sample page, we directly use the raw Uri string (with query options) to fetch the entities from the Northwind OData service. Whenever a new `Category` item is selected, we rebuild the query Uri string in the `SelectedIndexChanged` event of the `DropDownList` control and also repopulate the `XmlDataSource` control so that the new Product list will be presented on the page UI.

For each `XmlDataSource` control, we have specified a XSLT file, which helps transform the Atom XML format OData query response into the target XML format (expected by the `DropDownList` and `GridView` Controls). Both files use the similar XSLT code logic, which first locates the entity elements (via XPath) within the Atom XML response document, and then converts them into a simplified XML element list.

As we can see, with such a raw OData query Uri + XSLT approach, we can generate an OData-driven ASP.NET page without using any strong-typed client proxy.

There's more...

The preceding sample page (`ProductsByCategoryWithXSLT.aspx`) still uses ASP.NET DataBound Controls (such as the `DropDownList` and `GridView` Controls) to render the HTML page UI. If you want to generate the HTML content completely through XSLT, you can try using the ASP.NET `Xml` control instead. For more information on this, you can refer to the `ODataXSLT2HTMLPage.aspx` page in the sample code of this recipe.

See also

▸ *Filtering OData query results by using query options* recipe in *Chapter 2, Working with OData at Client Side*

▸ *Building data-driven ASP.NET Web Form pages with OData* recipe in *Chapter 4, Using OData in Web Application*

Building AJAX style data-driven web pages with jQuery

Nowadays, with the support of AJAX (Asynchronous JavaScript and XML)-based web script technologies, more and more web applications are developed with rich interactive and high responding web pages, which do not require lots of post-backs for data refreshing or user interactions. jQuery is one of the most popular AJAX script libraries which greatly simplify the rich client-side script programming in HTML-based web pages. In this recipe, we will introduce how to take advantage of the jQuery script library for building OData-enabled AJAX style web pages.

Getting ready

The sample page here still uses the Northwind OData service as data source and provides an AJAX-style UI for exploring the `Categories` and `Products` information (see the following screenshot).

Categories: Confections ▼				
ID	**Product Name**	**Supplier ID**	**Unit Price**	**Discontinued**
16	Pavlova	7	17.4500	false
19	Teatime Chocolate Biscuits	8	9.2000	false
20	Sir Rodney's Marmalade	8	81.0000	false

You can download the jQuery script library from its official site or directly import it through Microsoft AJAX CDN (refer to the following links).

Downloading jQuery at `http://docs.jquery.com/Downloading_jQuery`

Microsoft Ajax Content Delivery Network at `http://www.asp.net/ajaxlibrary/cdn.ashx`

The source code for this recipe can be found in the `\ch04\ODataWithJQuerySln` directory.

How to do it...

1. Create a new ASP.NET web application which contains the Northwind OData service (with the `Categories` and `Products` entity sets exposed).

2. Import the jQuery script library (downloaded to local disk) into the web application.

    The jQuery library used here is of version `1.4.4` and is put in the **scripts** subfolder in the sample web application (see the following screenshot).

3. Create a new **HTML Page** in the web application (see the following screenshot)

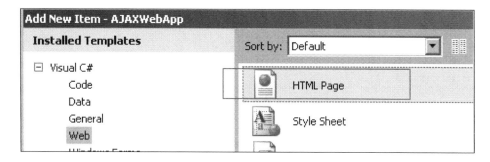

4. Open the `.htm` page file and add the following HTML content:

    ```
    <html>
    <head>
        <title></title>
        <script src="scripts/jquery-1.4.4.min.js"></script>
    ```

```
            <script src="scripts/ProductsByCategory.js"></script>
    </head>
    <body>
        <div>
            Categories: <select id='lstCategories'></select>
        </div>
        <hr />
        <div>
            <table>
                <thead>
                    <tr>
                        <th>ID</th>
                        <th>Product Name</th>
                        <th>Supplier ID</th>
                        <th>Unit Price</th>
                        <th>Discontinued</th>
                    </tr>
                </thead>
                <tbody id='tbbProducts'>
                </tbody>
            </table>
        </div>
    </body>
</html>
```

5. Create the main application script file (named `ProductsByCategory.js`) and put it in the same folder as the jQuery script file.

6. Add the function for loading the `Category` list in the `ProductsByCategory.js` file (see the following `loadCategories` function).

```
function loadCategories() {
    var svc_url = "../NWDataService.svc/Categories?$select=Categor
yID,CategoryName";
    $.ajax({
        type: "GET",
        url: svc_url,
        dataType: "json",
        success: function (resp) {
            var categories = resp.d;
            $.each(categories, function (i, category) {
                // Construct dropdown item
                var item = $("<option>");
                item.attr("value", category.CategoryID);
                item.text(category.CategoryName);
                // Add Item into dropdownlist
```

```
            $("#lstCategories").append(item);
        });
        // Load the Products for default Category
        $("#lstCategories").attr("selectedIndex", 0);
        loadProductsByCategory($("#lstCategories").val());
    },
    error: function () {
        alert("Failed to retrieve Category items!");
    }
    });
}
```

7. Add the function for loading the `Product` list based on the selected `Category` item (see the following `loadProductsByCategory` function).

```
function loadProductsByCategory(_categoryID) {
    //alert("load products of category == " + _categoryID);

    var svc_url = "../NWDataService.svc/Categories(" + _categoryID
+ ")/Products";
    $.ajax({
        type: "GET",
        url: svc_url,
        dataType: "json",
        success: function (resp) {
            var products = resp.d;
            // Clear the table
            var tBody = $("#tbbProducts");
            tBody.html("");

            // Add table row for each Product
            $.each(products, function (i, product) {
                var tRow = $("<tr>");
                var tColID = $("<td>" + product.ProductID + "</
td>");
                var tColName = $("<td>" + product.ProductName +
"</td>");
                var tColSupID = $("<td>" + product.SupplierID +
"</td>");
                var tColUnitPrice = $("<td>" + product.UnitPrice +
"</td>");
                var tColDiscontinued = $("<td>" + product.
Discontinued + "</td>");
                tRow.append(tColID);
                tRow.append(tColName);
                tRow.append(tColSupID);
```

```
                        tRow.append(tColUnitPrice);
                        tRow.append(tColDiscontinued);
                        tBody.append(tRow);
                });

            },
            error: function () {
                alert("Failed to retrieve Category items!");
            }
        });
    }
```

8. Add the page initialization script at the bottom of the `ProductsByCategory.js` file (see the following code snippet).

```
$(document).ready(function () {

    $("#lstCategories").bind("change", function () {
        var categoryID = $(this).val();
        loadProductsByCategory(categoryID);
    });

    loadCategories();
});
```

How it works...

In the sample page, all application-specific code is defined in the `ProductsByCategory.js` file while the `.htm` page only contains the HTML content. Whenever the sample page is rendered in web browser, the initializing script code is executed, which calls the `loadCategories` function to populate the `Category` list. Then, if a certain `Category` item is selected, the `loadProductsByCategory` function is called so as to display the associated `Product` list.

Both `loadCategories` and `loadProductsByCategory` functions use the `$.ajax` function (provided by the jQuery library) to perform OData queries against the Northwind OData service. When invoking the `$.ajax` function, we supply the Uri string of the OData query, the data type we expect (XML or JSON), and a callback function for processing the response data (in case, the request succeeds). For detailed information on using the `$.ajax` function, you can refer to the following document:

jQuery.ajax() at `http://api.jquery.com/jQuery.ajax/`

By using some HTTP sniffer tools or web browsers' debug extensions, we can check the underlying HTTP requests issued by the jQuery library (see the following screenshot).

There's more...

In this sample, we put the AJAX web page in the same web application with the Northwind OData service. This is because web page script function (such as $.ajax in jQuery library) cannot directly access a remote service due to the **XSS** (Cross-site scripting) restriction (see the following reference).

http://en.wikipedia.org/wiki/Cross-site_scripting

In case you want to access a remote service via AJAX script code, you can build a proxy service in the local web application, which acts as the connector between the AJAX web page and the remote service.

See also

▶ *Building data-driven ASP.NET Web Form pages with OData* recipe in *Chapter 4, Using OData in Web Application*

▶ *Consuming OData service with datajs script library* recipe in *Chapter 4, Using OData in Web Application*

Consuming OData service with datajs script library

From the previous recipe, we can find that it is quite simple and straight for us to query OData service through existing AJAX script libraries (like jQuery). However, if we want to perform edit and update operations against OData service, it would be a bit complicated for us to construct the raw OData requests (of Atom XML or JSON format) via normal AJAX script code. Then, is there a more convenient means for us to perform all **CRUD** operations against the OData service within AJAX script code? Fortunately, there is already a full-fledged cross-browser script library called **datajs** which can help achieving this goal. In this recipe, we will use some typical OData CRUD cases to demonstrate the usage of datajs script library in AJAX web pages.

Getting ready

Here we will create an AJAX web page which allows user to view, create, and delete `Category` items (against the Northwind OData service) by using the datajs script library. To simplify the HTML UI generation code, we will also use the jQuery script library here. The following screenshot shows the main UI of the sample web page:

You can get the datajs script library from the following CodePlex workspace:

datajs - JavaScript Library for data-centric web applications at
`http://datajs.codeplex.com/`

The source code for this recipe can be found in the `\ch04\DatajsODataSln` directory.

How to do it...

1. Create a new ASP.NET web application, which contains the Northwind OData service.

2. Add the datajs and jQuery script libraries into the web application. The datajs library used here is of 1.0.2 version (see the following screenshot).

3. Create the main HTML page (`Categories.htm`) in the web application.

4. Fill the following HTML content into the `Categories.htm` page:

```
<head>
    <title></title>
    <script src="scripts/jquery-1.4.4.min.js"></script>
    <script src="scripts/datajs-1.0.2.min.js"></script>
    <script src="scripts/Categories.js"></script>
</head>
<body>
    <h1>All Categories</h1>
    <table>
        <thead>
            <tr>
                <th>ID</th>
                <th>Name</th>
                <th>Description</th>
                <th>Product Count</th>
                <th>Delete</th>
            </tr>
        </thead>
        <tbody id="tbbCategories">
        </tbody>
    </table>
    <h1>Add New Category</h1>
    <fieldset>
        Name:    <input id="txtName" type="text"
value="NewCategory" /><br />
        Description:    <textarea id="txtDescription">Description
of New Category</textarea><br />
```

```
          <input type="button" value="Create"
onclick="addNewCategory();" />
     </fieldset>
</body>
```

5. Create the main script file (`Categories.js`) and put it in the same folder as the datajs script library.

6. Add the script code for querying all the `Category` items in the `Categories.js` file (see the following `showAllCategories` function).

```
function showAllCategories() {
     OData.read("../NorthwindOData.svc/
Categories?$expand=Products",
          function (data, request) {

               var tbb = $("#tbbCategories");
               tbb.html("");
               for (var i = 0; i < data.results.length; ++i) {
                    var tRow = $("<tr>");
                    tRow.append("<td>" + data.results[i].
CategoryID + "</td>");
                    tRow.append("<td>" + data.results[i].
CategoryName + "</td>");
                    tRow.append("<td>" + data.results[i].
Description + "</td>");
                    tRow.append("<td>" + data.results[i].Products.
length + "</td>");
                    tRow.append("<td><input type='button'
value='Delete' onclick='deleteCategory(" + data.results[i].
CategoryID + ");' /></td>");
                    tbb.append(tRow);
               }
          });
}
```

7. Add the script code for creating a new `Category` item in the `Categories.js` file (see the following `addNewCategory` function).

```
function addNewCategory() {
     if (!confirm("Are you sure to create the new Category item?"))
return false;

     var name = $("#txtName").val();
     var desc = $("#txtDescription").val();

     var req = {
          requestUri: "../NorthwindOData.svc/Categories",
```

```
        method: "POST",
        data: { CategoryName: name, Description: desc, Picture:
null }
    };

    OData.request(
            req,
            function (data) {
                alert("Creation completed.");
                window.location.reload();
            },
            function (err) {
                alert("Error: " + err.message + " - " + JSON.
stringify(err));
            }
        );
}
```

8. Add the script code for deleting the `Category` item in the `Categories.js` file (see the following `deleteCategory` function).

```
function deleteCategory(categoryID) {
    if (!confirm("Are you sure to delete this Category item?"))
return false;

    var req = {
        requestUri: "../NorthwindOData.svc/Categories(" +
categoryID + ")",
        method: "DELETE"
    };

    OData.request(
            req,
            function (data) {
                alert("Deleting completed.");
                window.location.reload();
            },
            function (err) {
                alert("Error: " + err.message + " - " + JSON.
stringify(err));
            }
        );
}
```

In addition, the script file will add the following code to call the `showAllCategories` function when the sample page is loaded in web browser.

```
$(document).ready(function () {
    showAllCategories();
});
```

How it works...

Although the sample page still uses the jQuery library for presenting the HTML page UI, all OData service accessing related code relies on the datajs library. As shown in the preceding functions, the datajs library has provided a well-defined object model for performing various kinds of OData operations. By using the `OData.read` function, we can query the OData service with the Uri string supplied in the first parameter. And the `OData.request` function provides more advanced options for sending OData requests (such as `Create`, `Update`, `Delete`, and so on) against the target service. Before invoking the `OData.request` function, we need to construct a JSON object which contains all necessary request properties including query Uri, request method (such as `GET`, `POST`), and data entity objects (like the `Category` entity object supplied in the `addNewCategory` function).

For more information about using the datajs library, you can refer to the following web documentation:

datajs documentation at `http://datajs.codeplex.com/documentation`

See also

► *Building data-driven ASP.NET Web Form pages with OData* recipe in *Chapter 4, Using OData in Web Application*

► *Building AJAX style data-driven web pages with jQuery* recipe in *Chapter 4, Using OData in Web Application*

Using OData service in Silverlight data access application

So far we have discussed several cases of developing a data-driven web application with OData. All of them use HTML pages as the main web UI and most of them are driven by JavaScript code. However, for .NET web developers, we have another nice choice for building rich, interactive web applications—Silverlight. The fact that Silverlight adopts both XAML-based UI framework (like what WPF uses) and strong-typed .NET programming languages makes it the preferred choice especially when you're already familiar with XAML syntax and general .NET Framework based programming.

In this recipe, we will demonstrate how to use the OData service for developing a Silverlight data access application.

Getting ready

The sample Silverlight application we will build here allows users to explore the `Customers`, `Orders`, and `Order_Details` data by using the Northwind OData service. The application consists of two Silverlight pages, and users can navigate between them so as to switch between different data views (see the following screenshot).

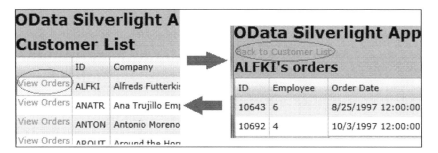

Make sure you have the latest version of Silverlight Developer Runtime and Silverlight Tools for Visual Studio installed. You can get them from the Silverlight official site at `http://www.silverlight.net/downloads`.

The source code for this recipe can be found in the `\ch04\ODataSilverlightSln` directory.

How to do it...

1. Launch the **New Project** wizard and select the **Silverlight Application** template (see the following screenshot).

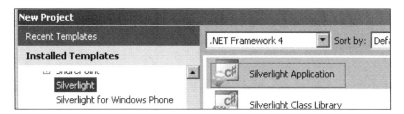

2. In the **New Silverlight Application** dialog, choose to create a new **ASP.NET Web Application Project** for hosting the Silverlight application (see the following screenshot).

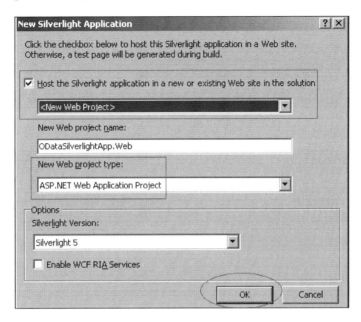

3. Click on the **OK** button to create the **Silverlight Application** project.

4. Add the Northwind OData service into the Silverlight host web application (see the **ODataSilverlightApp.Web** project shown in the following screenshot).

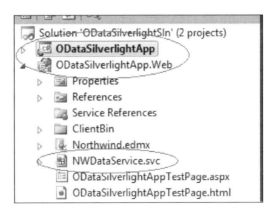

5. Add the OData client proxy in the **ODataSilverlightApp** project (see the following screenshot).

6. Define a helper class for creating data context object of OData client proxy (see the following code snippet).

```
public class ODataHelper
{
    static Uri _svcUri = new Uri("NWDataService.svc", UriKind.
Relative);
    static NWDataSvc.NorthwindEntities _ctx = null;

    public static NWDataSvc.NorthwindEntities GetServiceContext()
    {
        if (_ctx == null)
        {
            _ctx = new NWDataSvc.NorthwindEntities(_svcUri);
        }
        return _ctx;
    }
}
```

7. Create the following Silverlight pages in the **ODataSilverlightApp** project:

   ❑ MainPage.xaml—the navigation container page

   ❑ CustomerList.xaml—the page for displaying Customer list

   ❑ CustomerOrders.xaml—the page for displaying Order list of a selected customer

 The MainPage.xaml page is pre-generated by Visual Studio when you create the Silverlight application.

The following screenshot shows the **ODataSilverlightApp** project structure after creating the preceding three pages:

8. Define the XAML content for the `MainPage.xaml` page (see the following XAML fragment).

```
<Grid x:Name="LayoutRoot" Background="LightGray">
        <StackPanel>
                <TextBlock  FontSize="20" FontWeight="Bold">
                    OData Silverlight Application
                </TextBlock>
                <sdk:Frame x:Name="NavFrame"
                                Source="/CustomerList.xaml" >
                </sdk:Frame>
        </StackPanel>
    </Grid>
```

9. Define the XAML content for the `CustomerList.xaml` page (see the following XAML fragment).

```
<navigation:Page x:Class="ODataSilverlightApp.CustomerList"
......
            Loaded="Page_Loaded">
    <Grid x:Name="LayoutRoot">
            <StackPanel>
                    <TextBlock FontSize="20" FontWeight="Bold">Customer
List</TextBlock>
                    <sdk:DataGrid Name="dgCustomers"
                                    AutoGenerateColumns="false"
IsReadOnly="True" Height="200" >
                        <sdk:DataGrid.Columns>
                            <sdk:DataGridTemplateColumn>
                                <sdk:DataGridTemplateColumn.CellTemplate>
                                <DataTemplate>
                                    <HyperlinkButton
NavigateUri="{Binding CustomerID, StringFormat='/CustomerOrders.
xaml?customerID=\{0\}'}"
```

```
                                                        Content="View
Orders" TargetName="NavFrame" />
                            </DataTemplate>
                        </sdk:DataGridTemplateColumn.CellTemplate>
                    </sdk:DataGridTemplateColumn>
                        <sdk:DataGridTextColumn Binding="{Binding
CustomerID}" Header="ID"></sdk:DataGridTextColumn>
                        <sdk:DataGridTextColumn Binding="{Binding
CompanyName}" Header="Company"></sdk:DataGridTextColumn>
                        <sdk:DataGridTextColumn Binding="{Binding
ContactName}" Header="Contact"></sdk:DataGridTextColumn>
                        <sdk:DataGridTextColumn Binding="{Binding
Address}" Header="Address"></sdk:DataGridTextColumn>
                        <sdk:DataGridTextColumn Binding="{Binding
Phone}" Header="Phone"></sdk:DataGridTextColumn>
                    </sdk:DataGrid.Columns>
                </sdk:DataGrid>
            </StackPanel>
        </Grid>
</navigation:Page>
```

10. Add the code for loading the `Customer` list in the code-behind file of the `CustomerList.xaml` page (see the following `Page_Loaded` function).

```
private void Page_Loaded(object sender, RoutedEventArgs e)
{
    var ctx = ODataHelper.GetServiceContext();

    var customers = new DataServiceCollection<NWDataSvc.
Customer>(ctx);
    customers.LoadCompleted += (obj, args) =>
    {
        if (customers.Continuation != null)
        {
            customers.LoadNextPartialSetAsync();
        }
        else
        {
            dgCustomers.ItemsSource = customers;
            dgCustomers.UpdateLayout();
        }
    };

    customers.LoadAsync(ctx.Customers.AsQueryable());
}
```

11. Define the XAML content of the `CustomerOrders.xaml` page (see the following XAML fragment).

```
<navigation:Page
......
Loaded="Page_Loaded">
    <Grid x:Name="LayoutRoot">
        <StackPanel>
            <HyperlinkButton NavigateUri="/CustomerList.xaml"
TargetName="NavFrame">Back to Customer List</HyperlinkButton>
            <TextBlock Name="lblTitle"  FontSize="16"
FontWeight="Bold" />
            <sdk:DataGrid Name="dgOrders" ItemsSource="{Binding}"
                          AutoGenerateColumns="false"
IsReadOnly="True"
                          Height="150" SelectionChanged="dgOrders_
SelectionChanged">
                <sdk:DataGrid.Columns>
                    <sdk:DataGridTextColumn Binding="{Binding
OrderID}" Header="ID"></sdk:DataGridTextColumn>
                    <sdk:DataGridTextColumn Binding="{Binding
EmployeeID}" Header="Employee"></sdk:DataGridTextColumn>
                    <sdk:DataGridTextColumn Binding="{Binding
OrderDate}" Header="Order Date"></sdk:DataGridTextColumn>
                    <sdk:DataGridTextColumn Binding="{Binding
RequiredDate}" Header="Required Date"></sdk:DataGridTextColumn>
                    <sdk:DataGridTextColumn Binding="{Binding
ShippedDate }" Header="Shipped Date"></sdk:DataGridTextColumn>
                </sdk:DataGrid.Columns>
            </sdk:DataGrid>
            <TextBlock Name="lblSubTitle"  FontSize="14"
FontWeight="Bold">
                Detailed Items of selected Order:
            </TextBlock>
            <sdk:DataGrid Name="dgOrderDetails"
ItemsSource="{Binding Path=Order_Details}"
                          AutoGenerateColumns="true"
IsReadOnly="True"
                          Height="150" >
            </sdk:DataGrid>
        </StackPanel>
    </Grid>
</navigation:Page>
```

12. Add the code for refreshing the `Order` list (based on selected `Customer`) in the code-behind file of the `CustomerOrders.xaml` page (see the following code snippet).

```
private void Page_Loaded(object sender, RoutedEventArgs e)
{
    var id = NavigationContext.QueryString["customerID"];
    if (string.IsNullOrEmpty(id)) NavigationService.Navigate(new
Uri("/CustomerList.xaml"));

    lblTitle.Text = id + "'s orders";

    var ctx = ODataHelper.GetServiceContext();
    var orders = new DataServiceCollection<NWDataSvc.Order>(ctx);
    orders.LoadCompleted += (obj, args) =>
    {
        if (orders.Continuation != null)
        {
            orders.LoadNextPartialSetAsync();
        }
        else
        {
            LayoutRoot.DataContext = orders;
            dgOrders.UpdateLayout();
        }
    };

    var query = ctx.Orders.Expand("Order_Details").Where(o =>
o.CustomerID == id).AsQueryable();

    orders.LoadAsync(query );
}

private void dgOrders_SelectionChanged(object sender,
SelectionChangedEventArgs e)
{
    dgOrderDetails.DataContext = dgOrders.SelectedItem;
}
```

13. Build the solution and launch the Silverlight test page (within the **ODataSilverlightApp.Web** project) in the web browser.

How it works...

There are three Silverlight pages in the sample application. The `MainPage.xaml` page acts as a navigation container, which uses the `Frame` control to host other pages (so that users can switch between the `CustomerList.xaml` and `CustomerOrders.xaml` pages within the same container page).

Both `CustomerList.xaml` and `CustomerOrders.xaml` pages use the Visual Studio generated OData proxy to fetch entity objects from the Northwind OData service. And for data binding consideration, we use instances of the `DataServiceCollection<T>` class to hold the returned entity objects so that they can be directly bound to the Silverlight `DataGrid` Controls.

In addition, all the OData queries are executed in an asynchronous manner here. This is because all network access APIs (such as `WebRequest` class, Web Service, or WCF client proxies) are by design asynchronous only. This can help preventing the Silverlight (web browser host) UI from being frozen by long-running network access code.

There's more...

In this sample, the OData service is hosted in the same web application as the Silverlight web page. This is because Silverlight also has cross-domain network access restriction (like JavaScript) in the web browser. In order to allow cross-domain network access from Silverlight clients, the service (resource) host needs to provide a cross-domain policy file (see the following reference for more information).

Network Security Access Restrictions in Silverlight at `http://msdn.microsoft.com/en-us/library/cc645032%28v=VS.95%29.aspx`

See also

  ▶ *Performing WPF data binding with OData service data* recipe in *Chapter 2, Working with OData at Client Side*

  ▶ *Building data-driven ASP.NET Web Form pages with OData* recipe in *Chapter 4, Using OData in Web Application*

Consuming WCF Data Service in PHP pages

As one of the most popular web development technologies, PHP is widely used for building various intranet and Internet web applications. It is no doubt that PHP has built-in APIs for consuming XML Web Services and processing XML or JSON-based response content. Though this book is .NET oriented, since IIS 7 has provided built-in extensions for hosting PHP web applications, we will also take the opportunity to introduce how to consume WCF Data Service in PHP web pages.

Getting ready

Here we will build two PHP web pages, which present the `Categories` and `Products` information from the Northwind OData service.

Since we will use IIS 7 for hosting the sample PHP web pages, make sure the local IIS 7 server has the FastCGI extensions for PHP installed (refer to the following article for detailed configuration steps).

Enable FastCGI Support in IIS 7 at `http://learn.iis.net/page.aspx/246/using-fastcgi-to-host-php-applications-on-iis`

Alternatively, you can also use the Web Platform Installer to help you do all the trivial installation and configuration tasks (refer to the following link).

Install PHP for Windows Here! at `http://www.microsoft.com/web/platform/phponwindows.aspx`

The source code for this recipe can be found in the `\ch04\ODataInPHPWebSln` directory.

How to do it...

1. Create a new ASP.NET web application, which contains the Northwind OData service.

2. Fire the **File | Add | New Web Site** menu to launch the **Add New Web Site** wizard (see the following screenshot).

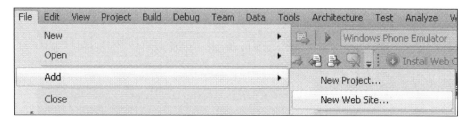

3. Create new **ASP.NET Empty Web Site** as the container of PHP pages (see the following screenshot).

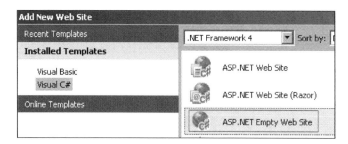

4. Create the following two PHP pages in the PHP container website:

   ❏ CategoryList.php—used for displaying the Category list

   ❏ ProductsByCategory.php—used for displaying the Product list of a given category

 Since Visual Studio doesn't have a built-in item template for PHP web pages, you can create two .txt files first, and then change their extensions to .php.

5. Add the HTML content and PHP code for the CategoryList.php page (see the following code fragment).

```php
<?php
$svc_url = 'http://localhost:18165/NWDataService.svc/Categories?$s
elect=CategoryID,CategoryName';
$xml = simplexml_load_file($svc_url);
$xml->registerXPathNamespace('m', 'http://schemas.microsoft.com/
ado/2007/08/dataservices/metadata');
$xml->registerXPathNamespace('d', 'http://schemas.microsoft.com/
ado/2007/08/dataservices');
?>

<html>
<body>

<h1>Category List</h1>
<form id='formCategories' name='formCategories' method='post'
action='ProductsByCategory.php' >
<b>Categories:</b>

<select id='lstCategories' name='categoryID'
onchange='sync_selected_item();'>
<?php

$elms = $xml->xpath('//m:properties');
foreach ($elms as $elm)
{
   $id = $elm->xpath('d:CategoryID');
   $name = $elm->xpath('d:CategoryName');

   echo "<option value='" . $id[0] . "'>" . $name[0] ."</option>";
}
?>
</select>
```

```
<input id='hdCategoryName' type='hidden' name='categoryName'  />
<input type='submit' value='Show Products' />
</form>

<script type='text/javascript'>
function sync_selected_item(){
  var list = document.getElementById('lstCategories');
  var hd = document.getElementById('hdCategoryName');

  var idx = list.selectedIndex;
  var txt = list.options[idx].text;
  hd.value = txt;
}
sync_selected_item();
</script>
</body>
</html>
```

6. Add the HTML content and PHP code for the `ProductsByCategory.php` page (see the following code fragment).

```php
<?php
$categoryID = $_POST["categoryID"];
$categoryName = $_POST["categoryName"];

$svc_url = 'http://localhost:18165/NWDataService.svc/
Products?$filter=CategoryID eq ' . $categoryID;

$xml = simplexml_load_file($svc_url);
$xml->registerXPathNamespace('m', 'http://schemas.microsoft.com/
ado/2007/08/dataservices/metadata');
$xml->registerXPathNamespace('d', 'http://schemas.microsoft.com/
ado/2007/08/dataservices');
?>

<html>
<body>
<a href='CategoryList.php'>Back to Category List</a>
<h1>Products under &quot; <?php echo $categoryName ?>  &quot;
category</h1>

<table>
<thead>
  <td>ID</td>
  <td>Name</td>
  <td>Unit Price</td>
```

```
    <td>Discontinued</td>
</thead>
<?php
$elms = $xml->xpath('//m:properties');

foreach ($elms as $elm)
{
   $id = $elm->xpath('d:ProductID');
   $name = $elm->xpath('d:ProductName');
   $uprice = $elm->xpath('d:UnitPrice');
   $discontinued = $elm->xpath('d:Discontinued');

   echo "<tr>";
   echo "<td>" . $id[0] ."</td>";
   echo "<td>" . $name[0] ."</td>";
   echo "<td>" . $uprice[0] ."</td>";
   echo "<td>" . $discontinued[0] ."</td>";
   echo "</tr>";
}
?>

</body>
</html>
```

7. Deploy the PHP website into IIS 7. Make sure the target IIS 7 server has installed the FastCGI extension for PHP (refer to the *Getting ready* section). And you can use the **Publish Web Site** wizard as we've discussed in the *Hosting a WCF Data Service in IIS server* recipe in *Chaper 3, OData Service Hosting and Configuration*.

8. Launch the PHP pages (from the IIS 7 website) in the web browser. The following screenshot shows the web browser output by browsing the `CategoryList.php` page:

By clicking on the **Show Products** button, we're redirected to `ProductsByCategory.php` which will display the `Product` list based on the selected `Category` item (see the following screenshot).

Back to Category List

Products under " Confections " category

ID	Name	Unit Price	Discontinued
16	Pavlova	17.4500	false
19	Teatime Chocolate Biscuits	9.2000	false
20	Sir Rodney's Marmalade	81.0000	false

How it works...

Like classic ASP (Active Server Page) pages, PHP web pages combine the server-side code and HTML markup together in the page content. At the beginning of each of the preceding sample PHP pages, we add declare and initialize some global variables, and objects used within the entire page. Some other code blocks are embedded within the HTML markup so as to dynamically generate certain HTML UI elements.

For the OData service consumption part, we have utilized the SimpleXML library, which is a built-in PHP extension for processing XML data. Unlike those well-known DOM or SAX-based XML processing APIs, the SimpleXML library provides some special but simple functions for converting XML text into strong-typed PHP objects which can be further queried by application code. In the sample pages, we first load the OData query result (in Atom XML format) by supplying the raw query Uri. Then, we use XPATH to extract all entity elements and present each of them inside the HTML output. For more information about the SimpleXML library, you can refer to the following reference manual:

PHP-->SimpleXML at `http://cn2.php.net/simplexml`

There's more...

At the time of writing this recipe, the OData SDK for PHP has been announced on the OData official site. Therefore, for advanced OData service accessing scenarios in PHP web development, it is recommended to use this full-fledged library. You can get more information about the OData SDK for PHP from the following site:

`http://odataphp.codeplex.com/`

See also

▶ *Hosting a WCF Data Service in IIS server* recipe in *Chapter 3, OData Service Hosting and Configuration*

▶ *Building data-driven ASP.NET Web Form pages with OData* recipe in *Chapter 4, Using OData in Web Application*

5
OData on Mobile Devices

In this chapter, we will cover:

- ▶ Accessing OData service with OData WP7 client library
- ▶ Consuming JSON-format OData service without OData WP7 client library
- ▶ Creating Panorama-style, data-driven Windows Phone applications with OData
- ▶ Using HTML5 and OData to build native Windows Phone application
- ▶ Accessing WCF Data Service in Android mobile application
- ▶ Accessing WCF Data Service in iOS application

Introduction

With the continuous evolution of mobile operating systems, smart mobile devices (such as smartphones or tablets) play increasingly important roles in everyone's daily work and life. The **iOS** (from Apple Inc., for iPhone, iPad, and iPod Touch devices), **Android** (from Google) and **Windows Phone 7** (from Microsoft) operating systems have shown us the great power and potential of modern mobile systems.

In the early days of the Internet, web access was mostly limited to fixed-line devices. However, with the rapid development of wireless network technology (such as 3G), Internet access has become a common feature for mobile or portable devices. Modern mobile OSes, such as iOS, Android, and Windows Phone have all provided rich APIs for network access (especially Internet-based web access). For example, it is quite convenient for mobile developers to create a native iPhone program that uses a network API to access remote RSS feeds from the Internet and present the retrieved data items on the phone screen. And to make Internet-based data access and communication more convenient and standardized, we often leverage some existing protocols, such as XML or JSON, to help us. Thus, it is also a good idea if we can incorporate OData services in mobile application development so as to concentrate our effort on the main application logic instead of the details about underlying data exchange and manipulation.

In this chapter, we will discuss several cases of building OData client applications for various kinds of mobile device platforms. The first four recipes will focus on how to deal with OData in applications running on Microsoft Windows Phone 7. And they will be followed by two recipes that discuss consuming an OData service in mobile applications running on the iOS and Android platforms. Although this book is .NET developer-oriented, since iOS and Android are the most popular and dominating mobile OSes in the market, I think the last two recipes here would still be helpful (especially when the OData service is built upon WCF Data Service on the server side).

Accessing OData service with OData WP7 client library

What is the best way to consume an OData service in a Windows Phone 7 application? The answer is, by using the OData client library for Windows Phone 7 (**OData WP7 client library**). Just like the WCF Data Service client library for standard .NET Framework based applications, the OData WP7 client library allows developers to communicate with OData services via strong-typed proxy and entity classes in Windows Phone 7 applications. Also, the latest **Windows Phone SDK 7.1** has included the OData WP7 client library and the associated developer tools in it.

In this recipe, we will demonstrate how to use the OData WP7 client library in a standard Windows Phone 7 application.

Getting ready

The sample WP7 application we will build here provides a simple UI for users to view and edit the **Categories** data by using the Northwind OData service. The application consists of two phone screens, shown in the following screenshot:

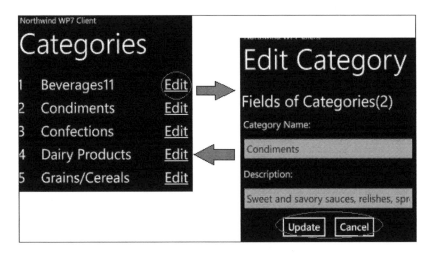

Make sure you have installed Windows Phone SDK 7.1 (which contains the OData WP7 client library and tools) on the development machine. You can get the SDK from the following website:

```
http://create.msdn.com/en-us/home/getting_started
```

The source code for this recipe can be found in the \ch05\ODataWP7ClientLibrarySln directory.

How to do it...

1. Create a new ASP.NET web application that contains the Northwind OData service.
2. Add a new **Windows Phone Application** project in the same solution (see the following screenshot).

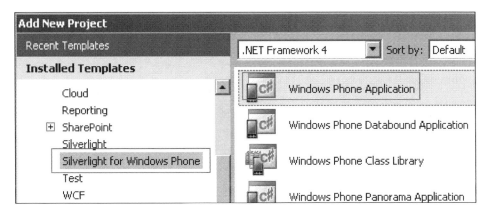

3. Select **Windows Phone OS 7.1** as the **Target Windows Phone OS Version** in the **New Windows Phone Application** dialog (see the following screenshot).

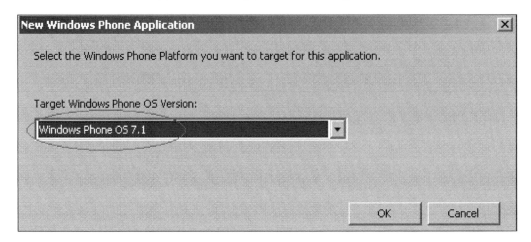

4. Click on the **OK** button, to finish the WP7 project creation.

The following screenshot shows the default WP7 project structure created by Visual Studio:

5. Create a new **Windows Phone Portrait Page** (see the following screenshot) and name it `EditCategory.xaml`.

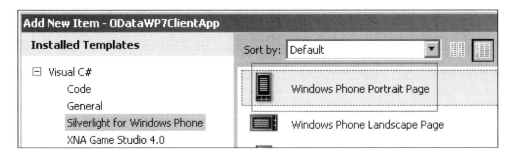

6. Create the OData client proxy (against the Northwind OData service) by using the Visual Studio Add Service Reference wizard.

7. Add the XAML content for the `MainPage.xaml` page (see the following XAML fragment).

```xml
<Grid x:Name="ContentPanel" Grid.Row="1" Margin="12,0,12,0">
    <ListBox x:Name="lstCategories" ItemsSource="{Binding}">
        <ListBox.ItemTemplate>
            <DataTemplate>
                <Grid>
                    <Grid.ColumnDefinitions>
                    <ColumnDefinition Width="60" />
                    <ColumnDefinition Width="260" />
                    <ColumnDefinition Width="140" />
                    </Grid.ColumnDefinitions>
                        <TextBlock Grid.Column="0"
                            Text="{Binding Path=CategoryID}"
                            FontSize="36" Margin="5"/>
                        <TextBlock Grid.Column="1"
                            Text="{Binding Path=CategoryName}"
                            FontSize="36" Margin="5"
                            TextWrapping="Wrap"/>
                        <HyperlinkButton Grid.Column="2"
                            Content="Edit"
                                HorizontalAlignment="Right"
                            NavigateUri="{Binding Path=CategoryID,
                            StringFormat='/EditCategory.xaml?
                            ID={0}'}"
                            FontSize="36"  Margin="5"/>
                </Grid>
            </DataTemplate>
        </ListBox.ItemTemplate>
    </ListBox>
</Grid>
```

8. Add the code for loading the `Category` list in the code-behind file of the `MainPage.xaml` page (see the following code snippet).

```csharp
public partial class MainPage : PhoneApplicationPage
{
    ODataSvc.NorthwindEntities _ctx = null;
    DataServiceCollection<ODataSvc.Category> _categories = null;

    ......

    private void PhoneApplicationPage_Loaded(object sender,
        RoutedEventArgs e)
```

```
    {
        Uri svcUri = new
            Uri("http://localhost:9188/NorthwindOData.svc");
        _ctx = new ODataSvc.NorthwindEntities(svcUri);
        _categories = new
            DataServiceCollection<ODataSvc.Category>(_ctx);

        _categories.LoadCompleted += (o, args) =>
        {
            if (_categories.Continuation != null)
                _categories.LoadNextPartialSetAsync();
            else
            {
                this.Dispatcher.BeginInvoke(
                    () =>
                    {
                        ContentPanel.DataContext = _categories;
                        ContentPanel.UpdateLayout();
                    }
                );
            }
        };

        var query = from c in _ctx.Categories
                    select c;

        _categories.LoadAsync(query);
    }
}
```

9. Add the XAML content for the EditCategory.xaml page (see the following XAML fragment).

```
<Grid x:Name="ContentPanel" Grid.Row="1" Margin="12,0,12,0">
    <StackPanel>
        <TextBlock Text="{Binding Path=CategoryID,
            StringFormat='Fields of Categories({0})'}"
            FontSize="40" Margin="5" />
        <Border>
            <StackPanel>
                <TextBlock Text="Category Name:" FontSize="24"
                    Margin="10" />
                <TextBox x:Name="txtCategoryName"
                    Text="{Binding Path=CategoryName,
                    Mode=TwoWay}" />
```

```xml
            <TextBlock Text="Description:"
                FontSize="24" Margin="10" />
            <TextBox x:Name="txtDescription"
                Text="{Binding Path=Description,
                    Mode=TwoWay}" />
        </StackPanel>
    </Border>
    <StackPanel Orientation="Horizontal"
        HorizontalAlignment="Center">
        <Button x:Name="btnUpdate"  Content="Update"
            HorizontalAlignment="Center"
            Click="btnUpdate_Click" />
        <Button x:Name="btnCancel" Content="Cancel"
            HorizontalAlignment="Center"
            Click="btnCancel_Click" />
    </StackPanel>
</StackPanel>
</Grid>
```

10. Add the code for editing the selected `Category` item in the code-behind file of the `EditCategory.xaml` page.

    In the `PhoneApplicationPage_Loaded` event, we will load the properties of the selected `Category` item and display them on the screen (see the following code snippet).

```csharp
private void PhoneApplicationPage_Loaded(object sender,
RoutedEventArgs e)
{
    EnableControls(false);

    Uri svcUri = new Uri("http://localhost:9188/NorthwindOData.
svc");
    _ctx = new ODataSvc.NorthwindEntities(svcUri);

    var id = int.Parse(NavigationContext.QueryString["ID"]);
    var query = _ctx.Categories.Where(c => c.CategoryID == id);

    _categories = new
        DataServiceCollection<ODataSvc.Category>(_ctx);
    _categories.LoadCompleted += (o, args) =>
    {
        if (_categories.Count <= 0)
        {
            MessageBox.Show("Failed to retrieve Category item.");
            NavigationService.GoBack();
        }
```

```
        else
        {
            EnableControls(true);
            ContentPanel.DataContext = _categories[0];
            ContentPanel.UpdateLayout();
        }
    };

    _categories.LoadAsync(query);
}
```

The code for updating changes (against the `Category` item) is put in the `Click` event of the **Update** button (see the following code snippet).

```
private void btnUpdate_Click(object sender, RoutedEventArgs e)
{
    EnableControls(false);

    _ctx.UpdateObject(_categories[0]);
    _ctx.BeginSaveChanges(
        (ar) =>
        {
            this.Dispatcher.BeginInvoke(
                () =>
                {
                    try
                    {
                        var response = _ctx.EndSaveChanges(ar);
                        NavigationService.Navigate(new
                            Uri("/MainPage.xaml", UriKind.Relative));
                    }
                    catch (Exception ex)
                    {
                        MessageBox.Show("Failed to save
                            changes.");
                        EnableControls(true);
                    }
                }
            );
        },
        null
    );
}
```

11. Select the WP7 project and launch it in **Windows Phone Emulator** (see the following screenshot).

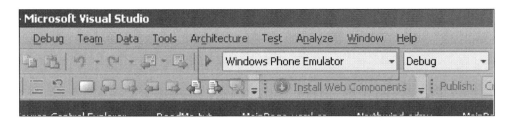

Depending on the performance of the development machine, it might take a while to start the emulator.

Running a WP7 application in Windows Phone Emulator is very helpful especially when the phone application needs to access some web services (such as WCF Data Service) hosted on the local machine (via the Visual Studio test web server).

How it works...

Since the OData WP7 client library (and tools) has been installed together with Windows Phone SDK 7.1, we can directly use the Visual Studio Add Service Reference wizard to generate the OData client proxy in Windows Phone applications. And the generated OData proxy is the same as what we used in standard .NET applications. Since Windows Phone applications also use XAML-based pages (similar to Silverlight) for UI presentation, the data querying and binding code logic of the WP7 sample application (in this recipe) looks quite similar to the *Using OData service in Silverlight data access application* recipe in *Chapter 4, Using OData in Web Application*. Similarly, all network access code (such as the OData service consumption code in this recipe) has to follow the asynchronous programming pattern in Windows Phone applications.

There's more...

In this recipe, we use the Windows Phone Emulator for testing. If you want to deploy and test your Windows Phone application on a real device, you need to obtain a Windows Phone developer account so as to unlock your Windows Phone device. Refer to the following walkthrough:

App Hub - windows phone developer registration walkthrough available at
`http://go.microsoft.com/fwlink/?LinkID=202697`

See also

> ▸ *Using Visual Studio to generate strong-typed OData client proxy* recipe in *Chapter 2, Working with OData at Client Side*
>
> ▸ *Editing and deleting data through WCF Data Service client library proxy* recipe in *Chapter 2, Working with OData at Client Side*
>
> ▸ *Using OData service in Silverlight data access application* recipe in *Chapter 4, Using OData in Web Application*

Consuming JSON-format OData service without OData WP7 client library

By using the **OData WP7 client library**, it is quite simple and straightforward to consume an OData service in Windows Phone applications. But, what if we do not want to use the OData WP7 client library and still want to query data entities from OData services? This might be the case if we want to avoid involving additional components/libraries (such as the OData client library) in our WP7 application. Well, we can use the `WebClient` class to issue raw OData query requests and manually parse the Atom XML format responses via LINQ to XML APIs. Then, what about JSON-format responses?

In this recipe, we will demonstrate how to build a WP7 OData client which consumes JSON format query responses without using the OData WP7 client library.

Getting ready

In this recipe, we will build a simple WP7 application that retrieves the `Category` list (in JSON format) from the Northwind OData service and displays it on the phone screen.

Make sure you have installed the Windows Phone SDK 7.1 (which contains the OData WP7 client library and tools) on the development machine. You can get the SDK from the following website: `http://create.msdn.com/en-us/home/getting_started`

The source code for this recipe can be found in the `\ch05\SimpleODataWP7Sln` directory.

How to do it...

1. Create a new ASP.NET web application that contains the Northwind OData service.

2. Create a new Windows Phone application (use Windows Phone OS 7.1).

 You can refer to the *Accessing OData service with OData WP7 client library* recipe in this chapter for detailed information.

3. Add the following assembly references in the Windows Phone application:
   - ❑ System.Runtime.Serialization.dll
   - ❑ System.Servicemodel.Web.dll

4. Create some helper classes for deserializing the JSON-format OData response (see the following code snippet).

```
// For deserialize the response body
public class CategoriesResponse
{
    public List<CategoryObj> d { get; set; }
}


// For deserialize each Category entity
public class CategoryObj
{
    public string __metadata { get; set; }
    public int CategoryID { get; set; }
    public string CategoryName { get; set; }
    public string Description { get; set; }


}
```

5. Add the XAML content for the `MainPage.xaml` page (auto-generated in the project).

The following is the main XAML fragment of the `MainPage.xaml` page in the sample application:

```
<StackPanel x:Name="TitlePanel" Grid.Row="0"
    Margin="12,17,0,28">
    <TextBlock x:Name="ApplicationTitle"
        Text="Northwind Data Client"
        Style="{StaticResource PhoneTextNormalStyle}"/>
    <TextBlock x:Name="PageTitle" Text="Categories"
        Margin="9,-7,0,0"
        Style="{StaticResource PhoneTextTitle1Style}"/>
</StackPanel>

<Grid x:Name="ContentPanel" Grid.Row="1"
    Margin="12,0,12,0">
```

```
                    <ListBox x:Name="lstCategories"
                           ItemsSource="{Binding }">
                  <ListBox.ItemTemplate>
                      <DataTemplate>
                          <StackPanel Orientation="Horizontal"
                                 Margin="5">
                              <TextBlock Text="{Binding
                                  Path=CategoryID}"
                                  FontSize="54" Width="80"
                                  Height="80" />
                              <StackPanel Orientation="Vertical">
                                  <TextBlock  Text="{Binding
                                      Path=CategoryName}"
                                      FontSize="36" Margin="3" />
                                  <TextBlock Text="{Binding
                                      Path=Description}"
                                      FontSize="14" />
                              </StackPanel>
                          </StackPanel>
                      </DataTemplate>
                  </ListBox.ItemTemplate>
              </ListBox>
          </Grid>
      </Grid>
```

6. Add the code for loading the `Category` list (from the Northwind OData service) in the code-behind file of the `MainPage.xaml` page.

   All the OData query and response processing code will be put in the `PhoneApplicationPage_Loaded` event (see the following code snippet).

```
private void PhoneApplicationPage_Loaded(object sender,
RoutedEventArgs e)
{
    WebClient wc = new WebClient();
    wc.Headers[HttpRequestHeader.Accept] = "application/json";
    Uri queryUri = new
        Uri("http://localhost:12040/NWDataService.svc/Categories?
        $select=CategoryID,CategoryName,Description");

    wc.OpenReadCompleted +=
        (src, args) =>
    {
        using (var responseStream = args.Result)
        {
```

```
DataContractJsonSerializer ser = new
    DataContractJsonSerializer
    (typeof(CategoriesResponse));
var responseObj = ser.ReadObject(responseStream) as
    CategoriesResponse;

if (responseObj != null)
{
    LayoutRoot.DataContext = responseObj.d;
    lstCategories.UpdateLayout();
}
else
{
    MessageBox.Show("Failed to retrieve Category
        list.");
}
    }
};

wc.OpenReadAsync(queryUri);
}
```

7. Launch **Windows Phone Application** in **Windows Phone Emulator** (use the *Ctrl* + *F5* or *F5* shortcuts).

    The following screenshot shows the main screen of the sample phone application:

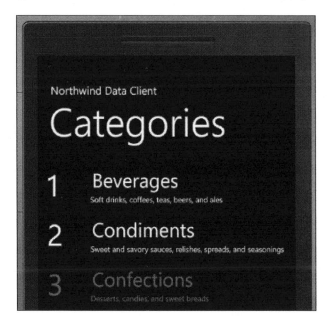

How it works...

The previous sample page uses the `OpenReadAsync` method of the `WebClient` class to send the raw OData query (which ensures the asynchronous network access). Also, we have specified the `Accept` HTTP header, so that the service will return a JSON-format response. After the response data arrives, we use the `DataContractJsonSerializer` class to deserialize the JSON-format response into strong-typed objects (based on the `CategoriesResponse` and `CategoryObj` helper classes we have defined).

By using Fiddler to capture the underlying HTTP response content (see the following screenshot), we find that the JSON object graph of the OData response exactly matches the helper classes we defined here.

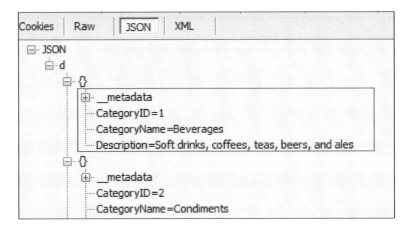

And it is recommended that we use Fiddler to inspect the JSON response data of an OData service before we define the helper classes for data serialization/deserialization between OData response and .NET objects.

Although we can use the `WebClient` + `DataContractJsonSerializer` approach to access an OData service, it is still quite cumbersome. In most cases, the OData WP7 client library is the preferred choice for consuming an OData service in Windows Phone applications.

See also

▶   *Accessing OData service with OData WP7 client library* recipe

Creating Panorama-style, data-driven Windows Phone applications with OData

Windows Phone 7 brings out the new **Panorama** UI style to improve the user navigation experience on the phone screen. Unlike standard applications that are designed to fit within the confines of the phone screen, WP7 applications with Panorama UI style offer a unique way to view data and resources by using a long horizontal canvas that extends beyond the confines of the screen. For WP7 data-driven applications, Panorama-style UI is extremely useful for presenting data that can be divided into multiple groups or partitions. In this recipe, we will show you how to use an OData service as the data source for building a WP7 Panorama-style, data-driven application.

Getting ready

Here, we will build a Panorama-style WP7 application to present the Northwind Categories and Products data (by using the Northwind OData service). In the application, each Category and its associated Product list will be displayed in a separate Panorama page, so that the user can swipe the phone screen, to navigate between them (see the following screenshot).

Make sure you have installed Windows Phone SDK 7.1 (which contains the OData WP7 client library and tools) on the development machine. You can get the SDK from the website `http://create.msdn.com/en-us/home/getting_started`.

The source code for this recipe can be found in the `\ch05\ ODataWP7PanoramaSln` directory.

How to do it...

1. Create a new ASP.NET web application that contains the Northwind OData service.
2. Create a new Windows Phone application (use Windows Phone OS 7.1).

 You can refer to the *Accessing OData service with OData WP7 client library* recipe in this chapter for detailed information.

3. Add the assembly reference, `Microsoft.Phone.Controls.dll`, in the Windows Phone Application.
4. Create the OData client proxy (against the Northwind OData service) by using the Visual Studio Add Service Reference wizard.
5. Add the XML namespaces for the `Panorama` Control in the XAML file of the `MainPage.xaml` page (see the following XAML fragment).

```
<phone:PhoneApplicationPage
    x:Class="ODataWP7PanoramaApp.MainPage"
    . . .
    xmlns:controls="clr-namespace:Microsoft.Phone.
        Controls;assembly=Microsoft.Phone.Controls"
    xmlns:shell="clr-namespace:Microsoft.Phone.
        Shell;assembly=Microsoft.Phone"
. . .
>
```

6. Add the `Panorama` Control under the default `Grid` container Control in the XAML file of the `MainPage.xml` page (see the following XAML fragment).

```
<Grid x:Name="LayoutRoot" Background="Transparent">
    <controls:Panorama x:Name="MainPanel" Background="Purple"
        Title="OData Panorama Demo"
        ItemsSource="{Binding}" >
        <controls:Panorama.HeaderTemplate>
            <DataTemplate>
                <TextBlock Text="{Binding Path=CategoryName}"
                    FontSize="54" FontWeight="Bold" />
            </DataTemplate>
```

```xml
        </controls:Panorama.HeaderTemplate>
        <controls:Panorama.ItemTemplate>
            <DataTemplate>
                <StackPanel>
                    <TextBlock Text="{Binding Path=CategoryName,
                        StringFormat='Products under {0}:'}"
                        FontSize="32" Margin="10" />
                    <ListBox ItemsSource="{Binding
                        Path=Products}">
                        <ListBox.ItemTemplate>
                            <DataTemplate>
                                <StackPanel
                                    Orientation="Horizontal">
                                    <TextBlock Text="{Binding
                                        Path=ProductID}"
                                        Margin="10,5,15,5"
                                        Width="50" />
                                    <TextBlock Text="{Binding
                                        Path=ProductName}"
                                        Margin="5" />
                                </StackPanel>
                            </DataTemplate>
                        </ListBox.ItemTemplate>
                    </ListBox>
                </StackPanel>
            </DataTemplate>
        </controls:Panorama.ItemTemplate>

        <controls:PanoramaItem>
            <ProgressBar IsIndeterminate="True" />
        </controls:PanoramaItem>
    </controls:Panorama>
</Grid>
```

7. Add the code for loading the `Category` and `Product` entities in the code-behind file of the `MainPage.xaml` page (see the following code snippet).

```csharp
public partial class MainPage : PhoneApplicationPage
{
    ......

    private void PhoneApplicationPage_Loaded(object sender,
        RoutedEventArgs e)
    {
        var svcUri = new
            Uri("http://localhost:11904/NWDataService.svc");
```

```
        var ctx = new NorthwindEntities(svcUri);

        var Categories = new DataServiceCollection<Category>(ctx);
        Categories.LoadCompleted += (o, args) =>
        {
            if (args.Error != null)
            {
                MessageBox.Show("Failed to retrieve data.");
                return;
            }

            if (Categories.Continuation != null)
                Categories.LoadNextPartialSetAsync();
            else
            {
                this.Dispatcher.BeginInvoke(() =>
                {
                    MainPanel.Items.Clear();
                    MainPanel.DataContext = Categories;
                });
            }
        };

        var query = ctx.Categories.Expand("Products");
        Categories.LoadAsync(
            query
        );
    }

    ......
```

How it works...

There is only one page (MainPage.xaml) in the same WP7 project. This page uses the Panorama Control (in the Microsoft.Phone.Controls assembly) provided by Windows Phone SDK to present the OData entities. When the application starts and displays the MainPage.xaml page, the PhoneApplicationPage_Loaded event is fired so as to retrieve the Category and Product lists from the Northwind OData service. After the data entities get loaded, we directly assign the data container (of the DataServiceCollection<T> class) to the Panorama Control's DataContext property (so as to trigger data binding). According to the data binding template in the XAML file, each Category entity (and its associated Product entities) will be bound to a separate PanoramaItem Control (inside the Panorama Control). Thus, users can flick the phone screen to explore each Category (and Products under the Category), one by one.

If you prefer using code instead of data binding, you can also programmatically create the `PanoramaItem` Controls based on the `Category` entity collection (see the following code snippet).

```
void PopulatePanoramaItemsWithCode
    (DataServiceCollection<NorthwindModel.Category> categories)
{
    foreach (var category in categories)
    {
        var panelItem = new PanoramaItem();

        panelItem.Content = new CustomUserControl();
        panelItem.DataContext = category;

        MainPanel.Items.Add(panelItem);
    }
}
```

For more information about the WP7 `Panorama` Control, you can refer to the following MSDN reference:

Panorama Control Overview for Windows Phone available at `http://msdn.microsoft. com/en-us/library/ff941104(v=vs.92)`

See also

▶ *Accessing OData service with OData WP7 client library* recipe

Using HTML5 and OData to build native Windows Phone application

When we say HTML5 and OData, you might think that we're probably going to create a data-driven web application (which uses HTML5 for UI presentation and uses JavaScript for accessing a backend OData service). This is partially true, since we do create some HTML5 web pages and use JavaScript for OData query and data population. However, this time we will use HTML and JavaScript to build a native Windows Phone application. How come? The latest Windows Phone 7.5 system has provided the IE 9 mobile web browser (also the corresponding `WebBrowser` Control for development usage), which is fully HTML 5-enabled. Thus, it is possible for us to develop a native WP7 application by using HTML 5. In this recipe, we will demonstrate how to create a native WP7 data-driven application by using HTML 5 and OData.

Getting ready

The sample WP7 application here will still display the Category and Product data by using the Northwind OData service. The following is the main app screen of the sample application in Windows Phone Emulator:

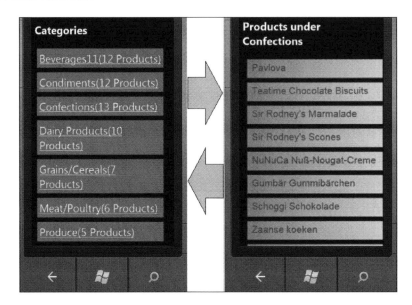

Make sure you have installed Windows Phone SDK 7.1 (which contains the OData WP7 client library and tools) on the development machine. You can get the SDK from the website `http://create.msdn.com/en-us/home/getting_started`.

The source code for this recipe can be found in the `\ch05\WP7ODataHTML5Sln` directory.

How to do it...

1. Create a new ASP.NET web application that contains the Northwind OData service.

2. Add the `jquery` and `datajs` script libraries into the web application (see the following screenshot).

3. Create the HTML 5 page (ODataHTML5.htm) in the web application and put the following HTML content in it:

```html
<!DOCTYPE html>
<html>
<head>
    <meta name="viewport" content="width=device-width,
        initial-scale=1.0, maximum-scale=1.0, user-scalable=0;">
    <link rel="Stylesheet" href="styles/defaultstyles.css" />
    <script type="text/javascript"
        src="scripts/jquery-1.4.4.min.js" ></script>
    <script type="text/javascript"
        src="scripts/datajs-1.0.2.min.js" ></script>
    <script type="text/javascript"
        src="scripts/app_code.js" ></script>
</head>
<body>
<div id="categoryPanel">
</div>
<div id="productPanel">
</div>
</body>
</html>
```

4. Create the CSS file (defaultstyles.css) and put the following styles in it (see the following style definition):

```css
body
{
    background-color:#000000; color:#ffffff;
}
#categoryPanel
{
    float:left; width:100%; margin:0px;
}
#productPanel
{
    width:100%; margin:0px;
}
.category_item
{
    float:left; width:90%; margin:5px; padding:5px;
    font-size:18pt; text-decoration:underline;
    background-color:#aa00ff;
}
```

5. Create the application script file (`app_code.js`) and put it in the same folder as the jQuery and datajs libraries.

6. Add the code for querying and populating OData entities in the `app_code.js` file.

The following is the function for populating the `Category` list:

```
function showCategories() {
    var cp = $("#categoryPanel");
    var pp = $("#productPanel");

    cp.html("");
    cp.append("<h2>Categories</h2>");

    OData.read("http://localhost:49409/NorthwindOData.svc/
        Categories?$expand=Products",
        function (data, request) {

            $.each(data.results, function (i, category) {
                var divCategory = $("<div
                    class='category_item'>");
                divCategory.append(category.CategoryName);
                divCategory.append(" (" +
                    category.Products.length + " Products)");

                cp.append(divCategory);

                divCategory.bind("click", function () {
                        showProductsOfCategory(category);
                });

            });

        });

    cp.show();
    pp.hide();
}
```

The following `showProductsOfCategory` function is used to populate the `Product` list of the selected `Category` item:

```
function showProductsOfCategory(_category) {
```

```
. . . . . .
var canvas = document.createElement("canvas");
canvas.width = 480;
canvas.height = Math.max(800, 70 *
    _category.Products.length);

var context = canvas.getContext("2d");

$.each(_category.Products, function (i, product) {
    var x = 10;
    var y = i * 50 + 5;
    var gradient = context.createLinearGradient(x, y, 310,
        y + 40);
    gradient.addColorStop(0, '#0099AA');
    gradient.addColorStop(1, '#00FFFF');
    context.fillStyle = gradient;
    context.fillRect(x, y, 300, 40);

    context.font = "16pt Arial";
    context.fillStyle = "#333333";
    context.fillText(product.ProductName, 20, y + 25);

});

. . . . . .
}
```

The following initialization code is put at the end of the app_code.js file:

```
$(document).ready(function () {
    showCategories();
});
```

7. Launch the ODataHTML5.htm page in IE 9 (or any other HTML 5-enabled web browser) and make sure it works.

8. Create a new Windows Phone application (use Windows Phone OS 7.1).

 You can refer to the *Accessing OData service with OData WP7 client library* recipe in this chapter for detailed information.

9. Copy the `ODataHTML5.htm` page and its referenced `.js` and `.css` files (reserve the folder structure) from the web application into the Windows Phone application.

    The following screenshot shows the WP7 project structure after copying the files:

    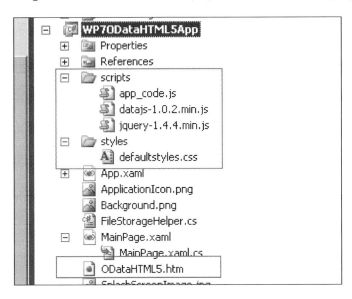

10. Make sure the `.htm`, `.js`, and `.css` files have their **Build Action** property set to **Content** in Visual Studio Solution Explorer (see the following screenshot).

    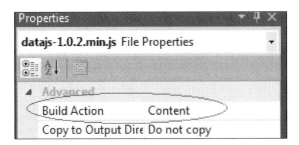

11. Create a helper class to copy the `ODataHTML5.htm` file and its referenced resource files into the **Local Data Storage** of the WP7 application (see the following `FileStorageHelper` class).

```
public class FileStorageHelper
{
    static string[] FOLDER_LIST = { "scripts", "styles" };
    static string[] FILE_LIST =
    {
        "ODataHTML5.htm",
        @"scripts\jquery-1.4.4.min.js",
```

```csharp
        @"scripts\datajs-1.0.2.min.js",
        @"scripts\app_code.js",
        @"styles\defaultstyles.css"
    };

    public static void EnsureLocalFiles()
    {
        using (var store =
            IsolatedStorageFile.GetUserStoreForApplication())
        {
            foreach (var dir in FOLDER_LIST)
            {
                if (!store.DirectoryExists(dir))
                {
                    store.CreateDirectory(dir);
                }
            }

            foreach (var file in FILE_LIST)
            {
                if (!store.FileExists(file))
                {
                    var sr = Application.GetResourceStream(new
                        Uri(file, UriKind.Relative));
                    using (BinaryReader br = new
                        BinaryReader(sr.Stream))
                    {
                        byte[] data =
                            br.ReadBytes((int)sr.Stream.Length);

                        using (var ifs = store.CreateFile(file))
                        {
                            ifs.Write(data, 0, data.Length);
                        }
                    }
                }
            }
        }
    }
}
```

12. Add a `WebBrowser` Control (set the `IsScriptEnabled` property to `True`) within the XAML content of the `MainPage.xaml` page (see the following XAML fragment).

```
<phone:PhoneApplicationPage
......
Loaded="PhoneApplicationPage_Loaded">

    <Grid x:Name="LayoutRoot" Background="Transparent">
        <phone:WebBrowser x:Name="wbMain"  IsScriptEnabled="True"
/>
    </Grid>
</phone:PhoneApplicationPage>
```

13. Add the file initialization and page loading code in the code-behind file of the `MainPage.xaml` page (see the following `PhoneApplicationPage_Loaded` function).

```
private void PhoneApplicationPage_Loaded(object sender,
RoutedEventArgs e)
{
    // Ensure HTML5 page files are copied to Local Data Storage
    FileStorageHelper.EnsureLocalFiles();

    // Load the HTML5 page in WebBrowser Control
    wbMain.Navigate(new Uri("ODataHTML5.htm", UriKind.Relative));
}
```

How it works...

Currently, the HTML5 support on the Windows Phone 7.5 system relies on the IE 9 mobile web browser and its corresponding `WebBrowser` Control. In this sample, we first create the HTML5 web page (which presents the data from the Northwind OData service) within an ASP.NET web application, and then copy the web page files (from the web application) into the WP7 application. The WP7 application only has one page (the default `MainPage.xaml` page), which uses the `WebBrowser` Control to load the HTML5 page (`ODataHTML5.htm`). We need to turn on the `IsScriptEnabled` property of the `WebBrowser` Control, so that the JavaScript code in the HTML page can correctly function. In addition, because the WP7 `WebBrowser` Control can only load local files from **Local Data Storage**, we have created a helper class (the `FileStorageHelper` class) to help copy the HTML5 page and its associated resource files into the Local Data Storage.

In case you do not want to put the web page files into the WP7 application (and copy them to Local Data Storage), you can also directly let the WebBrowser Control load the web page from a remote web application (see the following code snippet).

```
private void PhoneApplicationPage_Loaded(object sender,
RoutedEventArgs e)
{
    // We can also directly load the remote page into
    //WebBrowser Control
    // In this case, we do not need to copy HTML page resources
    //locally
    wbMain.Navigate(new
        Uri("http://localhost:49409/ODataHTML5.htm"));
}
```

There's more...

For more information about programming WP7 applications with WebBrowser Control and Local Data Storage, you can refer to the following MSDN references:

▸ *WebBrowser Control for Windows Phone* available at http://msdn.microsoft. com/en-us/library/ff431812(v=VS.92).aspx

▸ *Local Data Storage for Windows Phone* available at http://msdn.microsoft. com/en-us/library/ff626522(v=VS.92).aspx

See also

▸ *Consuming OData service with datajs script library* recipe in *Chapter 4, Using OData in Web Application*

▸ *Accessing OData service with OData WP7 client library* recipe

Accessing WCF Data Service in Android mobile application

Ever since 2009, the Android OS has become increasingly popular in the smartphone device market. As the Android OS is based on the open source Linux operating system and uses Java as its primary programming language, it is quite normal for many smart devices, such as mobile phones or tablets, to tend to use Android as their operating system.

Also, the number of applications available to Android clients grows extremely quickly. As of October 2011, there were more than 300,000 apps available for Android, and the estimated number of applications downloaded from the Android Market as of December 2011 exceeded 10 billion. Therefore, it would be quite interesting and useful if we can easily incorporate OData (especially the **WCF Data Service**-based implementation) to build data access application for Android devices.

In this recipe, we will show you how to build a simple OData client application through the **OData4j** library for Android devices.

Getting ready

We will build an Android application that displays the `Category` and `Product` information from the Northwind OData service. The application consists of two screens (see the following screenshot), one for displaying the Category list and another for displaying the Product list belonging to a certain Category. The following is a screenshot of the sample Android application:

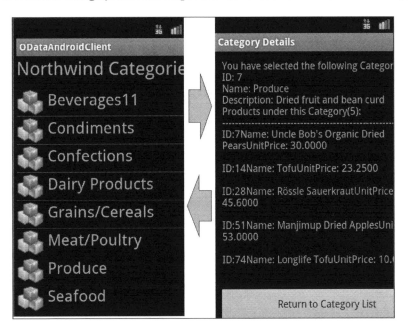

Before we start, it is necessary to set up a proper development environment with the following tools and components installed:

> Java SE (JRE and SDK), Version J2SE v1.6, available at `http://www.oracle.com/technetwork/java/javase/downloads/index.html`

> Eclipse IDE for Java Developers, Version Eclipse v3.7.1, available at `http://www.eclipse.org/downloads/`

- Android SDK and add-on tools for Eclipse, Version Android SDK v2.3.3, available at `http://developer.android.com/sdk/installing.html`

- OData4j library, Version OData4j v0.5, available at `http://code.google.com/p/odata4j/`

In addition, the following is a good article online (posted by *Allen Noren*) that introduces setting up an Android development environment:

`http://fyi.oreilly.com/2009/02/setting-up-your-android-develo.html`

The source code for this recipe can be found in the `\ch05\ODataAndroidClient` directory.

How to do it...

1. Start the Eclipse IDE (`eclipse.exe`).

2. Fire **File | New | Project ...**.

3. Select the **Android Project** type in the **New Project** dialog (see the following screenshot).

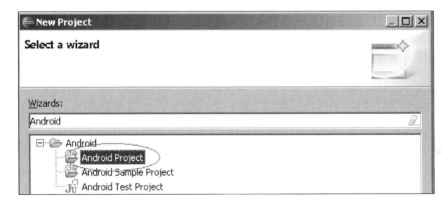

4. In the **New Android Project** dialog, select **Android 2.3.3** (only) as the **Build Target** (see the following screenshot).

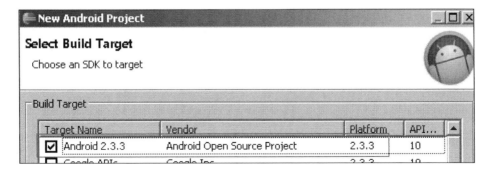

5. Specify the **Application Info** properties (see the following screenshot) and click on the **Finish** button to create the project.

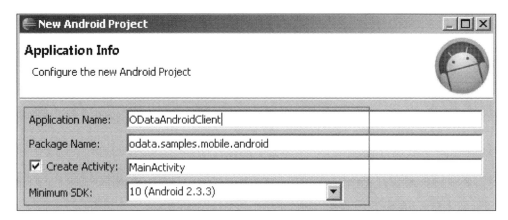

6. Fire **Project | Properties**.

7. Select the **Java Build Path** node and use the **Add External JARs...** button (on **Libraries** tab) to import the OData4j client library (see the following screenshot).

    Here we use the OData4j client library version 0.5 (`odata4j-0.5-clientbundle.jar` file).

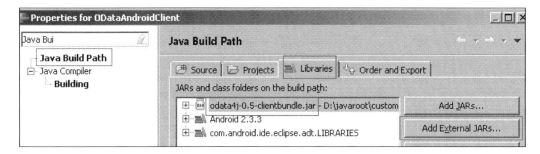

8. Define some helper class for data access and UI interaction (refer to the source code for complete class definition).

    The following `CategoryObj` and `ProductObj` classes (which contains some data properties) are used to map the OData entity objects:

```
public class CategoryObj implements Serializable  {

}
public class ProductObj implements Serializable{

}
```

The `CategoriesAdapter` class is used as a data source for UI data binding.

```
public class CategoriesAdapter extends
    ArrayAdapter<CategoryObj> {

. . . .
}
```

The following is the `CategoryListItemClickListener` class, which helps helps handle click events on a certain `Category` item:

```
public class CategoryListItemClickListener implements
    OnItemClickListener {

    . . . .
}
```

9. Add a function for retrieving the `Category` and `Product` entities in the `MainActivity` class (see the following `GetCategoryItems` function).

```
// Query Category list from Northwind based WCF DataService
    ArrayList<CategoryObj> GetCategoryItems(){
    String svcUri =
        "http://services.odata.org/Northwind/Northwind.svc/";
    ODataConsumer c = ODataConsumer.create(svcUri);

    ArrayList<CategoryObj> categoryList = new
        ArrayList<CategoryObj>();

    Enumerable<OEntity> cursor =
        c.getEntities("Categories").expand("Products").execute();
    for (OEntity entityObj : cursor)
    {
        CategoryObj cObj = new CategoryObj();
        cObj.CategoryID =  entityObj.getProperty
            ("CategoryID", Integer.class).getValue();
        cObj.CategoryName = entityObj.getProperty
            ("CategoryName", String.class).getValue();
        cObj.Description = entityObj.getProperty
            ("Description", String.class).getValue();

        List<OEntity> entityList = entityObj.getLink
            ("Products", OLink.class).getRelatedEntities();
        cObj.Products = new ArrayList<ProductObj>();

        for(OEntity pEntity: entityList){

            ProductObj pObj = new ProductObj();
            pObj.ProductID = pEntity.getProperty
                ("ProductID", Integer.class).getValue();
```

```
        pObj.ProductName = pEntity.getProperty
            ("ProductName", String.class).getValue();
        pObj.SupplierID = pEntity.getProperty
            ("SupplierID", Integer.class).getValue();
        pObj.UnitPrice = pEntity.getProperty
            ("UnitPrice", BigDecimal.class).getValue();


        cObj.Products.add(pObj);

    }

    categoryList.add(cObj);
    }


    return categoryList;
}
```

 Instead of using an OData service hosted in a local web application, here we use the sample Northwind OData service (read-only) over the Internet which is available at `http://services.odata.org/Northwind/Northwind.svc/`.

10. Add the code for data loading and presenting in the `onCreate` function of the `MainActivity` class (see the following code snippet).

```java
public class MainActivity extends Activity {
    /** Called when the activity is first created. */
    @Override
    public void onCreate(Bundle savedInstanceState) {
        super.onCreate(savedInstanceState);
        setContentView(R.layout.main);

        ListView lvCategories =
            (ListView)findViewById(R.id.lvCategories);

        // Add item click action listener
        lvCategories.setOnItemClickListener(
            new CategoryListItemClickListener(this)
        );

        // Populate category items on lstCategory
        ArrayList<CategoryObj> categoryList =
            GetCategoryItems();
        CategoriesAdapter adapter = new CategoriesAdapter
            (this, R.layout.list_item, categoryList);
        lvCategories.setAdapter(adapter);

    }
```

For the `Category` details screen, we will use code logic similar to the `MainActivity` class, to implement it. You can refer to the `SubActivity` class in the source code.

11. Open the `AndroidManifest.xml` file with **Android Manifest Editor**.

12. In the manifest editor, click on the **Add...** button and add a new **User Permission** of the **android.permission.INTERNET** type (see the following screenshot).

13. Save the changes and use **Run | Debug** or the *F11* key to start the application.

How it works...

The OData4j library uses a common `OEntity` class for representing various kinds of OData entity objects. We can use the `getProperty` method of the `OEntity` class to access each individual entity property (by specifying the property data type). If we want to access the child entity sets associated with a given entity object, we can use the `getLink` method to obtain an `OLink` instance (representing the association) and invoke the `getRelatedEntities` method to get the associated entity objects.

The Android application framework uses the `Activity` class to represent the phone screen UI element, and each `Activity` instance can contain child controls/elements called Widgets. In the sample application, the `MainActivity` class uses a `ListView` Widget for displaying the Category list. Although we use code to programmatically populate the `ListView` Widget (in the `MainActivity.onCreate` function), all the UI elements within the `MainActivity` have already been defined in an XML file (`main.xml`) under the `/res/layout` directory in the project (see the following screenshot).

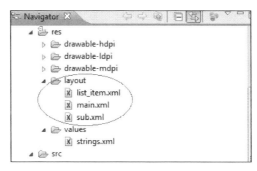

You can double-click on a .xml file (or right-click on the .xml file and choose a particular editor in the context menu) to edit the UI layout of each Widget.

For more information about Android development, you can refer to the tutorials on the Android Developer website (http://developer.android.com/training/index.html).

There's more...

Here, we use the OData4j library to build an OData client application for the Android platform. However, we can also use it for building a standard OData service, just like we do with WCF Data Service. You can get more information about the OData4j library from its Google Code workspace, available at http://code.google.com/p/odata4j/.

See also

> - *Building an OData service via WCF Data Service and ADO.NET Entity Framework* recipe in *Chapter 1, Building OData Services*

Accessing WCF Data Service in iOS application

iOS (formerly iPhone OS) is Apple Inc.'s mobile operating system. iOS has now been used in various Apple Inc. smart devices, such as the iPod Touch, iPad, and Apple TV. Also, as of October 4, 2011, Apple, Inc.'s App Store contained more than 500,000 iOS applications, resulting in more than 18 billion download times.

As iOS has become the core platform of Apple Inc.'s smart devices, it would be great if we can conveniently incorporate OData-compatible data services so as to build rich, Internet-based, data-driven applications for iPhone, iPod Touch, or iPad clients. Fortunately, we do not need to build everything from scratch. The **OData4ObjC** (OData for Objective-C) library has been developed by the open source community for facilitating the OData service access in applications for iOS or Mac OS X platforms.

In this recipe, we will show you how to create a simple iPhone application for displaying data entities retrieved from a WCF Data Service, by using the OData4ObjC library.

Getting ready

The iPhone application we will build here consists of a single screen, which displays Category information from the Northwind OData service. The following is what the main screen of the sample application looks like:

To develop iOS applications, we need to have the **XCode IDE**, available at `http://developer.apple.com/xcode/`, installed on a Mac OS X-equipped machine.

We also need the OData4ObjC library, which can be downloaded from `http://odata.github.com/OData4ObjC/`.

For this sample, we will use **XCode 4.2** (on **Mac OSX 10.7**) and the **OData4objC** library for **iOS v4.3**.

The source code for this recipe can be found in the `\ch05\iOSODataClient` directory.

How to do it...

1. Set up the Northwind OData service (created via the WCF Data Service) in a local IIS server.

 Make sure the service is accessible from the Mac OS X machine.

2. Launch the XCode IDE on the Mac OS X machine.

3. Start the new project wizard and choose the **Single View Application** template under **iOS | Application** (see the following screenshot).

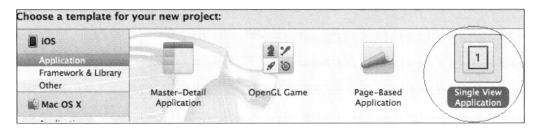

4. Specify the basic project settings (such as **Product Name**, **Class Prefix**, and **Device Family**) in the project options dialog (see the following screenshot).

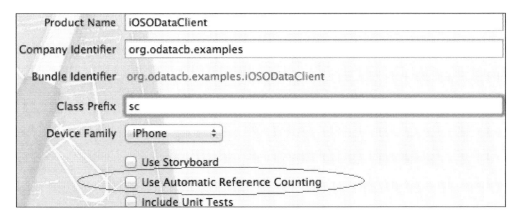

We choose **iPhone** as the **Device Family** value because we will create an iOS-based application for iPhone devices.

> Make sure the **Use Automatic Reference Counting** option is not checked here (because it is not compatible with the code generated by the OData4ObjC library).

5. Choose a project location (on the local Mac disk) and click on the **Create** button to finish project creation.

6. Use the odatagen utility (in the OData4ObjC library) to create the OData client proxy against the Northwind OData service.

    The following is the command syntax used to generate the sample OData client proxy:

    ```
    odatagen /uri=http://[servername]:[port]/NWDataService.svc /out=/
    Users/macuser/Desktop/ODataProxy
    ```

7. Add the generated OData proxy code (the .h and .m files) into the iOS project.

   The following screenshot shows the sample iOS project, which has included the OData client proxy code files (NorthwindEntities.h and NorthwindEntities.m).

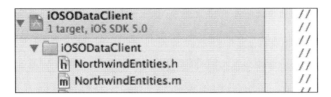

8. Add the code for querying Category entities in the viewDidLoad function of the scViewController class.

   The following is the complete code for the viewDidLoad function (in the scViewController.m file):

```
(void)viewDidLoad
{
    [super viewDidLoad];

    // Load Category list from OData service
    NorthwindEntities *proxy = [[NorthwindEntities alloc]
        initWithUri:@"http://192.168.1.4:9999/odataweb/
        nwdataservice.svc" credential:nil];

    QueryOperationResponse *response = [proxy
        execute:@"Categories"];

    NSMutableArray *categoryArray  = [response getResult];

    self.categoryList = categoryArray;

    [proxy release];
}
```

   For those member variables (such as the categoryList property) of the scViewController class, we should define them in the scViewController.h file (see the following code snippet).

```
@interface scViewController : UIViewController
<UITableViewDelegate, UITableViewDataSource>{
    NSMutableArray* categoryList;
}
@property (nonatomic,retain) NSMutableArray* categoryList;
```

   Here, we only need to define the categoryList variable (of the NSMutableArray* type) in the scViewController.h file.

In this recipe, the `scViewController` class also implements the `UITableViewDelegate` and `UITableViewDataSource` interfaces (protocols), which are necessary for the `TableView` Control used later.

9. Double-click on the `scViewController.xib` file to launch the **Interface Builder** tool in XCode.

10. Use **View | Utilities | Object Library** to display the **Object Library** panel.

11. Drag a `TableView` Control from the **Object Library** panel onto the **View** panel (see the following screenshot).

 You can use the search field on the **Object Library** panel to quickly find the `TableView` Control.

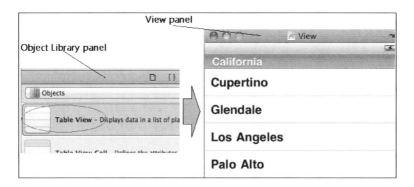

12. Select the `Table View` Control in the **Interface Builder** panel and open the **Connections Inspector** (by using **View | Utilities | Connections Inspector**).

13. Connect the **dataSource** and **delegate** outlets of the `TableView` Control to the `scViewController` class (which has implemented the required interfaces).

This can be done by clicking the small circle to the right of the **dataSource** outlet (the same for the **delegate** outlet) and dragging the blue line to the file's owner icon (see the following screenshot).

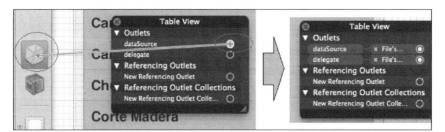

14. Implement the `numberOfRowsInSection` and `cellForRowAtIndexPath` functions of the `UITableViewDataSource` interface for the `scViewController` class (in the `scViewController.m` file).

The following is the implementation of these two functions in the sample:

```
// Customize the number of rows in the table view.
(NSInteger)tableView:(UITableView *)tableView numberOfRowsInSectio
n:(NSInteger)section {
    return [self.categoryList count];
}


// Customize the appearance of table view cells.
(UITableViewCell *)tableView:(UITableView *)tableView cellForRowAt
IndexPath:(NSIndexPath *)indexPath {

    static NSString *CellIdentifier = @"Cell";

    UITableViewCell *cell = [tableView
        dequeueReusableCellWithIdentifier:CellIdentifier];
    if (cell == nil) {
        cell = [[UITableViewCell alloc]
            initWithStyle:UITableViewCellStyleSubtitle
            reuseIdentifier:CellIdentifier];
    }

    // Extract the category object at the specific index
    NorthwindModel_Category* category = [self.categoryList
        objectAtIndex: [indexPath row]];

    // Configure the cell.
    UIImage *cellImage =
        [UIImage imageNamed:@"category_icon.jpg"];
    cell.imageView.image = cellImage;

    cell.textLabel.text = category.getCategoryName;
    cell.detailTextLabel.text = category.getDescription;

    return cell;
}
```

15. Build the entire project (by using the *Command + B* keys) and run it in the iPhone simulator (by using the *Command + R* keys).

How it works...

As we can see in the previous steps, the OData4ObjC library provides not only classes for accessing an OData service but also tools for generating strong-typed OData client proxy classes (by using the `odatagen` command-line tool).

Just like the `DataSvcUtil.exe` tool provided in the WCF Data Service client library, the `odatagen` utility accepts the service URI (through which it can get the metadata document) as a parameter and saves the generated OData proxy code to the specified output location. In the generated proxy code, there are one or more strong-typed classes representing the OData entity types (such as the `Category` entity of the Northwind OData service) exposed in the target OData service.

The code logic for performing OData queries is quite simple and straight. Just create an instance of the generated client context class (the `NorthwindEntities` class in this sample) and invoke the `execute` method (of the instance) to send the query.

In the sample application, we store the `Category` entities (returned by the OData query) in an `NSMutableArray` object (a member variable of the `scViewController` class). This object is then used as the data source for the `TableView` Control through the `UITableViewDataSource` interface implemented by the `scViewController` class. The `TableView` Control is a common UI element for presenting list- or collection-type data in iOS applications. Here, we just apply the default style on the `TableView` Control. You can also further customize the style to implement more complicated data collection presentation scenarios.

For more information about the `OData4ObjC` library and the `TableView` Control, you can look up the following references:

- *OData Client for Objective-C User Guide* available at `http://odata.github.com/ OData4ObjC/OData SDK for Objective-C User Guide.htm`

- *UITableView Tutorial* available at `http://www.iosdevnotes.com/2011/10/ uitableview-tutorial/`

See also

- *Building an OData service via WCF Data Service and ADO.NET Entity Framework* recipe in *Chapter 1, Building OData Services*

- *Hosting a WCF Data Service in IIS server* recipe in *Chapter 3, OData Service Hosting and Configuration*

6

Working with Public OData Producers

In this chapter, we will cover:

- ▶ Getting started with Netflix OData online catalog
- ▶ Manipulating Sharepoint 2010 documents through OData endpoint
- ▶ Using OData protocol for Windows Azure Table storage access
- ▶ Querying StackOverflow forums data with OData endpoint
- ▶ Tracking information of NuGet packages through OData feeds
- ▶ Exploring eBay online products catalog through OData service
- ▶ Consuming SSRS 2008 R2 report through OData feed

Introduction

So far we have gone through many cases of how to build OData services, or how to consume OData services in different kinds of client applications. However, some of you might be curious about whether there are any (or how many) public products or services which have already adopted OData in their data publishing and integration-related functionalities. Well, the answer is absolutely yes. And there are quite a few existing products or online services which have provided OData compatible interfaces for the clients to consume application data.

Among products or services owned by Microsoft, there are Sharepoint 2010, Windows Azure Storage service, SQL Server 2008 R2 Reporting Service, Dynamics CRM 2011, and so on, that have started to support OData. On the other hand, many online services such as Netflix. com, eBay.com, StackOverflow.com, Facebook, and so on, have also opened a part of their business data to consumers through OData-based service endpoints.

In this chapter, we will choose some of the previously mentioned applications or services as examples, and demonstrate how convenient it could be to build OData-based data access client applications for these existing applications and services.

Getting started with Netflix OData online catalog

When talking about any existing OData services available over the Internet, the Netflix online catalog service will often be mentioned and be used as the test service for dealing with OData related programming. Netflix is a well-known American Internet streaming media provider that opens public digital subscription and distribution services over the world. In order to take advantage of the OData ecosystem for increasing business data accessibility, Netflix has exposed the complete media/movie catalog data through OData endpoint over the Internet. In this recipe, we will show you how to query the OData-based Netflix catalog service in a .NET client application.

Getting ready

To make the complete service consuming process simple and clear, we will create a typical .NET console application for demonstration.

The source code for this recipe can be found in the `\ch06\NetflixODataSln` directory.

How to do it...

The following are the steps to create a sample application:

1. Create a new .NET console application as the OData client.
2. Launch Visual Studio Add Service Reference wizard and navigate to the following service address:

    ```
    http://odata.netflix.com/v2/Catalog/
    ```

3. By expanding the service node in the wizard dialog, we can have a quick look at all the available entity sets exposed in the Netflix OData service (see the following screenshot).

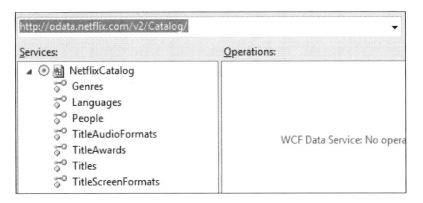

4. Define a helper function in the `Program.cs` file for creating the data context instance of the OData client proxy (see the following `GetODataContext` method).

```
static NetflixODataSvc.NetflixCatalog GetODataContext()
{
        var svcUri = new
            Uri("http://odata.netflix.com/v2/Catalog/",
            UriKind.Absolute);

        var ctx = new NetflixODataSvc.NetflixCatalog(svcUri);

        return ctx;
}
```

5. Add a function (in the `Program.cs` file) that uses LINQ expressions to perform the OData queries.

    The following `QueryNetflixGenres` function queries out the first 10 `Genre` entities from the Netflix catalog service:

```
static void QueryNetflixGenres()
{
    var ctx = GetODataContext();

        var first10genres = ctx.Genres.Take(10).ToList();

    foreach (var genre in first10genres)
    {
        Console.WriteLine("Genre Name:{0}", genre.Name);
    }
}
```

6. Add a function (in the `Program.cs` file) that uses raw a Uri string to perform the OData queries.

The following `QueryNetflixTitlesByGenre` function performs the same query as the `QueryNetflixGenres` function by using a raw query Uri string:

```
static void QueryNetflixTitlesByGenre(string genre)
{
    var ctx = GetODataContext();

        var queryUri = new Uri("Genres('" + genre +
        "')/Titles?$top=10", UriKind.Relative);

        var titles = ctx.Execute<NetflixODataSvc.Title>(queryUri);

    Console.WriteLine("First 10 titles under \"{0}\" genre",
    genre);
    foreach (var title in titles)
    {
        Console.WriteLine("=================================");
        Console.WriteLine("\tId:{0}",title.Id);
        Console.WriteLine("\tName:{0}", title.Name);
        Console.WriteLine("\tReleaseYear:{0}",
        title.ReleaseYear);
        Console.WriteLine("\tAverageRating:{0}",
        title.AverageRating);
    }
}
```

How it works...

As shown in the previous steps, the Netflix online catalog is a publicly opened OData endpoint that does not demand client authentication. After generating the strong-typed OData proxy through Visual Studio Add Service Reference wizard, we can use LINQ expression or raw query Uri string to perform OData queries against the service.

Alternatively, you can also use .NET `WebRequest` class or other HTTP network component to access the service by sending raw OData HTTP requests.

See also

▶ *Using Visual Studio to generate strong-typed OData client proxy* recipe in *Chapter 2, Working with OData at Client Side*

▶ *Accessing OData service via WebRequest class* recipe in *Chapter 2, Working with OData at Client Side*

Manipulating Sharepoint 2010 documents through OData endpoint

Microsoft Sharepoint is a web application platform designed for enterprises using Microsoft products (such as Windows Office, Active Directory, and so on) as the IT infrastructure. People can easily use Sharepoint Server to set up individual or team-wide internal portal website for team collaboration, project management, document repository, and so on.

In Sharepoint-based websites, almost all data are stored in the format of Sharepoint **Lists** and each *List* can contain one or more *List Items*. For example, an Announcement List can contain all the announcements published in the site; a Contact List can contain the contacts of all team members; a **Document Library** List can contain various kinds of documents and files.

For OData developers, there is a cool feature added in Sharepoint 2010, that is, all the Lists in a Sharepoint site can be accessed and manipulated through OData service endpoint. In this recipe, we will show you how to manipulate the documents in a Sharepoint 2010 Document Library by using OData service endpoint.

Here we will create a .NET console application, which uses a strong-typed OData proxy to perform `Query`, `Add` and `Delete` operations against a Document Library (within a Sharepoint 2010 Team Site).

Getting ready

Make sure you have a Sharepoint 2010 site available (and have sufficient access permissions on it) in your local environment.

The source code for this recipe can be found in the `\ch06\SharepointWithODataSln` directory.

How to do it...

Let's have a look at the following detailed steps:

1. Create a new .NET console application as the OData client.

2. Use the Visual Studio Add Service Reference wizard to create the OData proxy against the OData endpoint of the target Sharepoint 2010 site.

   For a given Sharepoint 2010 site, we can find the OData endpoint address (for the list data service) by using the following format Uri:

   ```
   http://[server name]:[port]/[site name]/_vti_bin/listdata.svc
   ```

By navigating to the endpoint address in the wizard dialog, we can preview all entity sets (representing the certain Sharepoint Lists) exposed by the service (see the following screenshot).

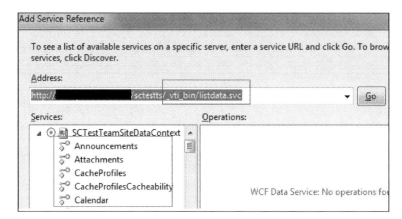

3. Define a helper function in the `Program.cs` file for creating the data context instance of the OData client proxy (see the following `GetODataContext` method).

```
static SPODataProxy.SCTestTeamSiteDataContext GetODataContext()
{
    var svcUri = new Uri("http://[sharepoint host
    name]/sctestts/_vti_bin/listdata.svc");
    var ctx = new
    SPODataProxy.SCTestTeamSiteDataContext(svcUri);
        ctx.Credentials =
        CredentialCache.DefaultNetworkCredentials;

    return ctx;
}
```

 As the sample Sharepoint server uses Windows authentication, we have specified the authentication credentials through the `Credentials` property on the data context object (in the `GetODataContext` method).

4. Add a function for querying all documents in a Document Library (see the following `ListSharedDocuments` function).

```
static void ListSharedDocuments()
{
    var ctx = GetODataContext();
```

```
        var query = from item in ctx.SharedDocuments
                    where item.ContentType == "Document"
                    select item;

foreach (var docItem in query)
{
    Console.WriteLine("=========={0}============",
    docItem.Name);
    Console.WriteLine("\tName: {0}", docItem.Name);
    Console.WriteLine("\tTitle: {0}", docItem.Title);
    Console.WriteLine("\tContentType: {0}",
    docItem.ContentType);
    Console.WriteLine("\tCreated: {0}", docItem.Created);
    Console.WriteLine("\tPath: {0}", docItem.Path);

}
}
```

5. Add a function for inserting an Office Word document into the same Document Library (see the following AddNewSharedDocumentsItem function).

```
static void AddNewSharedDocumentsItem()
{
    var ctx = GetODataContext();
        var strName = string.Format("NewDocument{0}",
        DateTime.Now.Ticks);
        var strPath = string.Format(
        "/sites/sctestts/Shared Documents/NewDocument{0}.docx",
        DateTime.Now.Ticks
        );

    var newDocItem = new SPODataProxy.SharedDocumentsItem()
    {
        Name= strName,
        Path= strPath,
    };

        ctx.AddToSharedDocuments(newDocItem);

        ctx.SetSaveStream(
         newDocItem,
         File.OpenRead(@"e:\temp\blankdoc.docx"),
         true,
         new DataServiceRequestArgs()
         {
             Slug = strPath
         }
        );

    ctx.SaveChanges();
}
```

6. Add a function for deleting some existing documents in the Document Library (see the following `DeleteSharedDocumentsItem` function).

```
static void DeleteSharedDocumentsItems()
{
    var ctx = GetODataContext();

    var items = (from item in ctx.SharedDocuments
                    where item.Name.StartsWith("NewDocument")
                    select item).ToArray();

    foreach (var item in items) ctx.DeleteObject(item);

    ctx.SaveChanges();
}
```

How it works...

The OData endpoint of Sharepoint 2010 sites is implemented with WCF Data Service. As shown in the previous code, the query and delete code logic is quite straightforward. We simply use the same code logic as we do when editing normal OData service entity sets. However, the code for adding a new document item is a bit more complicated since we need to supply the binary content of the new document item. To achieve this task, we need to leverage the **Binary Resource Stream** feature of WCF Data Service. This is done by using the `DataServiceContext.SetSaveStream` method which helps to associate a binary stream with the target OData entity object. We will talk more about the Binary Resource Stream feature of WCF Data Service in the *Exposing binary data on OData entity with Named Resource Stream* recipe in *Chapter 9, New Features of WCF Data Service 5.0 (OData V3)*.

There's more...

Including the OData endpoint feature, there are three main approaches available for .NET developers to access and manipulate data in Sharepoint 2010 sites. The other two are **Server-side Object Model** and **Client-side Object Model**.

Although the Server-side Object Model and Client-side Object Model provide much more advanced options for Sharepoint development, they also demand more requirements on the calling applications (compared to the OData endpoint approach). For example, you can only use Server-side Object Model on the server machines of the Sharepoint sites and both the Server-side Object Model and Client-side Object Model require us to add references against their corresponding assemblies before using them. For more information about Sharepoint programming with Server-side and Client-side Object Model, you can refer to the following MSDN references:

Using the SharePoint Foundation Server-side Object Model available at `http://msdn.microsoft.com/en-us/library/ee538251.aspx`

SharePoint 2010 Client Object Model available at `http://msdn.microsoft.com/en-us/library/ee537247.aspx`

See also

▸ *Using Visual Studio to generate strong-typed OData client proxy* recipe in *Chapter 2, Working with OData at Client Side*

▸ *Editing and deleting data through WCF Data Service client library* recipe in *Chapter 2, Working with OData at Client Side*

Using OData protocol for Windows Azure Table storage access

Microsoft has provided Windows Azure as the core Cloud computing platform for building and hosting applications in the Cloud. For applications developed for the Windows Azure platform, there are many different options for storing and managing application data. You can store your data as the common relational database through the SQL Azure service; or you can use Windows Azure storage (such as **Blob**, **Table** or **Queue** storage) to store your custom structured data. The Windows Azure Table storage provides a convenient means for developers to store collections of custom data entities. In Table storage, each collection is stored as a table and each entity object in collection is stored as a table row (with their properties stored as row fields/columns).

The Windows Azure SDK has already provided encapsulated class library and APIs for accessing Table storage data. However, what's amazing here is that the underlying communication of the Table storage access is based on OData protocol. In this recipe, we will demonstrate how we can manually make OData HTTP requests to access Windows Azure Table storage without using the Windows Azure SDK library.

Getting ready

Make sure you have a Windows Azure storage account available to test or you can use the local storage emulator provided by Windows Azure SDK (see the following reference).

Overview of Running a Windows Azure Application with the Storage Emulator available at `http://msdn.microsoft.com/en-us/library/windowsazure/gg432983.aspx`

The source code for this recipe can be found in the `\ch06\AzureStorageWithODataSln` directory.

How to do it...

The following are the steps for creating the sample application:

1. Create a new .NET console application.

2. Locate the OData endpoint address of the target Windows Azure Table storage account.

   The OData endpoint address of a given Windows Azure Table storage account is of the following format in which [account] is the actual name of the storage account:

   ```
   http://[account].table.core.windows.net/
   ```

3. Store the name and access key of the Windows Azure storage account through the appSettings section in the app.config file (see the following screenshot).

   ```
   <?xml version="1.0"?>
   <configuration>
     <appSettings>
       <add key="account" value="[account name]"/>
       <add key="key" value="[account key value]"/>
   ```

> For how to get the access key of a given Windows Azure storage account, you can refer to the following MSDN reference article:
>
> ```
> http://msdn.microsoft.com/en-us/library/
> windowsazure/hh531566.aspx
> ```

4. Define a helper function (in Program.cs file) for creating the WebRequest object and populating the HTTP headers for authentication (see the following code snippet).

   ```
   static HttpWebRequest
       GenerateODataWebRequestForAzureStorage(string url,
       string accountName, string accountKey)
   {
       var request = (HttpWebRequest)WebRequest.Create(url);

       request.Method = "GET";
           request.Headers.Add("x-ms-date",
           DateTime.UtcNow.ToString("R",
           CultureInfo.InvariantCulture));

       var resource = request.RequestUri.AbsolutePath;

       string stringToSign = string.Format("{0}\n/{1}{2}",
               request.Headers["x-ms-date"],
               accountName,
   ```

```
        resource
    );

var hasher = new
HMACSHA256(Convert.FromBase64String(accountKey));

string signedSignature =
Convert.ToBase64String(hasher.ComputeHash
(Encoding.UTF8.GetBytes(stringToSign)));
    string authorizationHeader = string.Format("{0} {1}:{2}",
    "SharedKeyLite", accountName, signedSignature);

    request.Headers.Add("Authorization", authorizationHeader);

return request;
}
```

5. Add a function (in `Program.cs` file) for querying the Table storage by using the `WebRequest` instance created by the helper function (see the following code snippet).

```
static void QueryTableItemsWithRawODataHttp()
{
    var accountName = ConfigurationManager.AppSettings["account"];
    var accountKey = ConfigurationManager.AppSettings["key"];

    var queryUrl = string.Format("http://{0}.table.core.windows.
    net/TestTable?$top=5", accountName);

    var request =
    GenerateODataWebRequestForAzureStorage(queryUrl,
    accountName, accountKey);

    var response = request.GetResponse();
    using (var sr = new
    StreamReader(response.GetResponseStream()))
    {
        var doc = XElement.Load(sr);

        var nsMetadata =
        "http://schemas.microsoft.com/ado/2007/
        08/dataservices/metadata";
        var nsSchema =
        "http://schemas.microsoft.com/ado/2007/08/dataservices";

        foreach (var elmItem in
        doc.Descendants(XName.Get("properties", nsMetadata)))
        {
```

```
            var name = elmItem.Descendants(XName.Get("Name",
            nsSchema)).First().Value;

            var partitionKey =
            elmItem.Descendants(XName.Get("PartitionKey",
            nsSchema)).First().Value;

            Console.WriteLine("Name:{0}, RowKey:{1}", name,
            partitionKey);
        }


    }
}
```

How it works...

In the sample code, we directly use raw OData HTTP requests (via `WebRequest` class) to query the `TestTable` table in the target Windows Azure Table storage. Each table stored in Windows Azure Table storage is like an OData entity set so that we can construct the query Uri for a certain table in the following format:

```
http://[account].table.core.windows.net/[table name]?[query options]
```

One thing worth noticing is that the OData endpoint of Windows Azure Table storage demands some HTTP headers from the client for authentication (for non-public tables). In the sample code of step 4 mentioned previously, we have supplied two HTTP headers (the `x-ms-date` header and the `Authorization` header) through the `WebRequest` object. The former contains the current UTC time and the latter is generated based on the account name and account key (hashed value) of the given storage account. The detailed information about the authentication header format can be found in the following MSDN document for Windows Azure storage service REST API.

Authentication Schemes available at `http://msdn.microsoft.com/en-us/library/windowsazure/dd179428.aspx`

There's more...

Although we can manually construct the OData HTTP requests for accessing Windows Azure Table storage, the encapsulated storage API provided in the Windows Azure SDK is still the preferred way to go in most cases. For example, the following code uses the storage API to query the same `TestTable` table (shown in the previous sample code's step 5) in a strong-typed manner.

```
static void QueryTableItemsWithStorageClientAPIs()
{
```

```
var account = GetStorageAccount();

var tableClient = account.CreateCloudTableClient();

    TableServiceContext ctx =
    tableClient.GetDataServiceContext();

    var allItems = ctx.CreateQuery<TestTableItem>(TABLE_NAME);

foreach (TestTableItem item in allItems)
{
    Console.WriteLine("Name:{0}, RowKey:{1}",item.Name,
    item.RowKey);
}
}
```

By using Fiddler, we can find that the storage API actually sends out the same OData HTTP requests as we've manually generated in this sample (see the following screenshot).

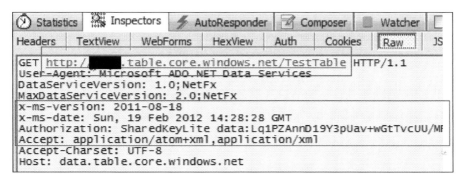

See also

► *Accessing OData service via WebRequest class* recipe in *Chapter 2, Working with OData at Client Side*

► *Deploying a WCF Data Service on Windows Azure host* recipe in *Chapter 3, OData Service Hosting and Configuration*

Query StackOverflow forums data with OData endpoint

StackOverflow (http://stackoverflow.com/) has become one of the biggest online communities which feature questions and answers on a wide range of topics in computer programming. As of January 2012, StackOverflow has about 967,000 registered users, and more than 2,000,000 questions. Users can easily use tags (such as C#, Java, PHP, JavaScript, jQuery, and so on) or custom search keywords to find their interested questions and topics in StackOverflow forums.

As a fully opened technical website, StackOverflow has opened its entire achieved knowledge database to the public. Users can freely get the information they need by downloading the data dumps from the Stack Exchange Data Explorer and then analyze them using whatever means they want.

Introducing Stack Exchange Data Explorer available at
http://blog.stackoverflow.com/2010/06/introducing-stack-exchange-data-explorer/

And if you're an OData developer, you definitely have more choices because you can use the OData endpoint exposed by the Stack Exchange Network to retrieve the same data. In this recipe, we will demonstrate how to use the OData endpoint to build a simple data analysis web page for the StackOverflow community.

Getting ready

Here, we will build a simple ASP.NET Web Form page, which uses two Chart controls to display the tag and post distribution information by using the Stack Overflow OData endpoint.

The source code for this recipe can be found in the \ch06\StackOverFlowODataSln directory.

How to do it...

Now, let's start building the sample web page using the following steps:

1. Create a new ASP.NET empty web application.
2. Generate a client proxy (via the Visual Studio Add Service Reference wizard) against the target OData endpoint.

   The OData endpoint for StackOverflow site is opened at the following location:

   http://data.stackexchange.com/stackoverflow/atom

By navigating to the endpoint address in the wizard dialog, we can preview the entity sets exposed in the OData endpoint (see the following screenshot).

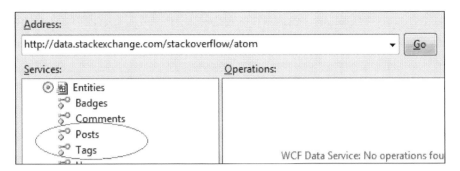

3. Create a new Web Form page (named `TagsReport.aspx`) in the web application.

4. Add the HTML content for the Web Form page (in the `TagsReport.aspx` file).

   Here shows the main HTML content of the page which consists of two ASP.NET Chart controls (one for displaying *Bar* chart and another for displaying *Pie* chart).

```
<form id="form1" runat="server">
    <div>
        <asp:Chart ID="tagsPie"
        runat="server" Height="400px"
        Width="530px" >
        <Series>
            <asp:Series Name="TagsSeries" ChartType="Pie"
            XValueMember="Key" YValueMembers="Value"
            Label="#VALX (#PERCENT)"  ToolTip="Percent of
            #VALX: #PERCENT"
            >
            </asp:Series>
        </Series>
        <ChartAreas>
            <asp:ChartArea Name="ChartArea1"
            AlignmentStyle="All" >
                <AxisY Title="Post Count">
                </AxisY>
                <AxisX Interval="1" Title="TagName" >
                    <LabelStyle Interval="1" Angle="20" />
                </AxisX>
                <Area3DStyle Enable3D="True"></Area3DStyle>
            </asp:ChartArea>
        </ChartAreas>
    <Titles>
        <asp:Title Text="Tags Distribution By Pie Chart: "
        Font="Times New Roman, 22pt, style=Bold" />
    </Titles>
    </asp:Chart>
```

```
<asp:Chart ID="tagsBar" runat="server"
Height="400px" Width="530px" >
<Series>
    <asp:Series Name="TagsSeries" ChartType="Bar"
     XValueMember="Key"
     YValueMembers="Value" ChartArea="ChartArea1" >
    </asp:Series>
</Series>
<ChartAreas>
    <asp:ChartArea Name="ChartArea1"
     AlignmentStyle="All">
     <AxisY Title="Post Count">
        </AxisY>
        <AxisX Interval="1" Title="TagName">
            <LabelStyle Interval="1" />
        </AxisX>
        <Area3DStyle Enable3D="True" />
    </asp:ChartArea>
</ChartAreas>
<Titles>
    <asp:Title Text="Tags Distribution By Bar Chart:"
     Font="Times New Roman, 22pt, style=Bold" />
</Titles>
</asp:Chart>
</div>
</form>
```

5. Add a function for querying the StackOverflow **Tags** and **Posts** data in the page's code-behind file (see the following `GetStackOverflowTags` function).

```
Dictionary<string, int> GetStackOverflowTags()
{
    if (Cache["TAGS"] == null)
    {
        Uri svcUri = new
        Uri("http://data.stackexchange.com/stackoverflow/atom");
        StackOData.Entities ctx = new
        StackOData.Entities(svcUri);

        var tags = ctx.Tags.Take(10).ToArray();

        Dictionary<string, int> dictTags = new
        Dictionary<string, int>();
        foreach (var tag in tags)
        {
            var postCount = ctx.Posts.Where(p =>
            p.Tags.Contains(tag.TagName)).Count();
         dictTags.Add(tag.TagName, postCount);
        }
```

```
                Cache["TAGS"] = dictTags;
        }

        return Cache["TAGS"] as Dictionary<string, int>;
    }
```

6. Add the code for binding the **Tags** and **Posts** data to the Chart controls within the `Page_Load` event of the page (see the following code snippet).

```
protected void Page_Load(object sender, EventArgs e)
{

    var dictTags = GetStackOverflowTags();

    tagsPie.Series[0].CustomProperties = "PieLabelStyle=
    Outside";
    tagsPie.DataSource = dictTags;
    tagsPie.DataBind();

    tagsBar.DataSource = dictTags;
    tagsBar.DataBind();
}
```

7. Build the web application and launch the `TagsReport.aspx` page in web browser.

   The following screenshot shows the page output after the **Tags** and **Posts** data (from the StackOverflow OData endpoint) get populated:

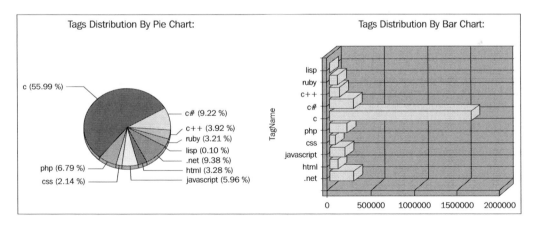

How it works...

In the sample page, we use the `Page_Load` event to query the **Tags** and **Posts** data from the StackOverflow OData endpoint. After retrieving the query result, we store them into the ASP.NET Cache storage (to avoid sequential service access) and bind the result data to the Chart controls. For simplicity, the sample code hasn't used an asynchronous pattern for data loading. Thus, it might take a while to load all the **Posts** data when the page is loaded at the first time.

There's more...

Compared to the StackOverflow online data explorer (at the location, `http://data.stackexchange.com/stackoverflow/query/new`), the OData endpoint gives developers much more flexibility and control for building custom data querying and analysis tools (by using the StackOverflow community data).

The sample page here has only utilized two entity sets (**Posts** and **Tags**) from the OData endpoint. If you want, you can use similar means to retrieve more complicated data output from all the entity sets exposed from the service. For example, in case you're interested in the trend of a certain new technology/topic discussed in the StackOverflow community, you can build an application to incrementally query on the new **Posts** created under that technology and perform your custom analysis over them.

See also

► *Using Visual Studio to generate strong-typed OData client proxy* recipe in *Chapter 2, Working with OData at Client Side*

Tracking information of NuGet packages through OData feeds

NuGet is a free, open source developer focused package management system for the .NET platform. With NuGet, .NET developers can easily find useful open source component libraries and integrate them into their .NET projects. Currently, you can use the Visual Studio NuGet package manager or directly go to `http://nuget.org/packages/` to look for any useful NuGet packages.

Well, what if we're only interested in some particular NuGet packages, or want to regularly monitor and track the update and status of those packages? This is useful not only if you just consume shared NuGet packages, but also if you publish your own components into the NuGet package collection.

No problem, NuGet provides a public data feed so that users can query information and track status of any NuGet package through the feed. And the more exciting point is that the NuGet data feed is fully OData compatible. In this recipe, we will demonstrate how we can use the OData feed to track the information of NuGet packages.

Getting ready

Here we will create a **WPF (Windows Presentation Foundation)** application that allows users to search for NuGet packages by using some keywords. The following screenshot shows the UI of the sample application:

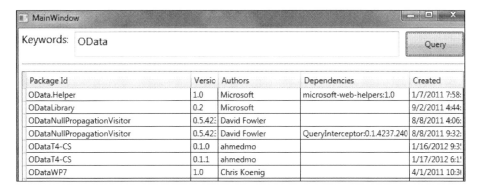

The source code for this recipe can be found in the `\ch06\NugetQueryWithODataSln` directory.

How to do it...

The following are the steps for building the sample WPF application:

1. Create a new WPF application as the OData client.

2. Generate the OData proxy (via the Visual Studio Add Service Reference wizard) against the NuGet data feed endpoint.

   The NuGet data feed endpoint can be found at:

   ```
   http://packages.nuget.org/v1/FeedService.svc/
   ```

By navigating to the endpoint address in the wizard dialog, we can find that the NuGet data feed only provides a single entity set–**Packages** (see the following screenshot).

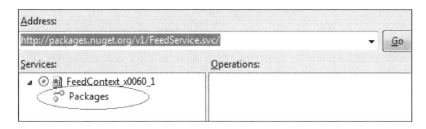

3. Compose the XAML content for the main WPF window (in `MainWindow.xaml` file).

The main window contains three key controls, one `TextBox` control for accepting search keywords, one `Button` control for submitting query requests and one `DataGrid` control for displaying query results (see the following XAML fragment).

```xaml
<StackPanel>
    <Grid>
        <Grid.ColumnDefinitions>
            <ColumnDefinition Width="80" />
            <ColumnDefinition Width="*" />
            <ColumnDefinition Width="100" />
        </Grid.ColumnDefinitions>
        <TextBlock Grid.Column="0" Text="Keywords:"
            HorizontalAlignment="Stretch"
            FontSize="16" Margin="5" />
        <TextBox Name="txtKeyword" Grid.Column="1"
         HorizontalAlignment="Stretch" FontSize="16"
         Margin="5" />
        <Button Name="btnQuery" Grid.Column="2"
         Content="Query"
         Height="37" HorizontalAlignment="Stretch"
         Margin="5"
         Click="btnQuery_Click" />
    </Grid>
    <Separator Margin="5" />
    <DataGrid Name="gridPackages"
     AutoGenerateColumns="False"
     HorizontalAlignment="Stretch"
     VerticalAlignment="Stretch" Margin="5"
     MinHeight="400">
    <DataGrid.Columns>
```

```xml
          <DataGridTextColumn Header="Package Id"
           Binding="{Binding Path=Id}" Width="3*" />
          <DataGridTextColumn Header="Version"
           Binding="{Binding Path=Version}" Width="0.5*" />
          <DataGridTextColumn Header="Authors"
           Binding="{Binding Path=Authors}" Width="1.5*" />
          <DataGridTextColumn Header="Dependencies"
           Binding="{Binding Path=Dependencies}" Width="2*"
           />
          <DataGridTextColumn Header="Created"
           Binding="{Binding Path=Created}" Width="1*" />
        </DataGrid.Columns>
      </DataGrid>
  </StackPanel>
```

4. Add a function for retrieving NuGet packages information (based on search keywords) from the data feed (see the following `QueryPackagesWithKeyword` function).

```csharp
void QueryPackagesWithKeyword(string kw)
{
    var ctx = new NugetOData.FeedContext_x0060_1(new
    Uri("http://packages.nuget.org/v1/FeedService.svc/"));

        var packages = from p in ctx.Packages
                       where p.Title.ToUpper().Contains(kw.
                       ToUpper())
                       select p;

    gridPackages.ItemsSource = packages.ToArray();
    gridPackages.UpdateLayout();
}
```

5. Add the code for invoking the `QueryPackagesWithKeyword` function in the `Click` event of the **Query** button (see the following code snippet).

```csharp
private void btnQuery_Click(object sender, RoutedEventArgs e)
{
    if (string.IsNullOrEmpty(txtKeyword.Text) ||
    txtKeyword.Text.Length < 3) return;

    QueryPackagesWithKeyword(txtKeyword.Text.Trim());
}
```

How it works...

As the NuGet data feed exposes all package-related information through the single **Packages** entity set, we just need to use some proper query options to filter out the certain packages we're interested in. In this sample, we filter the packages by using some keywords in the package name. Although we use LINQ style code to query the entity set, the underlying LINQ provider (provided by the WCF Data Service client library) automatically converts the LINQ query into the proper OData query Uri. By using Fiddler, we can find the raw OData query request sent to the target data feed endpoint (see the following screenshot).

See also

▶ *Using Visual Studio to generate strong-typed OData client proxy* recipe in *Chapter 2, Working with OData at Client Side*

▶ *Performing WPF data binding with OData service data* recipe in *Chapter 2, Working with OData at Client Side*

Exploring eBay online products catalog through OData service

eBay.com (managed by **eBay Inc.**) is an online auction and shopping website in which people and businesses buy and sell a broad variety of goods and services worldwide. When browsing over eBay.com, people can use the hierarchical product categories to search and find the certain product items they want. Now, eBay.com has also opened its complete products catalog through a Windows Azure hosted OData service. In this recipe, we will utilize this catalog service to build a simple application for exploring the product items on eBay.com.

Getting ready

Here, we will create an ASP.NET Web Form page to display available product items (from eBay. com) based on the selected category. The overall page UI looks like the following screenshot:

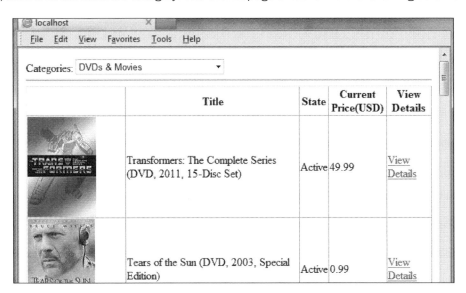

The source code for this recipe can be found in the \ch06\EBayODataSln directory.

How to do it...

Let's have a look at the following detailed steps:

1. Create a new ASP.NET empty web application.

2. Generate the OData proxy (via the Visual Studio Add Service Reference wizard) against the eBay products catalog service.

   The products catalog service is opened at the following base address:

   `http://ebayodata.cloudapp.net/`

3. Create a new Web Form page named `EBayItemsByCategory.aspx`.

4. Compose the HTML content of the `EBayItemsByCategory.aspx` page (see the following HTML fragment).

```
<form id="form1" runat="server">
    <div>
        Categories:
        <asp:DropDownList ID="lstCategories" runat="server"
         AutoPostBack="true"
```

```
            onselectedindexchanged=
            "lstCategories_SelectedIndexChanged" >
        </asp:DropDownList>
        <hr />
        <asp:GridView ID="gvItems" runat="server"
         AutoGenerateColumns="False" >
            <Columns>
                <asp:ImageField DataImageUrlField="GalleryUrl" >
                </asp:ImageField>
                <asp:BoundField DataField="Title"
                  HeaderText="Title" />
                <asp:BoundField DataField="SellingState"
                  HeaderText="State" />
                <asp:BoundField DataField="CurrentPrice"
                  HeaderText="Current Price(USD)" />
                <asp:HyperLinkField  Text="View Details"
                  HeaderText="View Details"
                  DataNavigateUrlFields="ViewItemUrl"
                  Target="_blank" />

            </Columns>
        </asp:GridView>

    </div>
</form>
```

5. Open the page's code-behind file (`EBayItemsByCategory.aspx.cs`) and add the code for populating the category list (in the `DropDownList` control) through the `Page_Load` event (see the following code snippet).

```
Uri _serviceUri = new Uri("http://ebayodata.cloudapp.net/");

protected void Page_Load(object sender, EventArgs e)
{
    if (!IsPostBack)
    {
        var ctx = new EBayOData.EBayData(_serviceUri);
        var categories =
        ctx.Categories
          .Where(c => c.Level == 1)
          .Select(c => new { Name = c.Name, Id = c.Id } )
          .ToList();

        lstCategories.DataTextField = "Name";
        lstCategories.DataValueField = "Id";
        lstCategories.DataSource = categories;
```

```
            lstCategories.DataBind();
        }
    }
```

6. Add the code for populating product items (in the `GridView` control) based on the selected category through the `SelectedIndexChanged` event of the `DropDownList` control (see the following code snippet).

```
protected void lstCategories_SelectedIndexChanged(object sender,
EventArgs e)
{
    var ctx = new EBayOData.EBayData(_serviceUri);
        var items =
        ctx.Items
         .Where(i => i.PrimaryCategoryId ==
          lstCategories.SelectedValue)
         .Take(20)
         .ToList();

    gvItems.DataSource = items;
    gvItems.DataBind();
}
```

How it works...

The sample page consists of two ASP.NET server controls; one is the `DropDownList` control for displaying the category list for selection; the other is the `GridView` control for presenting the products belong to the selected category. For simplicity, we have only retrieved the first level categories from the eBay catalog service while the actual `Categories` entity set contains much more records (organized in multiple levels). Also, since the sample page hasn't implemented paging for displaying all product items, we only retrieve the first 20 items under each category so as not to overwhelm the page.

The eBay catalog service provides much more than the `Categories` and `items` entity sets, which we have used here. They are as follows:

- Bidders
- Cross promotions
- Deals
- Feedback
- Items
- Shippings
- Transactions
- Users

This really opens the door for developers to easily build either online data tracking and query applications (such as for searching interested products or biddings) or offline data analysis applications (such as for discovering hot and popular products and trends) in an open and a standard way.

See also

▶ *Using Visual Studio to generate strong-typed OData client proxy* recipe in *Chapter 2, Working with OData at Client Side*

▶ *Building data-driven ASP.NET Web Form pages with OData* recipe in *Chapter 4, Using OData in Web Application*

Consuming SSRS 2008 R2 report through OData feed

So far we have explored several OData programming cases against some existing OData enabled products and online services. Now, let's have a look at another OData use case which does not require much programming skills. This time, the focus is on **Microsoft SQL Server Reporting Services** (**SSRS**).

SQL Server Reporting Services(SSRS) is a server-based reporting platform that provides comprehensive reporting functionality for a variety of data sources. With the services and tools of SSRS, IT professionals can easily create, deploy, and manage reports for their organizations. With the release of SQL Server 2008 R2, there comes a new feature through which we can export an existing SSRS report as a data feed, or you can even create a report whose primary purpose is to provide data in the form of data feed.

Yes, as you might have guessed, the data feed is fully OData compatible so that it can be consumed by various kinds of OData client application or tools. In this recipe, we will show you how we can use Microsoft Excel PowerPivot component to consume the OData feed exposed from SSRS reports.

Getting ready

Make sure the client machine has Excel 2010 and PowerPivot component installed. The PowerPivot component is available at the following site:

Microsoft PowerPivot available at `http://www.microsoft.com/en-us/bi/powerpivot.aspx`

For demonstration purpose, we will also need a sample report (accessible from client machine) published from a SQL Server Reporting Service (SSRS) instance of the 2008 R2 version.

How to do it...

The following are the steps for consuming the sample SSRS report:

1. Open the web browser and navigate to the sample SSRS report.

2. Click on the OData feed button on the right-hand side of the report page's toolbar to export the data feed (see the following screenshot).

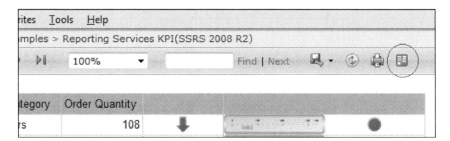

3. Save the data feed file (with the `.atomsvc` extension) prompted by the web browser into local disk (see the following screenshot).

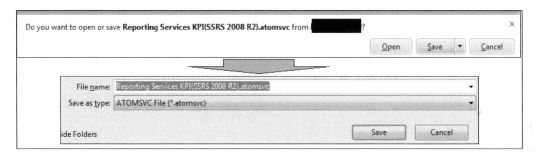

4. Launch Microsoft Excel 2010.

5. Select the **PowerPivot** tab and click on the **PowerPivot Window** ribbon to open a new PowerPivot specific window (see the following screenshot).

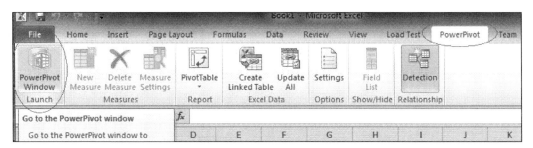

6. In the opened **PowerPivot Window**, select the **Home** tab and click the data feed button (looks similar to the SSRS report's data feed button) to launch the **Table Import Wizard** (see the following screenshot).

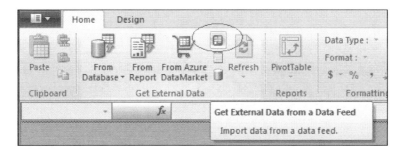

7. In the **Connect to a Data Feed** screen of the **Table Import Wizard**, supply the .atomsvc data feed file we have saved locally and give a **Friendly connection name** for this data feed (see the following screenshot).

> You can use the **Test Connection** button to verify if the target data source (data feed endpoint) is working correctly.

8. In the **Selected Tables and Views** screen of the **Table Import Wizard**, select the certain tables and views we want to import (from the target SSRS report feed) within the **Tables and Views** list view (see the following screenshot).

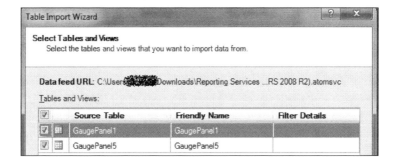

9. In the **Importing** screen of the **Table Import Wizard**, click on the **Finish** button to start the actual data importing progress.

    Depending on the amount of data to be loaded, it might take a while for the importing task to finish.

10. After the importing task finishes, check the importing result in the **Details** list view of the **Importing** screen (see the following screenshot).

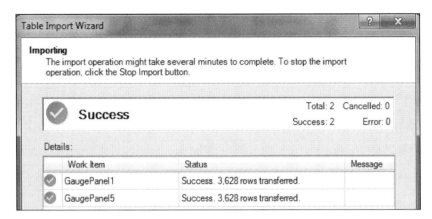

11. Close the **Table Import Wizard** and explore the imported tables and views (in the corresponding data sheets) in the **PowerPivot Window** (see the following screenshot).

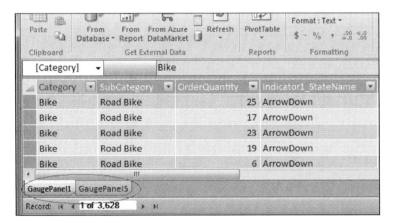

How it works...

As shown in the previous steps, the data feed of SSRS report is exposed as an .atomsvc file. If you open this file with a text or XML editor, you can find that the content of this file is just like the service document of a standard OData service. The sample data feed file here includes a single feed collection which points to the resource location of the target report data (see the following XML fragment).

```xml
<?xml version="1.0" encoding="utf-8" standalone="yes"?>
<service xmlns:atom="http://www.w3.org/2005/Atom"
xmlns:app="http://www.w3.org/2007/app" xmlns=
"http://www.w3.org/2007/app">
  <workspace>
    <atom:title>DrillDown Report</atom:title>
      <collection
      href="http://[server-
      name]/ReportServer?%2FReportProject%2FDrillDown%20
      Report&amp;
      rs%3ACommand=Render&amp;rs%3AFormat=ATOM&amp;
      rc%3ADataFeed=xAx0x0">
    <atom:title>Tablix1</atom:title>
    </collection>
  </workspace>
</service>
```

By using the resource location in the service document, the PowerPivot client can retrieve the detailed tables and rows of the target SSRS report and present them in the Excel worksheets.

There's more...

Although, we use Microsoft Excel PowerPivot component for the SSRS report feed consuming, you can surely use any other OData enabled tools or even build your own client applications in case you want to incorporate SSRS report through the OData based channel.

See also

▶ *Exploring an OData service through web browser* recipe in *Chapter 2, Working with OData at Client Side*

7

Working with Security

In this chapter, we will cover:

- ▶ Applying Windows authentication for OData service
- ▶ Using ASP.NET Forms authentication to secure OData service
- ▶ Securing OData service with HTTPS transport
- ▶ Implementing OData service authentication with custom HTTP Module
- ▶ Adding custom authorization with server-side processing pipeline
- ▶ Using Interceptors to control access for individual entity set
- ▶ Implementing role-based security for OData service

Introduction

Security is always a hot topic for any kind of distributed programming platform. For services that exchange important application data or expose functions for performing critical system operations, it is quite important to secure the communication between clients and services.

When dealing with security for a distributed service, we often encounter some common topics such as **authentication**, **authorization**, data protection, and so on. The OData protocol or WCF Data Service framework hasn't defined any kind of security protocol or infrastructure of its own, but rather relies on the security provisions of the data service host or the underlying transport layer. For example, for WCF Data Services hosted with the **ASP.NET/IIS** web application, we can leverage the built-in security support of ASP.NET and IIS host to secure the containing OData services. Also, as OData is naturally based on HTTP protocol, we can also take advantage of those existing HTTP enabled authentication and data securing mechanisms such as HTTPS/SSL secure transport.

In this chapter, we will discuss some common and easy to use means of implementing security protection for an OData service. We will start by demonstrating how to leverage built-in authentication methods (such as **Windows Authentication**, **Forms Authentication**, **HTTPS/SSL** protection) provided by the ASP.NET web application or IIS web server host, and then follow with some examples on how to implement custom authentication and authorization. At the end, we will provide a sample case of how to implement Role-based security by combining some of the features.

Applying Windows authentication for OData service

Windows authentication is one of the most common and popular authentication schemes used by client-server applications and services (such as IIS, SQL Server, Sharepoint Server, and so on) on the Microsoft Windows platform. When using Windows authentication, the client-side can explicitly supply the windows credentials or use the windows identity associated with the current security context to the server; while the server-side can use local Windows accounts or Active Directory accounts (Windows domain environment) to validate the authentication credentials sent from the client.

In this recipe, we will demonstrate how to apply Windows authentication for OData services hosted in an IIS server.

Getting ready

Here, we will use the Northwind sample OData service and configure it to use Windows authentication in an IIS 7 host. For deploying an OData service in IIS 7, you can refer to the *Hosting a WCF Data Service in IIS server* recipe in *Chapter 3, OData Service Hosting and Configuration*.

The source code for this recipe can be found in the `\ch07\ODataWindowsAuthWebSln` directory.

How to do it...

Now, let's have a look at the following steps to set up the Windows authentication:

1. Create a new ASP.NET web application which contains the Northwind OData service.

2. Add the **Windows Authentication** settings in the `web.config` file of the web application (see the following screenshot).

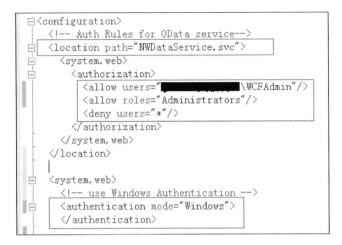

```
<configuration>
    <!-- Auth Rules for OData service-->
    <location path="NWDataService.svc">
        <system.web>
            <authorization>
                <allow users="          \WCFAdmin"/>
                <allow roles="Administrators"/>
                <deny users="*"/>
            </authorization>
        </system.web>
    </location>

    <system.web>
        <!-- use Windows Authentication -->
        <authentication mode="Windows">
        </authentication>
```

3. Deploy the web application into the IIS server (IIS 7).

4. Open IIS Manager and select the deployed web application (seen on the left-hand side).

5. In the **Feature** view, double click on the **Authentication** tab (see the following screenshot).

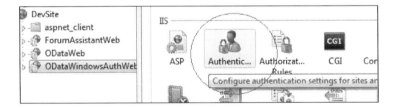

6. In the opened **Authentication** panel, disable the **Anonymous Authentication** option and enable the **Windows Authentication** option (see the following screenshot).

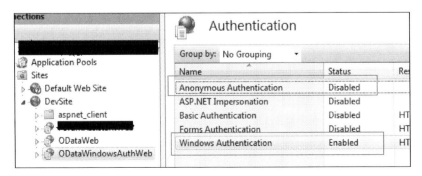

7. Create a new console application as the OData client.

8. Create the strong-typed OData proxy against the sample service.

9. Access the service by using a specific Windows account as the authentication credentials (see the following code snippet).

```
static void AccessWithNormalWindowsUserAccount()
{
    var svcUri = new Uri(SVC_URL);
    var ctx = new NWOData.NorthwindEntities(svcUri);

    ctx.Credentials = new System.Net.NetworkCredential(
                        "WCFUser",
                        "Password",
                        "[domain or machine name]"
                        );

    var categories = ctx.Categories.ToList();
    Console.WriteLine("There are {0} categories.",
        categories.Count);
}
```

10. Access the service by using the current security account as the authentication credentials (see the following code snippet).

```
static void AccessWithCurrentWindowsUserAccount()
{
    var svcUri = new Uri(SVC_URL);
    var ctx = new NWOData.NorthwindEntities(svcUri);

    ctx.Credentials =
    System.Net.CredentialCache.DefaultNetworkCredentials;

    var categories = ctx.Categories.ToList();
    Console.WriteLine("There are {0} categories.",
    categories.Count);
}
```

How it works...

In this sample, we apply Windows authentication on the OData service by enabling the built-in **Windows Authentication** module of the IIS server and setting the ASP.NET authentication mode as Windows (in the web.config file). Also, the <location> configuration element here (see the web.config fragment mentioned previously) helps restrict the access rules so that only those specified users (or roles) can access the sample OData service.

In case no authentication credentials are supplied or the authenticated client identity is not allowed to access the service, an **Access is denied** error will occur and the client side will get the corresponding error message (see the following screenshot) through exception details.

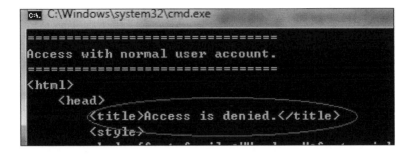

There's more...

In addition to IIS Manager, we can also use the `appcmd.exe` utility to configure the IIS authentication setting in the command-line prompt. For information about `appcmd.exe`, you can refer to the following document:

```
http://technet.microsoft.com/en-us/library/cc772200(v=ws.10).aspx
```

See also

▶ *Building an OData service via WCF Data Service and ADO.NET Entity Framework* recipe in *Chapter 1, Building OData Services*

▶ *Hosting a WCF Data Service in IIS server* recipe in *Chapter 3, OData Service Hosting and Configuration*

Using ASP.NET Forms authentication to secure OData service

Forms authentication is often used in Internet web applications for authenticating client users. ASP.NET web application also has built-in support on Forms authentication so that developers can easily use their own account database (such as SQL Server database, Active Directory or event custom file) for client authentication.

In this recipe, we will show you how we can take advantage of ASP.NET Forms authentication for securing an OData service.

Getting ready

We will still use the Northwind-based WCF Data Service as an example here and apply ASP.
NET Forms authentication to it. The following screenshot shows the overall project structure of
the sample web application in Visual Studio Solution Explorer:

The source code for this recipe can be found in the `\ch07\ODataFormsAuthSln` directory.

How to do it...

Let's start building the sample application now using the following steps:

1. Create a new ASP.NET web application that contains the Northwind OData service.

2. Open the `web.config` file, and add the configuration elements for enabling the
   Forms authentication (see the following configuration fragment):

```xml
<system.web>
  <authentication mode="Forms" >
    <forms loginUrl="Login.aspx"  requireSSL="false" >
      <credentials passwordFormat="Clear">
        <user name="user1" password="pwd4user1"/>
        <user name="user2" password="pwd4user2"/>
      </credentials>
    </forms>
  </authentication>
```

For simplicity, we directly define some hardcoded user accounts in
the `web.config` file instead of using additional account storage
such as the ASP.NET membership provider database.

3. Add the authorization settings for the OData service (in the `web.config` file) by using the `<location>` configuration element (see the following screenshot).

```
<configuration>
  <location path="NWDataService.svc" >
    <system.web>
      <authorization>
        <deny users="?" />
        <allow users="*"/>
      </authorization>
    </system.web>
  </location>
```

4. Create a **Generic Handler** (named `ODataFormsAuthHandler.ashx`) in the web application (see the following screenshot).

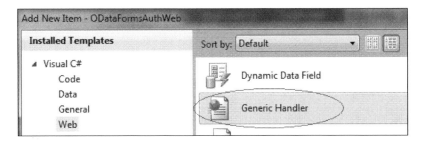

5. Add the code for performing Forms authentication programmatically in the code-behind file of the `ODataFormsAuthHandler.ashx` handler (see the following code snippet).

```
public class ODataFormsAuthHandler : IHttpHandler
{
    public void ProcessRequest(HttpContext context)
    {
        if (context.Request.HttpMethod == "POST")
        {
            var username = context.Request.Form["username"];
            var password = context.Request.Form["password"];

            if (FormsAuthentication.Authenticate(username,
            password))
            {
                FormsAuthentication.SetAuthCookie(username, true);
                context.Response.Write("<h1>Authentication
                succeed.</h1>");
            }
```

```
            else
            {
                context.Response.Write("<h1>Authentication
                failed.</h1>");
            }

            context.Response.Write("<h2>name: " + username + ",
            pwd: " + password + "</h2>");
            context.Response.Flush();
        }
    else
        {
            context.Response.Write("<h1>Only accept POST
            request for authentication.</h1>");
            context.Response.Flush();
        }
    }
    . . . . . .
}
```

6. Create a new console application as the OData client.

7. Create the strong-typed OData proxy against the sample service.

8. Add a helper function for performing Forms authentication against the `ODataFormsAuthHandler.ashx` handler in the service web application (see the following `GetAuthenticationCookie` function).

```
static string GetAuthenticationCookie(string username, string
    password)
{
    var request = (HttpWebRequest)WebRequest.
    Create("http://localhost:20162/ODataFormsAuthHandler.ashx");
    request.Method = "POST";
    request.ContentType = "application/x-www-form-urlencoded";

    using(var sw = new
    StreamWriter(request.GetRequestStream()))
    {
        sw.Write("username=" + username + "&password=" +
        password);
    }

    var response = (HttpWebResponse)request.GetResponse();

        return response.Headers[HttpResponseHeader.SetCookie];
}
```

9. Add the code for performing OData queries against the sample service (see the following `AccessODataService` function).

```
static void AccessODataService()
{
    var svcUri = new
    Uri("http://localhost:20162/NWDataService.svc");
    var ctx = new NWOData.NorthwindEntities(svcUri);

    // Injecting the cookie for forms authentication token
    ctx.SendingRequest +=
      (o, e) =>
      {
          var cookie = GetAuthenticationCookie("user1",
          "pwd4user1");
          e.RequestHeaders.Add(HttpRequestHeader.Cookie,
          cookie);
      };

    var categories = ctx.Categories.ToList();
    Console.WriteLine("There are {0} categories.",
    categories.Count);
}
```

How it works...

In the sample web application, we have enabled Forms authentication and used the `<authorization>` configuration section to restrict the access of the Northwind OData service (only authenticated users can access it). When you deploy the web application into the IIS server, make sure you have enabled the **Anonymous Authentication** (see the following reference) for the IIS application which is necessary for ASP.NET Forms authentication to work correctly.

Enable Anonymous Authentication (IIS 7) available at `http://technet.microsoft.com/en-us/library/cc731244(v=WS.10).aspx`

By default, web applications which use Forms authentication need a login page for client users to log on with their username/password credentials. However, such a user interactive approach does not work for a service applications such as Web Service or WCF Data Service. Therefore, we need to build an additional endpoint so that the service client (such as the OData client proxy) can use the endpoint to perform authentication programmatically.

In this sample, we create the `ODataFormsAuthHandler.ashx` handler which accepts the username/password credentials from the client and returns the generated authentication token (in HTTP response cookies). Thus, the OData client can programmatically access the handler to obtain the authentication token and hold it (in memory) for sequential OData service query requests. Also, when using the Visual Studio generated OData proxy to query the secured OData service, we can use the `SendingRequest` event of the data context class to supply the Forms authentication token (as the HTTP request cookie).

By the way, when the Forms authentication access rules are enabled, we will not be able to generate an OData client proxy through the Visual Studio Add Service Reference or `DataSvcUtil.exe` tool. In order to resolve this problem, we can either temporarily turn off the authorization rules when creating service proxy or manually download the metadata of the OData service and generate a service proxy against the local downloaded metadata.

There's more...

All the Forms authentication negotiation (based on the `ODataFormsAuthHandler.ashx` handler) between OData service and client are over plain HTTP transport. In a real production case, it is recommended that you use HTTPS/SSL transport so as to ensure the secure transfer of client user credentials and authentication tokens between the client and server.

See also

> ▸ *Building an OData service via WCF Data Service and ADO.NET Entity Framework* recipe in *Chapter 1, Building OData Services*

> ▸ *Securing OData service with HTTPS transport* recipe

Securing OData service with HTTPS transport

While trying to find a simple and quick means for securing an Internet faced web application, we will often consider HTTPS based transport as a good option. **HTTPS** is a combination of **Hypertext Transfer Protocol (HTTP)** with **SSL/TLS** protocol. It provides encrypted communication and secure identification of a network web server. As OData is naturally based on HTTP protocol, it is apparent that we can leverage HTTPS to implement transport layer security for our OData services. In this recipe, we will show you how to apply HTTPS transport security for OData services hosted in the IIS 7 server.

Getting ready

The next section will focus on the HTTPS/SSL configuration for the Northwind OData service deployed in IIS 7. You can refer to the _Hosting a WCF Data Service in IIS server_ recipe in _Chapter 3, OData Service Hosting and Configuration_ for details about deploying OData service into IIS 7.

The source code for this recipe can be found in the `\ch07\ODataHTTPsSln` directory.

How to do it...

The following are the detailed steps for securing an OData service:

1. Open IIS Manager.

2. Locate the website under which the OData service web application is deployed (see the following screenshot).

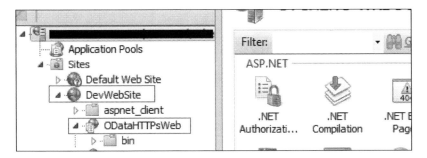

3. Right-click on the **DevWebSite** node and click on the **Edit Bindings...** context menu (see the following screenshot).

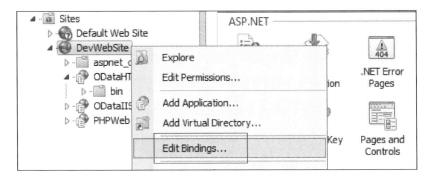

4. Click on the **Add...** button on the opened **Site Bindings** dialog (see the following screenshot).

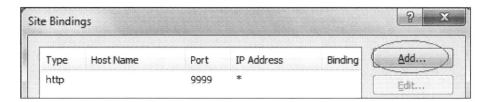

5. In the **Add Site Binding** dialog, specify the **Type**, **IP address**, **Port** and **SSL certificate** values for the HTTPS binding we want to add (see the following screenshot).

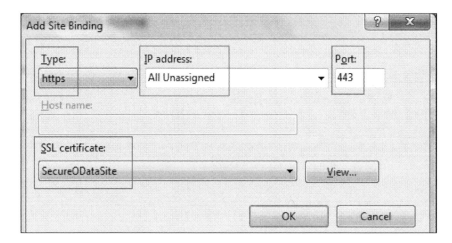

6. Click on the **OK** button and close all the opened dialogs.

7. Select the OData service web application and double click on the **SSL Settings** tab in the **Feature** panel (see the following screenshot).

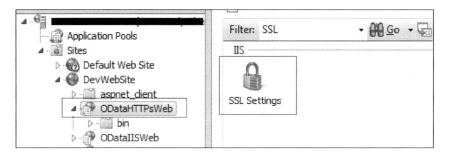

8. In the opened **SSL Settings** panel, turn on the **Require SSL** option so that the OData service web application can only be accessed via HTTPS transport (see the following screenshot).

SSL Settings

This page lets you modify the SSL settings for the content of a Web site or application.

☑ Require SSL

Client certificates:

⦿ Ignore

◯ Accept

◯ Require

9. Create a new console application as an OData client.

10. Generate the strong-typed OData proxy against the sample service.

 We can temporarily turn off the **HTTPS/SSL** option when generating the OData proxy in Visual Studio or command-line prompt.

11. Access the HTTPS secured service with the strong-typed OData proxy (see the following `AccessHTTPsSecuredODataService` function).

```
private static void AccessHTTPsSecuredODataService()
{
    // Register SSL certificate validation handler
    System.Net.ServicePointManager.
        ServerCertificateValidationCallback =
        (obj, cert, chain, errs) =>
        {
            // Ignore validation errors for testing certficate
            return true;
        };

    var svcUri = new
    Uri("https://localhost/ODataHTTPsWeb/NWDataService.svc");
    var ctx = new NWOData.NorthwindEntities(svcUri);

    var categories = ctx.Categories.ToList();
    Console.WriteLine("There are {0} categories.",
    categories.Count);
}
```

How it works...

In this sample, we use IIS Manager to configure the HTTPS transport for the OData service web application. The IIS server manages all HTTP and HTTPS transport channels at website level (as **Site Bindings**). When adding a new HTTPS **Site Binding** in IIS, we need to select a SSL Certificate. This certificate is used for the data security and server authentication over the HTTPS transport. For development/test purposes, we can use `makecert.exe` tool to generate a test certificate. The following is the command we have used for generating the sample SSL Certificate:

```
makecert -r -pe -n CN="SecureODataSite" -eku 1.3.6.1.5.5.7.3.1 -ss my
-sr localmachine -sky exchange -sp "Microsoft RSA SChannel Cryptographic
Provider" -sy 12
```

At web application level, we can use the **Require SSL** option to further control whether the web application can only be accessed via HTTPS transport or not.

At the client side, we create a console application which uses the strong-typed OData proxy to access the HTTPS secured service. One thing worth noticing is that the test certificate (created by `makecert.exe`) cannot pass the default SSL certificate validation on .NET based web clients (including `WebRequest` class, ASMX WebService client proxy, WCF client proxy, and so on). Therefore, we need to intercept the SSL certificate validation process (by using the `ServerCertificateValidationCallback` callback event of the `ServicePointManager` class) so as to suppress the default validation error.

By using Fiddler (or any other HTTP sniffer tools), we can capture the underlying transport communications and verify that the OData requests and responses are secured via the HTTPS channel (see the following screenshot).

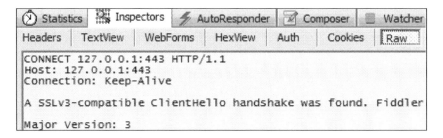

See also

> ▸ *Hosting a WCF Data Service in IIS server* recipe in *Chapter 3, OData Service Hosting and Configuration*

Implementing OData service authentication with custom HTTP Module

HTTP Module is an ASP.NET component that can intercept the HTTP requests (against ASP. NET web application resources) during the server-side processing pipeline. The IIS and ASP. NET infrastructure have provided many built-in HTTP modules, some of which are used for security authentication and authorization against incoming HTTP requests. Also, developers can also create their own HTTP modules to extend the default processing pipeline.

In most cases, we will use a ASP.NET/IIS based web application for hosting an OData service created via WCF Data Service. Therefore, it is certainly a good idea to leverage custom HTTP modules for extending the processing pipeline of OData services hosted in ASP.NET web applications. In this recipe, we will demonstrate how to apply custom authentication for a WCF Data Service through a custom HTTP Module.

Getting ready

The sample OData service used here is still based on the *Building an OData service via WCF Data Service and ADO.NET Entity Framework* recipe in *Chapter 1, Building OData Services*. We will create a custom HTTP Module that demands a custom HTTP header from the OData client for authentication.

The source code for this recipe can be found in the \ch07\CustomAuthODataSln directory.

How to do it...

The following are the detailed steps for creating the sample applications:

1. Create a new ASP.NET web application that contains the Northwind OData service.

2. Add a new **ASP.NET Module** (see the following screenshot) named CustomODataAuthModule in the web application.

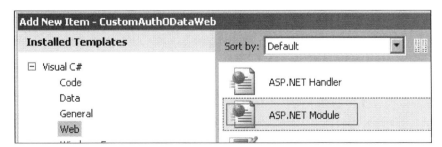

3. Open the `.cs` file of the `CustomODataAuthModule` class and add the authentication code in it (see the following code snippet).

```
public class CustomODataAuthModule : IHttpModule
{
......


    public void Init(HttpApplication context)
    {
        context.AuthenticateRequest += new
        EventHandler(context_AuthenticateRequest);
    }

    void context_AuthenticateRequest(object sender,
    EventArgs e)
    {
        var request = HttpContext.Current.Request;

        if (request.Path.Contains(".svc"))
        {
          var clientID = request.Headers["x-client-id"];

            if (string.IsNullOrEmpty(clientID) ||
               clientID.Length < 5)
            {
                throw new DataServiceException(401, "Invalid
                Client Authentication ID.");
            }
        }
    }
}
```

4. Open the `web.config` file of the web application and add the configuration elements for registering the `CustomODataAuthModule` HTTP Module.

The configuration elements used for registering the HTTP Module vary depending on whether we use the Classic or Integrated pipeline mode for the IIS 7 application pool. For Classic mode, we need to register the HTTP Module in the `<system.web>` section (see the following configuration fragment).

```
<system.web>
  <!-- For IIS6 or IIS 7 Classic Mode(also works for VS Test WebServer) -->
  <httpModules>
    <add name="CustomODataAuthModule"
         type="CustomAuthODataWeb.CustomODataAuthModule, CustomAuthODataWeb"/>
  </httpModules>
```

For the Integrated mode, we need to register the HTTP Module in the `<system.webServer>` section (see the following configuration fragment).

```
<system.webServer>
  <!-- For IIS 7 Integration Mode -->
  <modules>
    <add name="CustomODataAuthModule"
         type="CustomAuthODataWeb.CustomODataAuthModule, CustomAuthODataWeb"
  </modules>
</system.webServer>
```

5. Deploy the web application into IIS 7.

 For custom HTTP.modules or HTTP handlers, we can also use Visual Studio test web server (without the IIS server) for debugging and testing.

6. Create a new console application as OData client.

7. Generate the strong-typed OData proxy against the sample service.

8. Access the sample service by supplying the custom HTTP header for authentication (see the following code snippet).

```
static void AccessODataWithCustomAuthentication()
{
    var svcUri = new
    Uri("http://localhost:7908/NWDataService.svc/");
    var ctx = new ODataSvc.NorthwindEntities(svcUri);

        ctx.SendingRequest += (o, e) =>
        {
          e.RequestHeaders.Add("x-client-id",
          Environment.MachineName);
        };

    var categories = ctx.Categories.ToList();
    Console.WriteLine("There are {0} categories.",
    categories.Count);
}
```

How it works...

In the sample OData service, we create a custom HTTP Module which hooks up the `AuthenticateRequest` event (exposed on the `HTTP Module` class) of ASP.NET/IIS processing pipeline. The event handler simply looks for a custom HTTP header from the incoming request (against the `.svc` service document) and denies the request if the header is not supplied.

When dealing with HTTP Module registration, we need to use different configuration approaches based on the application pool pipeline mode used in the IIS 7 website or web application. The Integrated mode is newly provided in IIS 7. By using the Integrated mode, we can extend the .NET based HTTP Module to all requests (against ASP.NET or non ASP.NET specific resources) in IIS hosted web applications. For more information about **Integrated** and **Classic** mode and how they impact ASP.NET web applications hosting in IIS 7, you can refer to the following website:

Moving an ASP.NET Application from IIS 6.0 to IIS 7.0 available at
`http://msdn.microsoft.com/en-us/library/bb515251.aspx`

There's more...

The `AuthenticateRequest` event (of the `HTTP Module` class) we have used here is quite useful for implementing server-side request validation and interception. In addition, there are also many other useful events exposed in the ASP.NET processing pipeline through which we can implement various kinds of request interception functions based on our requirements. For more information on this, you can refer to the following article:

INFO: ASP.NET HTTP Modules and HTTP Handlers Overview available at `http://support.microsoft.com/kb/307985`

See also

▶ *Injecting custom HTTP headers in OData requests* recipe in *Chapter 2, Working with OData at Client Side*

▶ *Hosting a WCF Data Service in IIS server* recipe in *Chapter 3, OData Service Hosting and Configuration*

Adding custom authorization with server-side processing pipeline

As shown in the *Implementing OData service authentication with custom HTTP Module* recipe mentioned earlier, we can use ASP.NET HTTP Module to apply custom authentication or authorization code logic for OData services hosted in an IIS server. Such customization is based on the ASP.NET server-side processing pipeline, similar server-side extension interfaces can also be found in standard WCF service programming model. Then, is there any WCF Data Service specific server-side pipeline we can use for implementing custom security? The answer is of course, yes!

In this recipe, we will show you how to use the built-in extension object model of WCF Data Service to apply custom service authorization.

Getting ready

Here, we will use the Northwind OData service as an example and apply some custom authorization code logic to it. Although the authorization validation is still based on a custom HTTP header sent from client, this time we will use the WCF Data Service server-side pipeline (instead of HTTP Module) to implement the validation function.

The source code for this recipe can be found in the \ch07\ODataPipelineAuthSln directory.

How to do it...

The following are the detailed steps to implement the sample application:

1. Create a new ASP.NET web application that contains the Northwind OData service (named NorthwindOData.svc in this sample).

2. Open the code-behind file of the NorthwindOData.svc service.

3. Register an event handler for the ProcessingRequest event (against the ProcessingPipeline property) in the constructor of the service class (see the following code snippet).

```
public class NorthwindOData : DataService< NorthwindEntities >
{
    public NorthwindOData()
    {
        this.ProcessingPipeline.ProcessingRequest +=
        new
        EventHandler<DataServiceProcessingPipelineEventArgs>
        (ProcessingRequestHandler);
    }
}
```

4. In the `ProcessingRequest` event handler, add the code for validating the security token (custom HTTP header) from the incoming OData query request (see the following `ProcessingRequestHandler` function).

```
void ProcessingRequestHandler(object sender,
DataServiceProcessingPipelineEventArgs e)
{
    // Allow service root and metadata access for all users
    var svcUri = e.OperationContext.AbsoluteServiceUri;
    var opUri = e.OperationContext.AbsoluteRequestUri;
    if (opUri == svcUri ||
    opUri.PathAndQuery.Contains("$metadata")) return;

    // Check auth token
    var webContext = HttpContext.Current;
    var token = webContext.Request.Headers["auth-token"];

    if(string.IsNullOrEmpty(token) ||
    token.IndexOf("admin") == -1)
    {
        throw new DataServiceException(401, "Unauthorized
        OData Request!");
    }
}
......

}
```

5. Create a client application to consume the sample service.

For the OData client, we will use the similar code logic (supplying a custom HTTP header for authentication) as what we did in the *Implementing OData service authentication with custom HTTP Module* recipe mentioned earlier.

How it works...

In this sample, we use the `ProcessingPipeline` property of the `WCF Data Service` class to hook up the service processing pipeline. The `ProcessingRequest` event used here is raised before a certain WCF Data Service request gets processed at the server side. Therefore, it's a great point for us to perform custom authorization or other custom validation code logic. The event handler function takes a parameter of `DataServiceProcessingPipelineEventArgs` type, which allows us to access some context data of the incoming OData request. In the sample code, we use it to determine whether the incoming request is targeting the service root or metadata document. If so, we will pass the request, otherwise, we will perform validation against the request.

As the WCF Data Service is running within the ASP.NET runtime, we can also use `HttpContext.Current` property to access additional context information from the underlying HTTP request.

In addition, here we have only used the `ProcessingRequest` event of WCF Data Service server-side processing pipeline. Actually, there are some other events exposed by the pipeline through which we can implement other customization and extension code logic. For more information about these extension events, you can refer to the following MSDN website:

DataServiceProcessingPipeline class available at `http://msdn.microsoft.com/en-us/library/system.data.services.dataserviceprocessingpipeline.aspx`

See also

▶   *Implementing OData service authentication with custom HTTP Module* recipe

Using Interceptors to control access for individual entity set

OData services expose their primary data through entity sets so that client users can access the certain entity sets based their requirements. And from the other perspective, the OData service might want to expose different collections of entity set to different kinds of client users. Then, how can we implement such entity-set-specific access control?

Well, WCF Data Services has introduced another extension point called Interceptor which can help intercepting the service requests against an individual entity set exposed in the service. In this recipe, we will demonstrate how we can use Interceptors to apply access control for an individual entity set exposed in WCF Data Service.

Getting ready

In this sample, we will use some Interceptors to restrict the query and update access against the `Categories` entity set exposed in the Northwind OData service. Also, we assume that the service has enabled **Windows Authentication** so that we can perform the access control validation based on the Windows identity supplied from client. For how to apply Windows authentication, you can refer to the *Applying Windows authentication for OData service* recipe mentioned earlier.

The source code for this recipe can be found in the `\ch07\ODataQueryInterceptorAuthSln` directory.

How to do it...

The following are the detailed steps for creating the sample applications:

1. Create a new ASP.NET web application that contains the Northwind OData service.

   We need to expose at least the `Categories` entity set in the sample service and enable all built-in WCF Data Service access rules on it (see the following code snippet).

```
public class NorthwindOData : DataService< NorthwindEntities >
{
    public static void
    InitializeService(DataServiceConfiguration config)
    {
        config.DataServiceBehavior.MaxProtocolVersion =
        DataServiceProtocolVersion.V2;
            config.SetEntitySetAccessRule("Categories",
            EntitySetRights.All);
}
......
```

2. Define a `QueryInterceptor` function (for validating query requests against the `Categories` entity set) within the `WCF Data Service` class (see the following `onQueryCategories` function).

```
public class NorthwindOData : DataService< NorthwindEntities >
{
......

        [QueryInterceptor("Categories")]
        public Expression<Func<Category, bool>> OnQueryCategories()
        {
            var userId = HttpContext.Current.User.Identity.Name;

            if (ValidateUser(userId))
            {
                return c => true;
            }
                else
                {
                throw new DataServiceException(401, "Unauthorized
                    User!");
                }
        }


}
```

3. Define a `ChangeInterceptor` function (for validating update requests against the `Categories` entity set) within the `WCF Data Service` class (see the following `onChangeCategories` function).

```
[ChangeInterceptor("Categories")]
public void OnChangeCategories(Category product,
UpdateOperations operations)
{
    var userId = HttpContext.Current.User.Identity.Name;

    if (!ValidateUser(userId))
    {
        throw new DataServiceException(401, "Unauthorized
        User!");
    }
}
```

How it works...

In the sample service, we have applied two **Interceptors** for the `Categories` entity set. One is the `QueryInterceptor` function (defined by the `QueryInterceptorAttribute`) for validating the query requests, and another is the `ChangeInterceptor` function (defined by the `ChangeInterceptorAttribute`) for validating the update requests.

The `QueryInterceptor` function must return a lambda expression in the form of `Expression<Func<T,bool>>` where `T` represents the entity type of the target entity set. This lambda expression helps determine whether the entity object from target entity set should be returned to client or not. In this case, we simply throw out an instance of `DataServiceException` in case the client identity validation fails.

As for the `ChangeInterceptor` function, it must be a `void` function and accepts two parameters (one is an instance of the target entity type; another is an instance of `UpdateOperations` class). By using these two input parameters, we can determine *what* kind update operation is being made against *which* entity object. In the sample function, we also throw out a `DataServiceException` instance in case the validation fails.

At runtime, the Interceptor functions are called by WCF Data Service at the appropriate point during an OData request's processing lifecycle. Also, as Interceptor is per entity set based, when we want to customize the request processing logic against a specific entity set, it is more efficient to use an Interceptor rather than hook up the entire *server-side processing pipeline* of the target service.

See also

▶ *Applying basic access rules on WCF Data Service* recipe in *Chapter 3, OData Service Hosting and Configuration*

▶ *Applying Windows authentication for OData service* recipe

Implementing role-based security for OData service

So far we have discussed several different options to apply custom authentication or authorization code logic for an OData service including using HTTP Module, using WCF Data Service Interceptors, using a WCF Data Service server-side processing pipeline, and so on. Now, let's go one step further and try securing an OData service by using the combination of these options.

In this recipe, we will demonstrate how to implement the role-based security for an OData service (built via WCF Data Service) by using both HTTP Module and Interceptors.

Getting ready

A **role-based** security model is commonly used for implementing authorization logic in service applications. Role-based security has been supported since the earlier version of .NET Framework, and has been applied in many .NET development features such as ASP.NET, WCF, code access security, and so on. If you're not familiar with role-based security yet, you can have a look at the following website:

Role-based Security available at `http://msdn.microsoft.com/en-us/library/shz8h065.aspx`

The source code for this recipe can be found in the `\ch07\ODataRoleBasedSecuritySln` directory.

How to do it...

In this sample, we will apply role-based authorization control (based on our custom client authentication method) for the `Categories` and `Products` entity sets in the Northwind OData service. Now, let's have a look at the following steps to do it:

1. Create a new ASP.NET web application which contains the Northwind OData service.

   We need to at least expose the `Categories` and `Products` entity sets in the service.

2. Create an ASP.NET HTTP Module for populating the custom security context of each incoming OData request (see the following `RoleBasedAuthModule` class code).

```
public class RoleBasedAuthModule : IHttpModule
{
    ......

    public void Init(HttpApplication context)
    {
        context.AuthenticateRequest+=new
        EventHandler(OnAuthenticateRequest);
    }

    void OnAuthenticateRequest(object sender, EventArgs e)
    {
        var app = sender as HttpApplication;
        var request = app.Context.Request;
        var userId = request.Headers["odata-user-id"];

        if(string.IsNullOrEmpty(userId))
        {
            userId = "Anonymous";
        }

            var roles = GetRolesForUser(userId);

            var gPrincipal = new GenericPrincipal(
              new GenericIdentity(userId),
              GetRolesForUser(userId)
            );

            app.Context.User = gPrincipal;
    }

    #region -- Helper Methods --

    string[] GetRolesForUser(string userId)
    {
        if(userId == "Admin"){
            return new string[]{"Administrator", "User"};
        }
        else if (userId == "User")
        {
            return new string[] { "User" };
        }
```

```
        else
        {
            return new string[] { "" };
        }
    }
    #endregion
}
```

3. Register the HTTP Module (`RoleBasedAuthModule`) in the `web.config` file (see the following screenshot).

```
<system.webServer>
  <!-- For IIS 7 Integrated mode -->
  <modules>
    <add name="RoleBasedAuthModule"
        type="ODataServiceWeb.RoleBasedAuthModule, ODataServiceWeb"/>
  </modules>
```

4. Turn off the built-in ASP.NET authentication in the `web.config` file (see the following screenshot).

```
<configuration>
  <system.web>
    <authentication mode="None" />
```

5. Define the Interceptors for performing role-based access check in the `WCF Data Service` class

   Here are two sample `QueryInterceptor` functions, one for the `Categories` entity set; another for the `Products` entity set.

```
    [QueryInterceptor("Categories")]
    public Expression<Func<Category, bool>> OnQueryCategories()
{
    var user = HttpContext.Current.User;
    if (user.IsInRole("Administrator"))
        return (c) => true;
    else
        throw new DataServiceException(401, "Unauthorized
        User!");
}

    [QueryInterceptor("Products")]
    public Expression<Func<Product, bool>> OnQueryProducts()
{
```

```
        var user = HttpContext.Current.User;
        if (user.IsInRole("User"))
            return (p) => true;
        else
            throw new DataServiceException(401, "Unauthorized
            User!");
    }
```

6. Deploy the service web application into IIS server.

    We need to enable the **Anonymous Authentication** setting (see the following
    screenshot) for the IIS web application so as to suppress other built-in authentications.

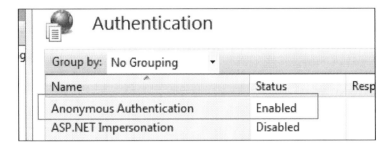

How it works...

In this sample, we use role-based authorization to grant different access control permissions
(based on the custom authentication identity) for different entity sets in the Northwind OData
service. The entire role-based security implementation consists of the following three parts:

▶ Validating the authentication token from each incoming service request

▶ Populating the security context for each service request

▶ Performing authorization check based on the roles associated in the security context
    data (for each service request)

The RoleBasedAuthModule HTTP Module is responsible for the former two parts. It first
validates the client identity by checking a custom HTTP header in the incoming request,
and then it creates a GenericPrincipal object (based on the client identity), which
encapsulates the security roles associated with the identity. When the processing flow
comes to the Interceptor functions, we simply extract the GenericPrincipal object from
HttpContext.Current.User property and perform the authorization check through the
IPrincipal.IsInRole method.

It is worth noticing that we have turned off the ASP.NET built-in authentication (in the `web.config` file) and enabled **Anonymous Authentication** in IIS authentication settings for the sample web application. This is necessary because we do not want to use any built-in authentication methods of ASP.NET or IIS server, but use our custom HTTP Module-based authentication.

There's more...

In this sample, we directly use the `GenericPrincipal` and `GenericIdentity` classes (under `System.Security.Principal` namespace) for populating the security context of each service request. If you want to store more complicated security context information, you can also implement your own principal and identity types based on the `IPrincipal` and `IIdentity` interfaces under the `System.Security.Principal` namespace.

See also

▶ *Implementing OData service authentication with custom HTTP Module* recipe

▶ *Using Interceptors to control access for individual entity set* recipe

8
Other OData Programming Tips

In this chapter we will cover:

- ▶ Using LINQPad to compose OData query code
- ▶ Exploring OData service with ODataExplorer
- ▶ Using OData service in Windows PowerShell script
- ▶ Exploring OData service with Microsoft Excel PowerPivot component
- ▶ Inspecting OData HTTP traffic through Fiddler web debugger
- ▶ Using Open Data Protocol Visualizer to inspect the object model of OData service
- ▶ Consuming OData service in Windows 8 Metro style application

Introduction

So far we've talked about many different aspects of OData programming with the .NET Framework platform, in the previous chapters. We have covered service-side development, client-side development, hosting and configuration, OData integration in web applications, OData integration in mobile apps, OData service security, and so on.

However, there are still many interesting and useful OData programming topics (which do not belong to any of the aspects discussed earlier) that haven't been covered yet.

In this chapter, we will take the opportunity to explore some special OData programming tips, which are also helpful to OData developers when developing or testing OData services.

Using LINQPad to compose OData query code

LINQPad is a free tool for querying data against various kinds of data sources which support .NET LINQ style query syntax. For example, we can use LINQPad to query a relational database through LINQ to SQL, we can use LINQPad to query a ADO.NET Entity Framework data model via LINQ to Entity, or we can also perform an XML document query via LINQ to XML. And with the query editor of LINQPad, we can easily compose and test our .NET or SQL-based query code interactively.

Currently, the latest version of LINQPad has started supporting .NET Framework 4.0 and OData-compatible data sources. In this recipe, we will discuss how to use LINQPad for composing and testing OData query code.

Getting ready

Before getting started, we need to download the latest version of LINQPad from the following official site:

`http://www.linqpad.net/`

The source code for this recipe can be found in the `\ch08\ODataLINQPadSln` directory.

How to do it...

Here we will use LINQPad 4 to compose some OData queries against the Northwind OData service. Let's take a look at the steps to do it.

1. Launch the LINQPad application. LINQPad is an XCOPY application so that we can directly launch the `LINQPad.exe` program downloaded to our local disk. The following screenshot shows the main UI of LINQPad:

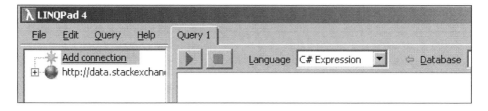

2. Click on the **Add connection** link button at the top of the left view.

3. In the **Choose Data Context** dialog, select **WCF Data Services (OData)** item from the **LINQPad Driver** list (see the following screenshot).

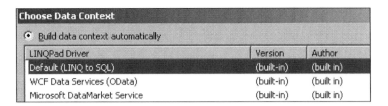

4. In the **WCF Data Services (OData) Connection** dialog, supply the OData service address in the **URI** field (see the following screenshot).

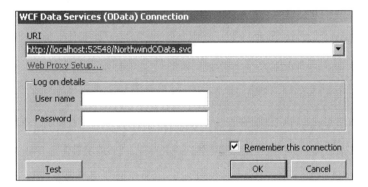

 You can specify authentication credentials in the **Log on details** panel in case the target service requires authentication.

5. Click on the **OK** button to save the service connection.

6. Use **File | New Query** to open a new query editor in the right panel of LINQPad.

7. Select **C# Expression** in the **Language** field (at the top of the query editor) and write the LINQ query expressions in the content area (see the following screenshot).

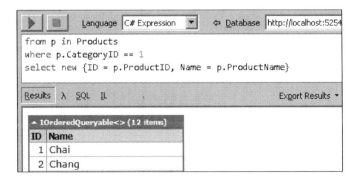

> Make sure the correct service connection is selected in the **Database** field (at the top of the query editor).

8. Click on the green triangle button (at the top-left corner of the query editor) to execute the query. The query result will be displayed in the bottom view of the query editor panel (see the previous screenshot).

9. Alternatively, select **C# Program** in the **Language** field and write the LINQ query code as a complete .NET code block or function (see the following screenshot).

```
Language  C# Program        ⇔ Database  http://localhost:

void Main()
{
    var categories = from c in Categories
    where c.CategoryName.Length >5
    select c;

    foreach(var c in categories){
        Console.WriteLine("{0}",  c.CategoryName);
    }
}
```

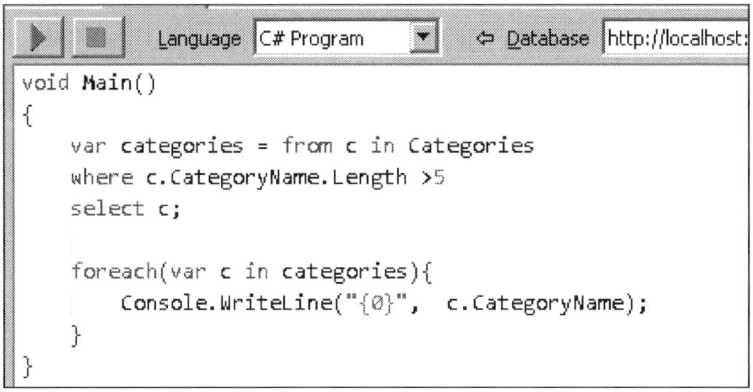

How it works...

LINQPad programmatically parses the query code in query editor panels and compiles them into the underlying execution code according to the target data source types. By selecting the **SQL** tab in the result view, we can get the data source specific query code generated by the tool. For a relational database, the raw SQL statements will be displayed while for an OData (WCF Data Services) source, the raw query Uri string will be displayed (see the following screenshot).

```
Language  C# Expression    ⇔ Database  http://localhost:52548/No

from p in Products
where p.CategoryID == 1
select new {ID = p.ProductID, Name = p.ProductName}

Results  λ  SQL  IL                    Analyze SQL ▼  Activate Autocompletion

ata.svc/Products()?$filter=CategoryID eq 1&$select=ProductID,ProductName
```

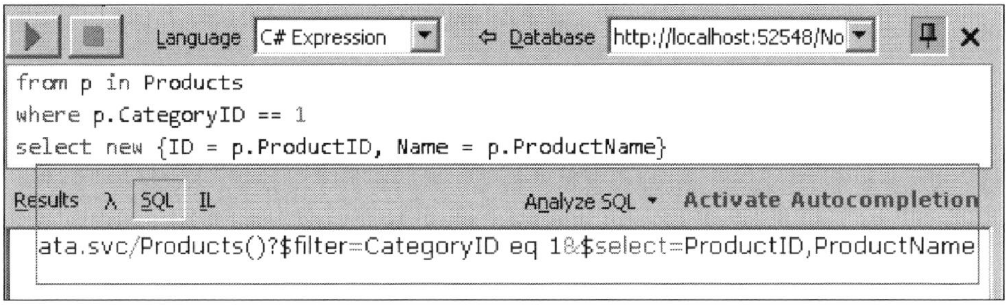

In addition, LINQPad will use separate .NET AppDomain to run each of the queries opened in the tool so that the processing and execution of all the queries will not interfere with each other. For more information about how LINQPad works, you can refer to the following page:

```
http://www.linqpad.net/HowLINQPadWorks.aspx
```

See also

▶   *Using Visual Studio to generate strong-typed OData client proxy* recipe in *Chapter 2, Working with OData at Client Side*

▶   *Filtering OData query results by using query options* recipe in *Chapter 2, Working with OData at Client Side*

Exploring OData service with ODataExplorer

Sometimes we might just want to quickly browse the data entities exposed in an OData service without using complicated and advanced queries. In such a case, a simple and easy-to-use GUI tool will be quite helpful.

ODataExplorer is a Silverlight-based utility which allows users to perform ad-hoc queries against OData services and view the data entities in a visualized manner. In this recipe, we will show you how to explore data entities from an OData service by using ODataExplorer.

Getting ready

Since ODataExplorer is a Silverlight-based application, make sure you have the Silverlight runtime installed on your local machine.

Refer to *Get Silverlight | Microsoft Silverlight* at `http://www.microsoft.com/getsilverlight/get-started/install/default.aspx`.

How to do it...

Now, let's go through the detailed steps to use ODataExplorer.

1.   Launch the web browser and navigate to the following URL address of the ODataExplorer tool:

```
http://www.silverlight.net/ODataExplorer
```

2. Alternatively, we can choose to install ODataExplorer locally (after it is loaded in the web browser) so as to directly launch it from the desktop or the **Start** menu the next time (see the following screenshot).

3. On the **OData Services** panel (on the left), click on the **Add New** button to add a new service reference (see the following screenshot).

4. In the **Add New OData Service** dialog, specify the **Workspace Name** and **Data Service Uri** fields for the target OData service (see the following screenshot).

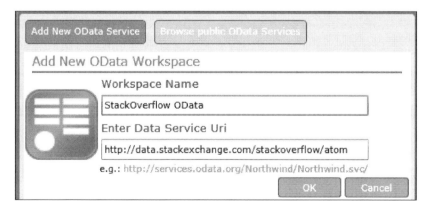

5. Click on the **OK** button to save the service reference.
6. Select the target service reference (we have added) in the **OData Services** panel.

7. Select an entity set in the **Collections** panel and use the GUI filters to apply OData query options (see the following screenshot). By default, the query result will be displayed in a visualized data grid view.

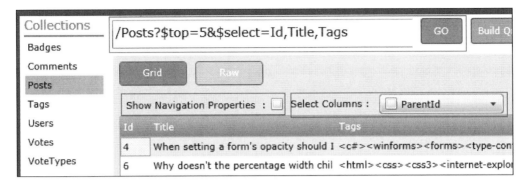

8. Click on the **Raw** button (beside the **Grid** button) to show raw data of the query result.

9. Select the data format (**XML** or **JSON**) and click on the **Go** button to view the raw HTTP headers and content (see the following screenshot).

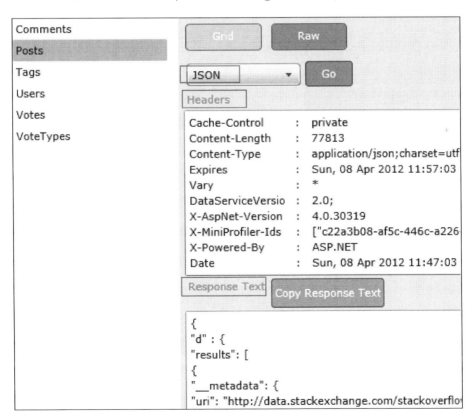

How it works...

Since ODataExplorer is a Silverlight-based application, it can only access remote OData services, which have a cross-domain policy file exposed for clients. If the target service does not have a cross-domain policy file, we will probably see the following error screen when accessing it from ODataExplorer (in the web browser):

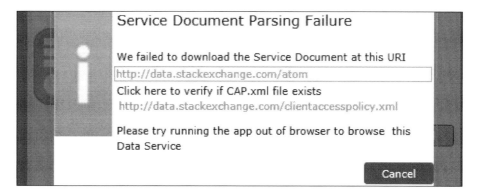

To work around this problem, we need to launch ODataExplorer through the **Out-of-Browser** mode (as shown in the second step previously).

There's more...

If you're interested in how ODataExplorer is implemented, you can get the complete source code of ODataExplorer from the following OData official site:

```
http://www.odata.org/developers/odata-sdk
```

See also

 ▶ *Using OData service in Silverlight data access application* recipe in *Chapter 4, Using OData in Web Application*

 ▶ *Querying StackOverflow forums data with OData endpoint* recipe in *Chapter 6, Working with Public OData Producers*

Using OData service in Windows PowerShell script

Windows PowerShell is a new task automation framework of the Microsoft Windows operating system. Windows PowerShell consists of a command-line shell and its associated scripting language built on top of it, and integrated with .NET Framework. With Windows PowerShell, IT professionals can automate administrative tasks just like they do with traditional bat or script files. And developers can use Windows PowerShell to perform many common management and testing tasks without creating dedicated utility programs.

Since Windows PowerShell is naturally coupled with .NET Framework, users can fully leverage the rich class library of .NET Framework in Windows PowerShell scripts. In this recipe, we will show you how to incorporate OData service in Windows PowerShell script code.

Getting ready

Make sure you have Windows PowerShell installed on your local machine. For Windows 2008 R2 and Windows 7, Windows PowerShell is already installed with the operating system. For Windows Server 2008 and Windows Vista, you can manually install it by following the *Windows Management Framework* reference at `http://go.microsoft.com/fwlink/?LinkId=177670`.

How to do it...

We will create a sample PowerShell script file to consume a local Northwind OData service. The following are the detailed steps to do it:

1. Create a new text file by using any text editor such as Notepad or Visual Studio text editor.

2. Add the following script code into the text file:

    ```
    #Construct the WebClient object
    $wc = New-Object System.Net.WebClient
    $wc.UseDefaultCredentials = $true

    #Query OData service with url
    $queryUri = "http://localhost:42203/NorthwindOData.svc/
    Categories(1)/Products?$top=5"
    [xml]$responseXML = $wc.DownloadString($queryUri)

    #Parse query result in XML format
    $entities = $responseXML.SelectNodes("//*[local-name() =
    'properties' ]")
    ```

```
ForEach($entity in $entities)
{
    $prodID = $entity.SelectSingleNode("./*[local-name() =
'ProductID']").InnerText;
    $prodName = $entity.SelectSingleNode("./*[local-name() =
'ProductName']").InnerText;
    $prodUnitPrice = $entity.SelectSingleNode("./*[local-name() =
'UnitPrice']").InnerText;

    $prodLine = [string]::Format("ID:{0}, Name:{1},
UnitPrice:{2}",  $prodID, $prodName,$prodUnitPrice)

    Write-Host $prodLine -foregroundcolor Green
}
```

3. Save the file with `.ps1` extension (such as `QueryOData.ps1`) into the local disk.

4. Launch the Windows PowerShell console (see the following screenshot) by using **Start | All Programs | Accessories | Windows PowerShell | Windows PowerShell** menu.

5. Navigate to the local directory which contains the saved sample script file.

6. Execute the sample script file (`QueryOData.ps1`) by typing the filename in the console (see the following screenshot).

 To execute the local Windows PowerShell script file, we have to prepend the `.\` path prefix before the filename due to security protection.

7. Check the execution output in the Windows PowerShell console window. The following screenshot shows the execution output of the sample `QueryOData.ps1` script file:

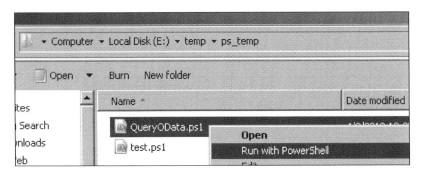

8. Alternatively, execute the script file from Windows Explorer by using the **Run with PowerShell** context menu (see the following screenshot).

How it works...

In the sample Windows PowerShell script file, we create an instance of the `System.Net.WebClient` class for communicating with the Northwind OData service. Since WCF Data Service returns response data in Atom XML format by default, we use an `XmlDocument` variable (declared with the `[xml]` keyword) to hold the response data (of the OData query). After the data is loaded into the `XmlDocument` object, we can simply use XPath to extract all entity elements from the XML DOM structure and inspect the properties of each entity object through the corresponding children elements.

Although it might be a bit cumbersome to parse an OData query response via XML API in Windows PowerShell script, the advantage is that we do not need to load any additional assembly references (for strong-typed OData client proxy).

See also

▶ *Accessing OData service via WebRequest class* recipe in *Chapter 2, Working with OData at Client Side*

Exploring OData service with Microsoft Excel PowerPivot component

In *Chapter 6, Working with Public OData Producers*, we have discussed how to use a Microsoft Excel PowerPivot component to consume the data feed generated by the SQL Server Reporting Service. Actually, the PowerPivot component can be used for exploring any services which have exposed their data through OData endpoints. In this recipe, we will take the Netflix online catalog service as example and demonstrate how to explore a standard an OData service with a Microsoft Excel PowerPivot component.

Getting ready

Make sure you have Microsoft Excel 2010 and PowerPivot component installed. You can download the PowerPivot installation package from the following site:

Microsoft Power Pivot at `http://www.microsoft.com/en-us/bi/powerpivot.aspx`

How to do it...

Now, let's have a look at the detailed steps to use the PowerPivot component.

1. Launch Microsoft Excel 2010 program.

2. Select the **PowerPivot** menu and click on the **PowerPivot Window** ribbon button (see the following screenshot).

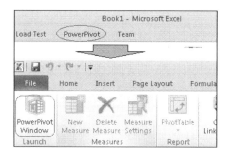

3. In the opened **PowerPivot for Excel** window, click on the button with the data feed icon (see the following screenshot) to start the import data wizard.

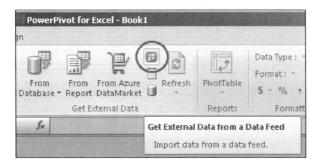

4. In the **Connect to a Data Feed** view of the **Table Import Wizard** dialog, specify **Data Feed Url** of the target OData service (see the following screenshot).

5. In **Select Tables and Views** of the **Table Import Wizard** dialog, select the entity sets we want to import in the **Tables and Views** list view (see the following screenshot).

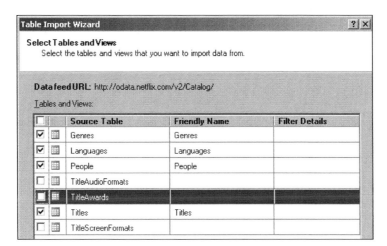

6. Click on the **Finish** button to start the actual data importing process.

7. Close the **Table Import Wizard** dialog after the data importing has finished.

8. View the imported entity sets through the corresponding worksheets in the **PowerPivot for Excel** window (see the following screenshot).

How it works...

In the **Table Import Wizard** dialog, when we supply **Data Feed Url** of the target OData service, the tool will access the URL (service base address) so as to get all exposed entity sets for users to select. After the actual data importing process starts, the PowerPivot tool sends HTTP-based OData query requests to the target service and loads the data from the selected entity sets one by one. By using Fiddler, we can inspect the underlying OData HTTP communications between the PowerPivot tool and the target service. The following screenshot shows the raw OData requests sent by the PowerPivot tool (captured in Fiddler), when we import entity sets from the Netflix online catalog service:

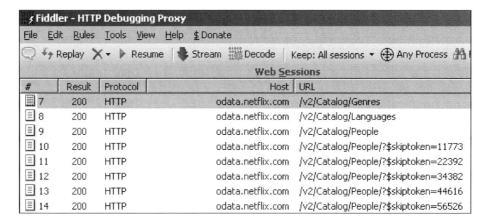

There's more...

Entity sets in an OData service might have relationships between each other. When we import entity sets from an OData service into a Microsoft Excel PowerPivot client, the relationships (between the imported entity sets) will get lost. To work around this problem, we can manually establish the relationships between the imported tables (corresponding to the OData entity sets) in a PowerPivot client. You can get more information about creating relationships between PowerPivot tables through the following tutorial:

Create Relationships Between Tables (Tutorial) at `http://technet.microsoft.com/en-us/library/gg413437.aspx`

See also

- ▶ *Consuming SSRS 2008 R2 report through OData feed* recipe in *Chapter 6, Working with Public OData Producers*
- ▶ *Inspecting OData HTTP traffic through Fiddler web debugger* recipe in *Chapter 8, Other OData Programming Tips*

Inspecting OData HTTP traffic through Fiddler web debugger

When developing OData services, we often need to inspect the underlying HTTP traffic between the client application and the target OData service for troubleshooting purposes. For example, we might want to check if the Atom XML or JSON-format data sent from the service is correct and expected, or we might want to check if the underlying HTTP response from the server includes some detailed error info when the client consuming code throws out some exceptions.

On the Microsoft Windows platform, Fiddler is a very popular tool for debugging and monitoring the HTTP traffic between web clients and servers. In this recipe, we will introduce how we can use Fiddler to inspect the underlying HTTP communication between OData services and client applications.

Getting ready

If you haven't installed Fiddler on your local machine yet, you can get it from the official site of Fiddler at `http://www.fiddler2.com/Fiddler2/version.asp`.

Also, you can quickly get started with Fiddler through the following help page at `http://www.fiddler2.com/Fiddler/help/`.

The source code for this recipe can be found in the `\ch08\ODataFiddlerSln` directory.

How to do it...

Now, let's go through the steps to use Fiddler for inspecting OData requests against the Northwind OData service.

1. Launch Fiddler by using **Start | All Programs | Fiddler**. Here we use version 2.3 of Fiddler for demonstration purposes. The following screenshot shows the Fiddler window which consists of a session list view on the left and a detailed inspection view on the right:

2. Run the OData client application, which accesses the Northwind OData service. The following is the main code logic of the sample OData client application:

```
var svcUri = new Uri("http://localhost:6909/NorthwindOData.svc/");
var ctx = new ODataSvc.NorthwindEntities(svcUri);

var categories = ctx.Categories.Take(6).ToList();

foreach (var c in categories)
{
    Console.WriteLine("Products for Category '{0}':",
c.CategoryName);
    var products = ctx.Products.Where(p => p.CategoryID ==
c.CategoryID).ToList();

    foreach (var p in products)
    {
        Console.WriteLine("ID:{0}, Name:{1}", p.ProductID,
p.ProductName);
    }
}
```

3. Watch the captured HTTP traffic (for the OData client-server communication) in the
    Web Sessions view of Fiddler (see the following screenshot).

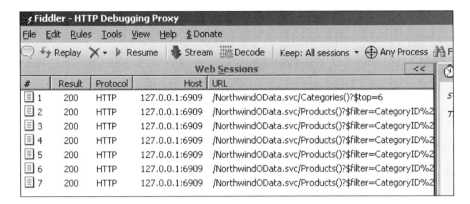

4. Double-click on a specific item in the **Web Sessions** view and inspect the detailed
    request/response payloads (of the selected item) through the **Inspectors** panel. The
    Inspectors panel consists of several tabs (such as **Headers**, **TextView**, **Raw**, **JSON**,
    XML, and so on), which can help inspecting the HTTP request/response data from
    different perspectives (see the following screenshot).

5. Click on the **Headers** tab in the **Inspectors** panel to look over the HTTP headers of
    the selected OData request/response session (see the following screenshot).

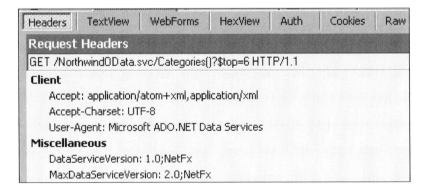

6. For an Atom XML format OData response, click on the **XML** tab in the **Inspectors** panel to look over the response content in the visualized structure (see the following screenshot).

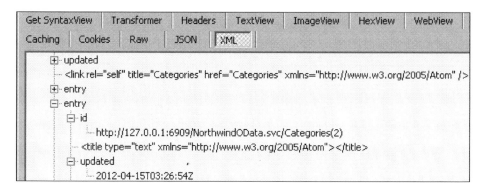

7. Alternatively, click on the **Raw** tab in the **Inspectors** panel to look over the entire request/response message (including both headers and content) in its raw text format.

How it works...

The Fiddler web debugger acts as an HTTP web proxy on the local machine (at `localhost` and port: `8888`) so that it can capture all HTTP traffic issued from WinINET-based applications. Other applications which support HTTP-based proxy can also leverage Fiddler for HTTP debugging by explicitly specifying Fiddler as the default HTTP proxy.

One special aspect is that when using IE web browser or .NET Framework-based client applications to access local services (hosted on local machine), we might find that Fiddler does not show the corresponding HTTP traffic sessions. This is because IE and .NET Framework are hardcoded to bypass all web proxies for HTTP requests targeting `localhost`. Don't worry, the following are some methods which can help work around this issue:

▸ Use the machine name or the DNS name of the local machine instead of `localhost` or `127.0.0.1`. For example, rather than entering `http://localhost:56789/odata.svc`, use `http://machinename:56789/odata.svc` instead.

▸ Use `ipv4.fiddler` or `ipv6.fiddler` to replace `localhost`. For example, rather than hitting `http://localhost:56789/odata.svc`, use `http://ipv4.fiddler:56789/odta.svc` instead.

▸ Add an alias for `127.0.0.1` to the Windows Hosts file and send requests to that alias. For example, rather than hitting `http://127.0.0.1/odata.svc`, use `http://[alias name]/odata.svc` instead. You can get more information about using Windows Hosts file in the Knowledge Base article at `http://support.microsoft.com/kb/228760`.

See also

▸ *Building an OData service via WCF Data Service and ADO.NET Entity Framework recipe in Chapter 1, Building OData Services*

Using Open Data Protocol Visualizer to inspect the object model of OData service

When using the Visual Studio Add Service Reference wizard to generate an OData proxy, the Visual Studio IDE will help us create some entity types based on the object model exposed by the target OData service.

In order to help developers easily inspect the object model of an OData service, Microsoft Data Modeling Group provides a Visual Studio extension component called **Open Data Protocol Visualizer** (**OData Visualizer**), which can help displaying the object model of OData services in a visualized approach.

In this recipe, we will demonstrate how we can use Open Data Protocol Visualizer to explore the data object model of an OData service in Visual Studio IDE.

Getting ready

Before getting started, we need to download and install the OData Visualizer extension. The extension package is available in **Visual Studio Gallery** at `http://visualstudiogallery.msdn.microsoft.com/f4ac856a-796e-4d78-9a3d-0120d8137722/`.

After the extension package is downloaded, we can simply double-click on the `OpenDataVisualizer.vsix` file (see the following screenshot) to install the extension into Visual Studio 2010.

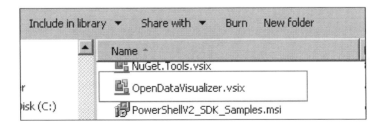

The source code for this recipe can be found in the `\ch08\ODataVisualStudioVisualizerSln` directory.

How to do it...

Now, let's go through the steps for inspecting the object mode of the *Netflix online catalog* service through OData Visualizer.

1. Create a new Console Application as the OData client.

2. Create the OData client proxy (via the Visual Studio Add Service Reference wizard) against the *Netflix online catalog* service at the location `http://odata.netflix.com/v2/Catalog/`.

3. Right-click on the generated OData proxy (under the **Service References** node in Visual Studio Solution Explorer) and select the **View in Diagram** context menu to launch OData Visualizer (see the following screenshot).

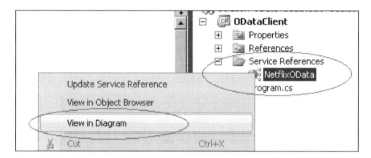

4. Switch to the opened designer surface of OData Visualizer. The OData Visualizer will show an empty designer surface with the following two sections:

   ❑ A hyperlink for activating **Open Data Protocol Model Browser**

   ❑ Some quick action links for displaying certain data model items (such as **Entity Types**, **Complex Types**, **Associations**, and so on) in the diagram

The following is how the initial designer surface looks like:

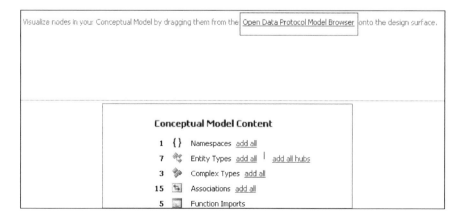

5. Click on the **add all** hyperlink beside the **Namespaces** item to add all **Entity Types** and **Complex Types** (including their **Associations**) into the designer surface. The following screenshot shows the designer surface after we click on the hyperlink. For demonstration purposes, we have collapsed all data type shapes in it.

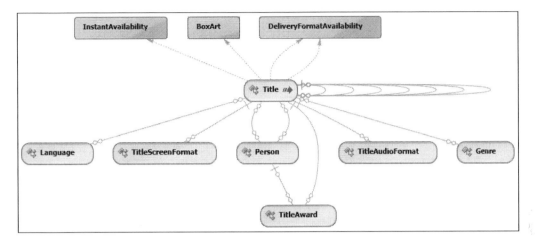

6. Right-click on the designer surface and select the **Expanded Shapes** context menu to show the details view of all data type shapes (see the following screenshot).

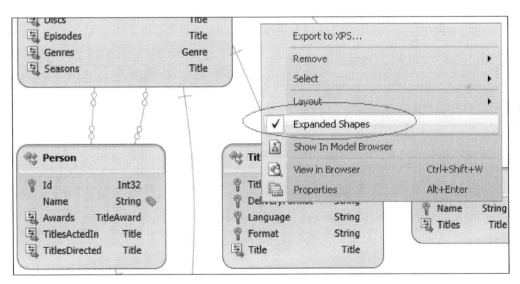

7. Alternatively, right-click on the designer surface and select the **Show In Model Browser** context menu (see the preceding screenshot) to show **Open Data Protocol Model Browser**.

8. In the **Open Data Protocol Model Browser**, navigate through all data types (included in the OData service object model) in a hierarchical structure (see the following screenshot).

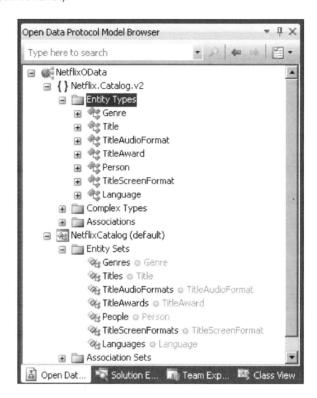

How it works...

As shown in the preceding steps, in order to use Open Data Protocol Visualizer in Visual Studio IDE, we need to create the OData client proxy through the **Visual Studio Add Service Reference** wizard first. This is because the Visual Studio generated OData proxy contains the entity data model information retrieved from the target service's metadata. If we click on the **Show All Files** button (with a red circle in the following screenshot) in **Solution Explorer** of Visual Studio, we can find the .edmx file (see the following screenshot), which contains the data entity model definition of the target OData service.

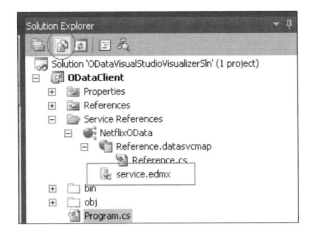

By opening the `.edmx` file with any XML or text editor, we can see the entity data model definition (in XML format) of the target OData service (see the following screenshot).

```
service.edmx  X  Source Control Explorer
  <edmx:Edmx Version="1.0" xmlns:edmx="http://schemas.microsoft.c
    <edmx:DataServices xmlns:m="http://schemas.microsoft.com/ado/
      <Schema Namespace="Netflix.Catalog.v2" xmlns:d="http://sche
        <EntityType Name="Genre">
          <Key>
            <PropertyRef Name="Name" />
          </Key>
          <Property Name="Name" Type="Edm.String" Nullable="false
          <NavigationProperty Name="Titles" Relationship="Netflix
        </EntityType>
        <EntityType Name="Title" m:HasStream="true">
```

For more information about the `.edmx` definition file, you can refer to the following MSDN reference:

.edmx File Overview (Entity Framework) at `http://msdn.microsoft.com/en-us/library/cc982042.aspx`

See also

► *Using Visual Studio to generate strong-typed OData client proxy* recipe in *Chapter 2, Working with OData at Client Side*

Consuming OData service in Windows 8 Metro style application

With the announcement of Windows 8 Developer Preview and Consumer Preview versions, more and more people have got in touch with the new Metro-style application design introduced by Microsoft. The Metro-style UI design is going to help developers build attractive, easy-to-use applications that will delight customers with their intuitive and common interaction model. Moreover, for Windows 8 Metro style application development, it now supports JavaScript + HTML5 as the first-class programming languages.

In this recipe, we will use the Windows 8 preview version as an example, and demonstrate how we can build a JavaScript + HTML5 based Metro style application, which shows the Movie collections from the *Netflix online catalog* service.

Getting ready

In order to build and run the sample application in this recipe, you must have a computer (or virtual machine) running Windows 8 and Visual Studio 2012 for Windows 8. Currently, you can get the preview version of both of them from the following site:

Windows Metro Style Apps Developer Downloads at `http://msdn.microsoft.com/en-us/windows/apps/br229516`

The sample application here is built with **Windows 8 Consumer Preview** and **Visual Studio 2012 Express beta for Windows 8**.

The source code for this recipe can be found in the **\ch08\ODataWin8MetroSln** directory.

How to do it...

The following are the steps to create the sample application:

1. Launch Visual Studio 2012 for Windows 8.
2. Click **File | New | Project** menu to open the **New Project** dialog.

3. In the **New Project** dialog, select the **Blank Application** project template under the **JavaScript | Windows Metro style** category (see the following screenshot).

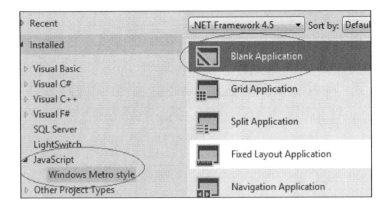

4. Click on the **OK** button to create the project. Visual Studio will help create all necessary project items with the structure shown in the following screenshot:

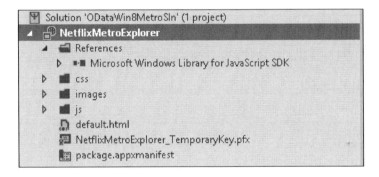

5. Define the HTML content for the `default.html` page. The following is the main HTML fragment (including script references and UI elements) of the `default.html` page:

```
<head>
......

    <link href="/css/default.css" rel="stylesheet">
    <script src="/js/default.js"></script>
    <script src="/js/dataAccess.js" ></script>
</head>
<body onload="loadGenres();">
    <div class="pageRoot">
        <h1>Netflix Movie Explorer(Win8 Metro + OData)</h1>
        <hr />
```

```
      <h2>Genres: <select id="lstGenres"
onchange="loadTitlesByGenre();" ></select></h2>
      <hr />
      <div id="lvMovies" data-win-control="WinJS.UI.ListView"
></div>
  </div>


  <!-- ListView Item Template -->
  <div id="movieListItemTemplate" data-win-control="WinJS.
Binding.Template">
      <div class="listItemContainer">
          <img src="#"
              data-win-bind="alt:Description;src:Picture" />
          <div>
              <h4 data-win-bind="innerText:Title"></h4>
              <h6 data-win-bind="innerText:Summary"></h6>
          </div>
      </div>
  </div>
</body>
```

6. Create a new JavaScript file (named `dataAccess.js`) and put it into the `/js` subdirectory, which contains all other built-in JavaScript files.

7. Add the code for populating the `Genre` list (from the *Netflix online catalog* service) in the `dataAccess.js` file (see the following `loadGenres` function).

```
function loadGenres() {
    var serviceUrl = "http://odata.netflix.com/v2/Catalog/
Genres?$top=50&$format=json";

    var headers = {
        "Accept": "application/json"
    };

    new WinJS.xhr({
        type: "GET",
        url: serviceUrl,
        headers: headers
    }).then(
        function (response) {
            var data = JSON.parse(response.responseText);
            var genres = data.d;
            var lst = document.getElementById('lstGenres');
```

```
                    lst.options.add(new Option("----  Please Select a
        Genre  ----"));
                    var i = 0;
                    for (i = 0; i < genres.length; ++i) {
                        lst.options.add(new Option(genres[i].Name));
                    }

                },
                function (error) {
                    Debug.writeln(error);
                }
            );
        }
```

8. Add the code for populating the `Movie` list (based on the selected `Genre` item) in the `dataAccess.js` file (see the following `loadTitlesByGenre` function).

```
function loadTitlesByGenre() {
    var lst = document.getElementById('lstGenres');
    if (lst.selectedIndex == 0) return;

    var currentGenre = lst.options[lst.selectedIndex].value;
    var queryOptions = "$filter=Type eq 'Movie'&$select=Id,Name,Sy
nopsis,ShortSynopsis,BoxArt&$top=40&$format=json";
    var serviceUrl = "http://odata.netflix.com/v2/Catalog/
Genres('" + currentGenre + "')/Titles?"+ queryOptions;
    var headers = {
        "Accept": "application/json"
    };

    new WinJS.xhr({
        type: "GET",
        url: serviceUrl,
        headers: headers
    }).then(
        function (response) {
            var entities = JSON.parse(response.responseText).d;
            var movies = new Array();

            var i = 0;
            for (i = 0; i < entities.length; ++i) {
                movies.push({
                    "Title": entities[i].Name,
                    "Summary": entities[i].ShortSynopsis,
                    "Description": entities[i].Synopsis,
                    "Picture": entities[i].BoxArt.MediumUrl
```

```
                        });


                      }

             var lv = document.getElementById('lvMovies').
      winControl;
             var movieList = new WinJS.Binding.List(movies);

             lv.itemDataSource = movieList.dataSource;
             lv.itemTemplate = document.getElementById('movieListIt
      emTemplate');

           },
           function (error) {
               Debug.writeln(error);
           }
        );
   }
```

9. Double-click on the `package.appxmanifest` file and select the **Capabilities** tab in the opened editor.

10. In the **Capabilities** tab, make sure the **Internet (Client)** option (within the **Capabilities** list) is checked (see the following screenshot).

11. Save all changes and launch the project (via the *F5* or *Ctrl + F5* key) in Visual Studio. The following screenshot shows the launched sample application, which displays the `Movie` list based on the selected `Genre` item:

How it works...

With the support of HTML5 + JavaScript based programming model, traditional web developers can also easily create Windows 8 Metro style applications just like they do for constructing web pages. In this sample, we have created a data-driven and rich interactive Netflix Movie Explorer application with only one HTML page and two custom script functions. Like normal HTML pages, we use the `onload` event of the `<body>` element to initialize the drop-down list for selecting the `Genre` item. And whenever the selected `Genre` item changes, we will retrieve the corresponding `Movie` items from the target service and display them in the `ListView` element (a built-in UI element of JavaScript-based Windows Metro style application).

In addition, when developing Windows 8 Metro style application, developers need to explicitly specify what kind of **Capabilities** the application needs. In this sample, since our Netflix Movie Explorer application needs to communicate with the *Netflix online catalog* service, the **Internet (Client)** capability is necessary for the application to work correctly.

For more information about Windows 8 Metro style design and development, you can go to the following site:

```
http://msdn.microsoft.com/en-us/windows/apps/br229512
```

There's more...

In this sample Metro-style application, we use plain JavaScript code for parsing the JSON-format OData query result. For a more complicated data access scenario, we can consider using the `datajs` script library to consume the OData service. You can refer to the recipe listed in the *See also* section for more information on this.

See also

- ▶ *Building AJAX style data-driven web pages with jQuery* recipe in *Chapter 4, Using OData in Web Application*
- ▶ *Consuming OData service with datajs script library* recipe in *Chapter 4, Using OData in Web Application*

9

New Features of WCF Data Service 5.0 (OData V3)

In this chapter we will cover:

- ▶ Upgrading existing OData service to WCF Data Service 5.0
- ▶ Using geospatial types in OData service
- ▶ Using Any and All operators to filter OData entities
- ▶ Updating OData entities through HTTP PATCH requests
- ▶ Resolving base URI of OData entity sets dynamically
- ▶ Exposing binary data on OData entity with Named Resource Stream
- ▶ Extending OData service functionalities with Service Actions

Introduction

In April 2012, Microsoft released **WCF Data Service 5.0** for **OData V3**. As the name indicates, this new version of WCF Data Service enables creation and consumption of data services for the Web according to Version 3 of the Open Data Protocol (OData), which facilitates data access and change via standard HTTP verbs. This release of WCF Data Services 5.0 includes **.NET Framework** server and client libraries as well as **Silverlight** client libraries.

Compared to **ADO.NET Data Service** and **WCF Data Service 4.0**, **WCF Data Services 5.0** adds support for many new features such as *Any/All query operator, Collection properties, Named Resource Streams, new primitive data types*, and so on.

In this chapter, we will go through some of the new features provided in WCF Data Service 5.0 and demonstrate how we can apply them in OData service and client development.

Upgrading existing OData service to WCF Data Service 5.0

With the release of WCF Data Service 5.0, which supports OData V3, we might want to start upgrading some of our existing OData services (built upon the WCF Data Service) to the new version so as to make both the service side and client side benefit from those new features, which have been added. In this recipe, we will take a tour of what we should do to upgrade an existing OData service application (built with WCF Data Service 4.0) to the new 5.0 version.

Getting ready

Before we start, we need to download and execute the **WCF Data Service 5.0 for OData V3** setup package, which will help install all the necessary assemblies and tools (for Visual Studio IDE and command line). You can get the setup package at the following location:

WCF Data Services 5.0 for OData V3 available at `http://go.microsoft.com/fwlink/p/?LinkId=248279`

The source code for this recipe can be found in the `\ch09\WCFDataServiceV5Sln` directory.

How to do it...

Now, let's have a look at the detailed upgrading steps:

1. Open the web application (which contains the WCF Data Service 4.0 based OData service) in Visual Studio 2010.

2. In the web application, update all WCF Data Service 4.0 specific assemblies (`System.Data.Services.dll` and `System.Data.Services.Client.dll`) to their WCF Data Service 5.0 counterparts (`Microsoft.Data.Services.dll` and `Microsoft.Data.Services.Client.dll`) in the assembly reference list (see the following screenshot).

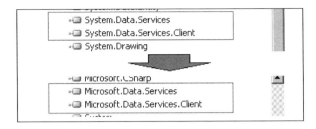

As shown in the previous screenshot, WCF Data Service 5.0 uses a different assembly file naming prefix from WCF Data Service 4.0.

 The new assemblies can be found in the WCF Data Service 5.0 installation path on the local machine. For example, `C:\Program Files\Microsoft WCF Data Services\5.0\bin\.NETFramework`.

3. Open the `.svc` file of the OData service and replace the `Factory` class (in the `<%@ ServiceHost %>` directive) to the WCF Data Service 5.0 specific one (see the following code fragment).

```
<%@ ServiceHost Language="C#"
    Factory="System.Data.Services.DataServiceHostFactory,
    Microsoft.Data.Services, Version=5.0.0.0, Culture=neutral,
    PublicKeyToken=31bf3856ad364e35"
. . . . . .   %>
```

4. Open the code-behind file of the OData service and set the `MaxProtocolVersion` property to `DataServiceProtocolVersion.V3` in the `InitializeService` function (see the following code snippet).

```
public class NorthwindOData : DataService< NorthwindEntities >
{
    public static void
        InitializeService(DataServiceConfiguration config)
    {
        config.DataServiceBehavior.MaxProtocolVersion =
            DataServiceProtocolVersion.V3;

        . . . . . .
    }
}
```

How it works...

WCF Data Service 5.0 uses `Microsoft.Data.Services` as the assembly file naming prefix, which is different from the `System.Data.Services` prefix used by the WCF Data Service 4.0 assemblies provided in .NET Framework 4.0. The reason for this is to simplify the side-by-side installation and make developers switch between different versions of WCF Data Service more conveniently.

WCF Data Service uses the `System.Data.Services.DataServiceHostFactory` class for activating the service instance at runtime (when the first request against the `.svc` file arrives). Therefore, we also need to update this class to the latest version (provided by WCF Data Service 5.0), so that the new service activation process can be applied.

In addition, by specifying the `MaxProtocolVersion` property to `DataServiceProtocolVersion.V3`, we have enabled the service to handle OData V3 (WCF Data Service 5.0) specific requests from the client. Also, even after we have upgraded the service to WCF Data Service 5.0, we can still use this property to restrict the service so that it only exposes **OData V2** (or earlier) features. You can get more information about WCF Data Service *versioning* at the following MSDN reference:

Data Service Versioning (WCF Data Services) available at `http://msdn.microsoft.com/en-us/library/ee473427(v=vs.103).aspx`

There's more...

The previous steps demonstrate how to upgrade a service application based on WCF Data Service. For client applications built upon the WCF Data Service Client library, the upgrade process is quite similar. The following are the basic steps:

1. Remove the existing OData proxy types and related assembly references (such as the `System.Data.Service.Client.dll`).

2. Regenerate the OData proxy through the Visual Studio Add Service Reference wizard.

Because the WCF Data Services 5.0 setup package will update the Add Service Reference tool in Visual Studio 2010, the regenerated OData proxy is automatically targeting the WCF Data Service 5.0 specific client library.

If you create the OData proxy through the `DataSvcUtil.exe` command-line tool, you should switch to the new version of this tool within the installation folder of WCF Data Service 5.0 (see the following screenshot).

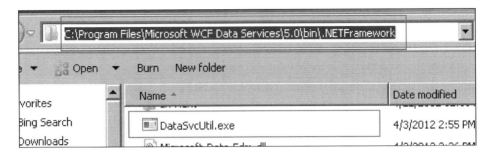

See also

▶ *Building an OData service via WCF Data Service and ADO.NET Entity Framework* recipe in *Chapter 1, Building OData Services*

Using geospatial types in OData service

WCF Data Service 5.0 (OData V3) has added support for some new primitive data types and the geospatial types are in this new type list. Geospatial data types have already been used in **SQL Server 2008 R2** and will probably be included as built-in types of the next version of the .NET Framework. And in this release, a dedicated spatial class library is provided so that OData services built upon WCF Data Service 5.0 can leverage geospatial primitive types (including **Geography** and **Geometry** types) to define their data object model.

In this recipe, we will show you how to build an OData service using the new geospatial types and apply the geospatial-specific query extensions at client side.

Getting ready

The sample OData service here will use a custom class instead of an ADO.NET Entity Framework data model as the data source. In the data source class, we will only expose a single entity set, which contains some `Address` records (which use the `GeographyPoint` spatial type).

Make sure you have installed WCF Data Service 5.0 components and updated your OData service and client projects correspondingly (refer to the *Upgrading existing OData service to WCF Data Service 5.0* recipe).

The source code for this recipe can be found in the `\ch09\ODataSpatialTypesSln` directory.

How to do it...

Now, let's go through the steps to create the sample application:

1. Create a new **Class Library** project (named SharedLib).

2. Add reference to the System.Spatial.dll assembly (from the installation folder of WCF Data Service 5.0) in the **Class Library** project.

3. Create a custom class (named TestSpatialOperations), which derives from the SpatialOperations class (under System.Spatial namespace) and override the spatial operations in the custom class.

    The following is the main code of the TestSpatialOperations class in this sample:

```
public class TestSpatialOperations: SpatialOperations
{
    public override double Distance(Geography operand1, Geography
                                    operand2)
    {
        var p1 = (GeographyPoint)operand1;
        var p2 = (GeographyPoint)operand2;

        // Call helper functions to calculate distance
        return GetDistanceByPoints(p1.Latitude, p1.Longitude,
            p2.Latitude, p2.Longitude);
    }

    public override double Distance(Geometry operand1, Geometry
        operand2)
    {
        throw new NotImplementedException();
    }
}
```

4. Create a new ASP.NET Empty Web Application project (in the same solution as the SharedLib Class Library project).

5. In the Web project, add reference to the SharedLib Class Library project.

> It is recommended that we use *project based reference* (if possible) instead of *file based reference* when referencing assemblies in Visual Studio projects.

6. Create a custom class (used as data source of the sample OData service), which exposes some spatial type objects via the `IQueryable<T>` interface.

The following `SimpleSpatialDataSource` class exposes a public property of the `IQueryable<AddressItem>` type:

```
public class SimpleSpatialDataSource
{
    static IList<AddressItem> _addresses;

    static SimpleSpatialDataSource()
    {
        _addresses = new List<AddressItem>();

        // Add some test records
        _addresses.Add(
            new AddressItem() {
                Name = "addr1",
                AddressLine = "Line of Address1",
                Location = GeographyPoint.Create(
                    47.7869921906598, -122.164644615406)
            }
        );
        _addresses.Add(
            new AddressItem() {
                Name = "addr2",
                AddressLine = "Line of Address2",
                Location =
                    GeographyPoint.Create(47.6867097047995,
                    -122.250185528911)
            }
        );

        ......
    }

    public IQueryable<AddressItem> Addresses
    {
        get { return _addresses.AsQueryable<AddressItem>(); }
    }
}
```

And the following is the definition of the `AddressItem` class:

```
[DataServiceKey("Name")]
public class AddressItem
{
```

```
public string Name { get; set; }
public string AddressLine { get; set; }
public GeographyPoint Location { get; set; }
}
```

7. Create a new WCF Data Service (named `SpatialDataService.svc`) and make sure it is updated to WCF Data Service 5.0.

8. In the code-behind file of the `SpatialDataService.svc` service, change the data source type (of the service class) to the `SimpleSpatialDataSource` class (see the following code snippet).

```
public class SpatialDataService : DataService<
    SimpleSpatialDataSource >
{
    . . . . . .
}
```

9. In the `InitializeService` function of the service class, register the custom implementation of the spatial operations to the WCF Data Service runtime.

    This can be done by assigning a new instance of the `TestSpatialOperations` class to the `SpatialImplementation.CurrentImplementation.Operations` property (see the following code snippet).

```
public static void InitializeService(DataServiceConfiguration
config)
{
    config.DataServiceBehavior.MaxProtocolVersion =
        DataServiceProtocolVersion.V3;
    config.SetEntitySetAccessRule("*", EntitySetRights.AllRead);

    // Register Spatial operations
    SpatialImplementation.CurrentImplementation.Operations =
        new TestSpatialOperations();
}
```

10. Create a new Console Application as the OData client.

11. Generate the OData proxy (via the Visual Studio Add Service Reference wizard) against the sample service.

12. Add a function for performing spatial type specific OData queries against the sample service (see the following `QuerySpatialDataService` function).

```
static void QuerySpatialDataService()
{
    var svcUri = new
        Uri("http://localhost:19749/SpatialDataService.svc/");
    var ctx = new ODataSvc.SimpleSpatialDataSource(svcUri);
```

```
        // Define a reference location for test
        var myLocation = GeographyPoint.Create(47.7201372000862,
            -121.189084876407);

        // Get all addresses order by distance to reference
        //location
        var allAddresses = ctx.Addresses.OrderBy(a =>
            a.Location.Distance(myLocation)).ToList();

        // Get nearby addresses from reference location
        var nearbyAddresses = ctx.Addresses.Where(a =>
            a.Location.Distance(myLocation) < 70).ToList();
    }
```

How it works...

In order to use the new spatial types provided in WCF Data Service 5.0, we need to add a reference to the `System.Spatial.dll` assembly. The current spatial class library of WCF Data Service 5.0 has not provided a default implementation of some common spatial calculation operations. That's why we need to create a custom implementation of the spatial operations and register them in the sample service's initialization code here. For reuse purpose, we define our custom implementation of the spatial operations (in the `TestSpatialOperations` class) in a separate **Class Library** project.

At the client side, we can directly use a Visual Studio generated OData proxy to perform spatial type specific queries. In this recipe we have performed two OData queries in the `QuerySpatialDataService` function. The first query retrieves all `AddressItem` entities and sorts them based on the distance to a fixed geographic location; the second query just retrieves all `AddressItem` entities that are nearby the fixed location (within a certain distance range). Both queries have used the `Distance` extension method for the `System.Spatial.Geography` class.

By using Fiddler, we can capture the raw OData query URI (translated from the LINQ queries) sent by the WCF Data Service client library (see the following screenshot).

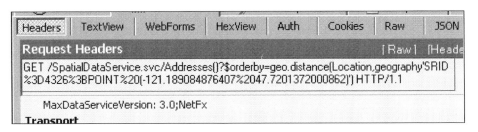

After formatting (use `UrlDecode` method) the URI captured in Fiddler, we can get the clear syntax of the two queries in the sample (see the following URI strings).

▶ `/SpatialDataService.svc/Addresses()?$orderby=geo.distanc`
`e(Location,geography'SRID=4326;POINT (-121.189084876407`
`47.7201372000862)')`

▶ `/SpatialDataService.svc/Addresses()?$filter=geo.distanc`
`e(Location,geography'SRID=4326;POINT (-121.189084876407`
`47.7201372000862)') lt 70.0`

When using the spatial operations (via LINQ query) against the Visual Studio generated OData proxy at the client side, we don't need to implement and register the spatial operations. This is because the WCF Data Service client library will handle the spatial operations and translate them into the OData query URI (which is then sent to and evaluated at server side).

 Note that if you call those operations in any other code (outside the LINQ queries against the OData proxy) at the client side, you still have to implement and register the spatial operations.

There's more...

At the time of this writing, the current ADO.NET Entity Framework (included in .NET Framework 4.0) does not support geospatial types as built-in primitive data properties. That's why we choose to build a custom data source class for the sample OData service here. However, the future release of ADO.NET Entity Framework will add built-in support for geospatial types. Then, it will be quite convenient for us to build geospatial-enabled OData service with the following structure:

▶ Using SQL Server 2008 R2 or 2012 as the raw data repository

▶ Using ADO.NET Entity Framework data model as the data connector

▶ Using WCF Data Service as the data publishing interface

See also

▶ *Using custom data objects as the data source of WCF Data Service* recipe in Chapter 1, Building OData Services

▶ *Upgrading existing OData service to WCF Data Service 5.0* recipe

Using Any and All operators to filter OData entities

When developing .NET-based OData client applications, we often use LINQ to query the entity sets exposed in OData services. At runtime, the WCF Data Service client library will translate the LINQ query into the corresponding OData query URI and send it to the service. WCF Data Service 5.0 comes with two new LINQ query operators supported by the client library; they are Any and All operators. These two operators are very useful when we want to filter entity objects based on some Collection type properties.

In this recipe, we will demonstrate how to use Any and All operators to filter entity objects returned in OData queries.

Getting ready

Make sure you have installed WCF Data Service 5.0 components and updated your OData service and client projects correspondingly (refer to *Upgrading existing OData service to WCF Data Service 5.0* recipe).

The source code for this recipe can be found in the \ch09\ODataNewLINQOperatorsSln directory.

How to do it...

In this recipe, we will use Any and All operators to filter the OData query against the Categories entity set exposed by Northwind OData service. Let's have a look at the detailed steps:

1. Create an ASP.NET web application which contains the Northwind OData service (based on WCF Data Service 5.0).

2. Create a new Console Application as the OData client.

3. Create the OData proxy (via Visual Studio Add Service Reference wizard) against the Northwind OData service.

4. Add a function which uses the Any operator to query the Categories entity set (see the following QueryODataServiceWithAnyOperator function).

   ```
   static void QueryODataServiceWithAnyOperator()
   {
       var svcUri = new
           Uri("http://localhost:20457/NorthwindOData.svc/");
       var ctx = new ODataSvc.NorthwindEntities(svcUri);

       var categories = from c in ctx.Categories
   ```

```
                        where c.Products.Any(p =>
                                p.ProductName.StartsWith("Ca"))
                        select c;

        foreach (var c in categories)
        {
            Console.WriteLine("Category: {0}", c.CategoryName);
            ctx.LoadProperty(c, "Products");
            foreach (var p in c.Products)
            {
                Console.WriteLine("\tProduct: {0}", p.ProductName);
            }
        }
    }
```

5. Add a function that uses the `All` operator to query the `Categories` entity set (see the following `QueryODataServiceWithAllOperator` function).

```
static void QueryODataServiceWithAllOperator()
{
    var svcUri = new Uri("http://localhost:20457/NorthwindOData.
    svc/");
    var ctx = new ODataSvc.NorthwindEntities(svcUri);

    var categories = ctx.Categories.Where(
                    c => c.Products.All(
                        p => p.ProductName.Length > 8
                        )
                    );

    foreach (var c in categories)
    {
        Console.WriteLine("Category: {0}", c.CategoryName);
        ctx.LoadProperty(c, "Products");
        foreach (var p in c.Products)
        {
            Console.WriteLine("\tProduct: {0}", p.ProductName);
        }
    }
}
```

How it works...

Both `Any` and `All` operators are used for applying filters against `Collection` type properties. In this recipe, we use these two operators to filter the `Categories` entity set (from the Northwind OData service) based on the `Products` property (of `Collection` type) of each `Category` entity. The `QueryODataServiceWithAnyOperator` function queries all `Category` entities each of which has some associated `Product` entities whose names start with some particular characters. And the `QueryODataServiceWithAllOperator` function queries all `Category` entities, which have all their associated `Product` entities with lengthy names.

When processing the `Any` operator, the WCF Data Service client library converts it to the proper OData extension syntax in the generated query URI. The following screenshot shows the raw query URI sent to the service (captured via Fiddler):

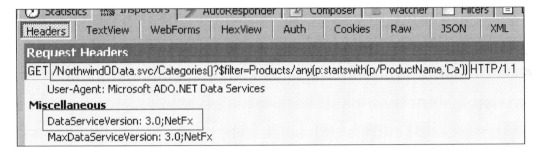

And the same process also applies to the query that uses the `All` operator (see the following screenshot).

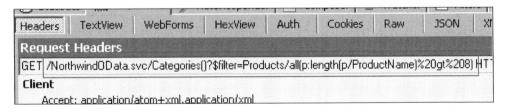

There's more...

Although WCF Data Service 5.0 (OData V3) has added support for `Any` and `All` operators, there are some LINQ query operators or methods that are not supported yet. For detailed information about how the WCF Data Service client library processes and executes LINQ-based queries, you can refer to the following MSDN reference:

LINQ Considerations (WCF Data Services) available at `http://msdn.microsoft.com/en-us/library/ee622463(v=vs.103).aspx`

See also

▸ *Filtering OData query results by using query options* recipe in *Chapter 2, Working with OData at Client Side*

▸ *Upgrading existing OData service to WCF Data Service 5.0* recipe

Updating OData entities through HTTP PATCH requests

The OData protocol supports two types of HTTP requests for updating service entities. They are as follows:

▸ **HTTP PUT** request

▸ **HTTP MERGE** request

By using HTTP PUT request, the server-side entity will be completely replaced by the entity sent by the client; while the HTTP MERGE request will only update the changed properties of the target entity on the server. In most cases, we will use the MERGE requests (the default option used by the WCF Data Service client library). However, MERGE is not a standard verb of the HTTP protocol. In order to adopt existing standards of HTTP as much as possible, OData V3 (WCF Data Service 5.0) has added a new type of update request based on the HTTP PATCH verb, which is newly added in HTTP standards.

In this recipe, we will introduce how to use HTTP PATCH request for updating OData entities.

Getting ready

In this recipe, we will use HTTP PATCH request (via the Visual Studio generated OData proxy) to update some `Category` entities in the Northwind OData service.

Make sure you have installed WCF Data Service 5.0 components and updated your OData service and client projects correspondingly (refer to *Upgrading existing OData service to WCF Data Service 5.0* recipe).

The source code for this recipe can be found in the `\ch09\ODataUpdateWithPatchSln` directory.

How to do it...

The following are the steps to create the sample application:

1. Create the ASP.NET web application which contains the Northwind OData service (updated to WCF Data Service 5.0).

   For demonstration, we need to at least expose the `Categories` entity set and enable all access rules on it (see the following `InitializeService` function).

   ```
   public static void InitializeService
       (DataServiceConfiguration config)
   {
       config.DataServiceBehavior.MaxProtocolVersion =
           DataServiceProtocolVersion.V3;
       config.SetEntitySetAccessRule("Categories",
           EntitySetRights.All);
   }
   ```

2. Create a new Console Application as the OData client.

3. Use the Visual Studio Add Service Reference wizard to generate the OData proxy (against the Northwind OData service) in the OData client.

4. Add the code for updating `Category` entities through HTTP PATCH requests in the OData client (see the following `UpdateEntityWithPatchOption` function).

   ```
   static void UpdateEntityWithPatchOption()
   {
       var svcUri = new Uri(SVC_URL);
       var ctx = new ODataSvc.NorthwindEntities(svcUri);

       var testCategory = ctx.Categories.FirstOrDefault();

       testCategory.Description = testCategory.Description + "2";

       ctx.UpdateObject(testCategory);

       ctx.SaveChanges(SaveChangesOptions.PatchOnUpdate);
   }
   ```

How it works...

In the sample OData client, we specify the `SaveChangesOptions.PatchOnUpdate` value when invoking the `SaveChanges` method of the `DataServiceContext` class generated in the OData proxy. The `SaveChangesOptions.PatchOnUpdate` is a new option added in WCF Data Service 5.0. By specifying this option, the WCF Data Service runtime will generate the underlying request (for updating OData entities) with HTTP PATCH verb. The following screenshot shows the raw HTTP request URI and headers (captured via Fiddler) of the update request sent in the sample OData client:

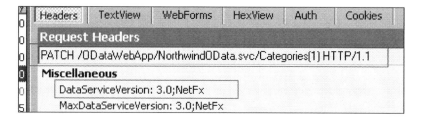

What if we change the OData client code and use the default option for the `SaveChanges` method call (see the following code snippet)?

```
static void UpdateEntityWithDefaultMergeOption()
{
    ......
    ctx.UpdateObject(testCategory);

    ctx.SaveChanges();
}
```

Then, the underlying update request will be changed to use HTTP MERGE verb. The following screenshot shows the HTTP MERGE request (captured via Fiddler) generated from the previous code:

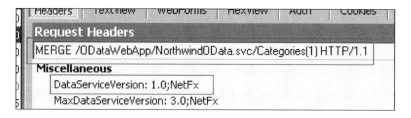

Actually, HTTP PATCH based update requests are handled in the same manner as HTTP MERGE based requests. Therefore, it doesn't matter which one we use in most cases. However, in case the OData hosting environment only allows standard HTTP verbs, the HTTP PATCH based approach will show its advantage. In addition, since HTTP PATCH is a new verb introduced in the HTTP protocol, it is also possible that some web servers or client components might not have added support for it yet.

See also

▶ *Editing and deleting data through WCF Data Service client library* recipe in *Chapter 2, Working with OData at Client Side*

▶ *Upgrading existing OData service to WCF Data Service 5.0* recipe

Resolving base URI of OData entity sets dynamically

When using the WCF Data Service client library based client proxy to access an OData service, we need to supply the base URI of the target service (in the constructor of the `DataServiceContext` derived class). Then, the client library will use this base URI to resolve the absolute address of each entity set exposed in the target service. For example, given the base URI of an OData service, `http://localhost:8888/MyODataService.svc/`, the client library will locate each entity set by following the address pattern, `http://localhost:8888/MyODataService.svc/[Entity Set Name]/`.

Now, with WCF Data Service 5.0, we can customize how the client library (OData proxy) resolves the entity set URI so as to implement some features such as dynamic address resolving. In this recipe, we will demonstrate how to use this feature in OData client application.

Getting ready

Make sure you have installed WCF Data Service 5.0 components and updated your OData service and client projects correspondingly (refer to the *Upgrading existing OData service to WCF Data Service 5.0* recipe).

The source code for this recipe can be found in the `\ch09\ODataEntitySetResolverSln` directory.

How to do it...

In this recipe, we will use Visual Studio generated OData proxy to query two entity sets from the Northwind OData service. And each entity set will be accessed from different locations through the dynamic URI resolving feature. The following are the detailed steps:

1. Create the ASP.NET web application which contains the Northwind OData service (updated to WCF Data Service 5.0).

    The service needs to expose two entity sets, they are `Categories` and `Products` (see the following screenshot).

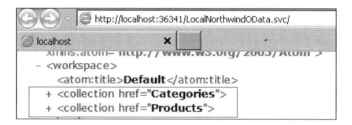

2. Create a new Console Application as the OData client.

3. Use the Visual Studio Add Service Reference wizard to generate the OData proxy against the sample service.

4. Define a function (in the `Program.cs` file), which dynamically resolves the URI address of a given entity set (see the following `ResolveEntitySetUriByName` function).

```
static Uri ResolveEntitySetUriByName(string name)
{
    switch(name)
    {
        case "Categories":
            // Use local service for Categories entity set
            return new Uri
                ("http://localhost:36341/
                LocalNorthwindOData.svc/Categories");
        case "Products":
            // Use Remote service for Products entity set
            return new Uri
                ("http://services.odata.org/
                Northwind/Northwind.svc/Products");
        default:
            throw new ArgumentException
                ("Invalid EntitySet Name!");
    }
}
```

5. Define a function (in the `Program.cs` file) to query the `Categories` and `Products` entity sets by using the dynamic URI resolving function (see the following `QueryODataWithDynamicUris` function).

```
static void QueryODataWithDynamicUris()
{
    var svcUri = new
        Uri("http://localhost:36341/LocalNorthwindOData.svc/");
    var ctx = new ODataSvc.NorthwindEntities(svcUri);

    // Register the Entity Set Uri Resolver
    ctx.ResolveEntitySet = ResolveEntitySetUriByName;

    var categories = ctx.Categories.ToList();
    foreach (var c in categories)
    {
        Console.WriteLine("Products of '{0}' Category:",
            c.CategoryName);
        var products = ctx.Products.Where(p => p.CategoryID ==
            c.CategoryID).ToList();
        foreach (var p in products)
        {
            Console.WriteLine("\t{0}", p.ProductName);
        }
    }
}
```

How it works...

As we have seen in the previous sample code, the URI resolving function (`ResolveEntitySetUriByName`) is the key point for driving the dynamic entity set address resolving functionality. We register this function through the `DataServiceContext.ResolveEntitySet` property right after the OData proxy is created. Whenever an OData query is executed, the client runtime will call the resolving function (if registered) to obtain the absolute URI address of the target entity set. In the `ResolveEntitySetUriByName` function here, we map the `Categories` entity set to the *local* Northwind OData service; while the `Products` entity set is mapped to the *remote* Northwind OData service on the Internet.

By using Fiddler to monitor the underlying OData HTTP requests, we can confirm that the `Categories` entity set is accessed from the *local* service while the `Products` entity set is accessed from the *remote* service (see the following screenshot).

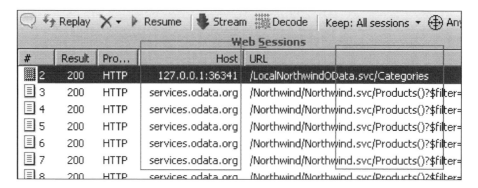

One thing worth noticing is that there are some cases in which the dynamic URI resolving function will be bypassed. For example, when we use the `Expand` query option to load some `Category` entities and their associated `Product` entities together (see the following code snippet), only a single OData request is sent so that the base URI address of the `Categories` entity set is used for loading both `Category` and `Product` entities.

```
var categories = ctx.Categories.Expand("Products").ToList();
```

See also

▸ *Using Visual Studio to generate strong-typed OData client proxy* recipe in *Chapter 2, Working with OData at Client Side*

▸ *Upgrading existing OData service to WCF Data Service 5.0* recipe

Exposing binary data on OData entity with Named Resource Stream

For OData entities which contain binary properties, WCF Data Service runtime will transfer the binary data in *base64 encoded* format. This works well for small binary data, however, it is not quite good for large binary data such as file content and picture data. To resolve this problem, **WCF Data Service 4.0 (OData V2)** has already utilized the *media link entry* (of the AtomPub protocol) to support raw stream-based binary resource associated with a certain OData entity. However, one entity can only have a single binary resource associated due to the AtomPub protocol limitation.

Fortunately, in WCF Data Service 5.0 (OData V3), an enhanced **Named Resource Stream** feature is introduced so that we can attach multiple raw binary resource streams to an OData entity. In this recipe, we will demonstrate how we can use a Named Resource Stream to expose raw binary data in OData service and consume them from the client.

Getting ready

Make sure you have installed WCF Data Service 5.0 components and updated your OData service and client projects correspondingly (refer to the *Upgrading existing OData service to WCF Data Service 5.0* recipe).

The source code for this recipe can be found in the `\ch09\ODataNamedStreamSln` directory.

How to do it...

For demonstration purposes, we will use the `Categories` entity set (in the Northwind OData service) as example, and attach two binary resource streams (for storing the `Logo` and `SmallLogo` image data) on each `Category` entity. The following are the detailed steps:

1. Create a new ASP.NET web application which contains the Northwind OData service (updated to WCF Data Service 5.0).

    We will only expose the `Categories` entity set in the sample service (see the following code snippet).

    ```
    public class NorthwindOData : DataService< NorthwindEntities >
    {
        public static void
            InitializeService(DataServiceConfiguration config)
        {
            config.DataServiceBehavior.MaxProtocolVersion =
                DataServiceProtocolVersion.V3;
            config.SetEntitySetAccessRule("Categories",
                EntitySetRights.All);
        }
    }
    ```

2. Create a new C# code file (named `Northwind.Extensions.cs`) to define a *partial class* for the `Category` entity type generated by the ADO.NET Entity Framework data model (see the following code snippet).

    ```
    using System.Data.Services.Common;

    namespace ODataWebApp
    {
        [NamedStream("Logo")]
    ```

```
[NamedStream("SmallLogo")]
public partial class Category
{}
}
```

The partial class (for the `Category` entity type) just defines two `NamedStreamAttribute` attributes (under `System.Data.Services.Common` namespace), which specify the names of the binary resource streams.

 By using partial class in a separate code file, we can prevent our custom code from being overwritten by the Visual Studio IDE when updating the ADO.NET Entity Framework data model.

3. Create a new class (named `SimpleNamedStreamProvider`) that implements the `IDataServiceStreamProvider2` interface (under the `System.Data.Services.Providers` namespace).

    The following is the declaration of the sample provider class:

```
public class SimpleNamedStreamProvider:
    IDataServiceStreamProvider2
{
    ......
}
```

4. Implement the Named Resource Stream specific functions within the `SimpleNamedStreamProvider` class (see the following code snippet).

```
public System.IO.Stream GetReadStream(object entity,
    ResourceProperty streamProperty, string etag, bool?
    checkETagForEquality,
    System.Data.Services.DataServiceOperationContext
    operationContext)
{
    Category c = entity as Category;
    if (c == null) throw new DataServiceException("Only support
        stream resource on Category entity.");

    var logoFilePath = string.Format("~/Images/{0}.{1}.png",
        c.CategoryID, streamProperty.Name);

    var stream = File.Open(
        System.Web.Hosting.HostingEnvironment.MapPath
        (logoFilePath),
```

```
                FileMode.Open
                );
        return stream;
}


public Uri GetReadStreamUri(object entity, ResourceProperty
        streamProperty,
        System.Data.Services.DataServiceOperationContext
        operationContext)
{    return null;    }


public string GetStreamContentType
    (object entity, ResourceProperty streamProperty,
    System.Data.Services.DataServiceOperationContext
    operationContext)
{

    if (entity is Category)
    {
        return "image/png";
    }
    throw new DataServiceException("Only support stream
        resource on Category entity.");
}


public string GetStreamETag
    (object entity, ResourceProperty streamProperty,
    System.Data.Services.DataServiceOperationContext
    operationContext)
{    return null;    }


public System.IO.Stream GetWriteStream(object entity,
    ResourceProperty streamProperty,
    string etag, bool? checkETagForEquality,
    System.Data.Services.DataServiceOperationContext
    operationContext)
{

    throw new DataServiceException("The stream resource is
        read-only!");
}
```

For other functions of the `IDataServiceStreamProvider2` interface, we can simply leave them as unimplemented (or we can just throw out a `NotImplementedException` exception in each unimplemented function).

5. Implement the `IServiceProvider` interface on the service class of the sample Northwind OData service (see the following code snippet).

```
public class NorthwindOData :
DataService< NorthwindEntities >, IServiceProvider
{
    ......

    public object GetService(Type serviceType)
    {
        if (serviceType == typeof(IDataServiceStreamProvider2))
        {
            return new SimpleNamedStreamProvider();
        }
        return null;
    }
}
```

6. Open the `web.config` file of the web application and enlarge the default message size limit (through the `<system.serviceModel>` section) for the sample OData service (see the following configuration fragment).

```
<system.serviceModel>
  <serviceHostingEnvironment
    aspNetCompatibilityEnabled="true"/>
  <services>
    <!-- For the sample Northwind OData service -->
    <service name="ODataWebApp.NorthwindOData">
<endpoint binding="webHttpBinding"
    bindingConfiguration="largeMessageBinding"
    contract="System.Data.Services.IRequestHandler"></endpoint>
    </service>
  </services>
  <bindings>
    <webHttpBinding>
      <!-- configure the maxReceivedMessageSize to the max
        value
          you want the service to receive-->
      <binding name="largeMessageBinding" transferMode="Streamed"
            maxReceivedMessageSize="2147483647"/>
    </webHttpBinding>
  </bindings>
</system.serviceModel>
```

7. Launch the sample web application and use the web browser to explore the Named Resource Streams exposed on the `Category` entities.

    The following screenshot shows the `Logo` and `SmallLogo` resource stream references contained in a certain `Category` entity:

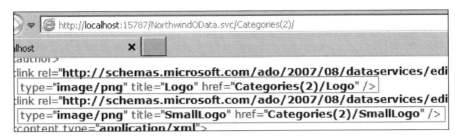

    If we navigate to the resource location indicated by the `href` attribute (see the previous screenshot), the web browser will download the image resource stream and display it in the browser window (see the following screenshot).

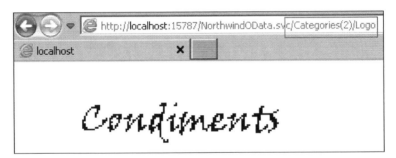

8. Alternatively, use a Visual Studio generated OData proxy to access the Named Resource Streams (`Logo` and `SmallLogo`) exposed on each `Category` entity.

    We can use the `GetReadStreamUri` and `GetReadStream` methods (of the `DataServiceContext` class) to retrieve the URI string and the actual binary data of the target binary resource (see the following code snippet).

```
var svcUri = new
    Uri("http://localhost:15787/NorthwindOData.svc/");
var ctx = new ODataSvc.NorthwindEntities(svcUri);

foreach (var category in ctx.Categories)
{
    var name = category.CategoryName;

    // Get Stream Resource Uri
    var logoUri = ctx.GetReadStreamUri(category, "Logo");
```

```
        var smallLogoUri = ctx.GetReadStreamUri(category,
        "SmallLogo");

        // Get Stream Resource data directly
        var response = ctx.GetReadStream(category, "Logo",
            new DataServiceRequestArgs() { });
        var imgLogo = Image.FromStream(response.Stream);

        var filePath = string.Format("{0}.Logo.png",
            category.CategoryID);
        imgLogo.Save(filePath);
}
```

How it works...

In the sample service, we use the `NamedStreamAttribute` attribute to declare the resource streams on the `Category` entity class (generated by the ADO.NET Entity Framework). This approach works for a **.NET Reflection** provider based OData service too. By inspecting the OData service metadata, we can find the definition of those properties (of `Edm.Stream` type) generated for the corresponding Named Resource Streams (see the following screenshot).

As we can see from the previous screenshot, a resource stream property has the same definition syntax as other primitive type properties in the metadata of an OData service.

Starting with **Entity Data Model (EDM) 2.2** (probably supported by the next version of .NET Framework), binary stream data type will be naturally supported by the ADO.NET Entity Framework data model.

The `IDataServiceStreamProvider2` interface (implemented by the `SimpleNamedStreamProvider` class) is specific to the Named Resource Stream feature of WCF Data Service 5.0 (OData V3). This interface derives from the `IDataServiceStreamProvider` interface, which is necessary for implementing the old binary stream provider of WCF Data Service 4.0. The code logic for implementing both of these interfaces is quite similar except that the `IDataServiceStreamProvider2` specific methods take an additional parameter (of `ResourceProperty` type) for identifying the target resource stream. The following table shows the methods we have implemented in the sample provider class so as to use the Named Resource Stream feature:

Member name	Description
GetReadStream	This method is invoked by the data service to return a named stream. We will return a FileStream based on the logo image of the requested Category entity.
GetReadStreamUri	This method is invoked by the data service to return the URI that is used to request a specific named stream for the media link entry. We will return null so as to let the runtime autogenerate the URI string.
GetStreamContentType	This method is invoked by the data service to return the Content-Type value of a specific named stream. We will simply return image/png for the logo image streams in this sample.
GetStreamETag	This method is used when you manage concurrency for the binary data. In this sample, we will simply return null so that the runtime will not track concurrency.
GetWriteStream	This method is invoked by the data service to obtain the stream that is used when receiving a named stream sent from the client. We will not implement it since the sample resource streams are read-only.

For more information about how to implement the `IDataServiceStreamProvider` interface (specific to the WCF Data Service 4.0 binary stream provider), you can refer to the following MSDN code sample:

Streaming Photo OData Service Sample available at `http://code.msdn.microsoft.com/Streaming-Photo-OData-7feb9239/sourcecode?fileId=22215&pathId=511955853`

In addition to creating the stream provider class, we also need to implement the `IServiceProvider` interface on the service class (of the OData service). As shown in the sample service class (`NorthwindOData` class), we simply return a new instance of the stream provider class in case the `IDataServiceStreamProvider2` interface is requested at the runtime.

It is worth noticing that we have specified some additional configuration elements within the web.config file of the sample web application. This is because WCF Data Service runtime uses the WebHttpBinding binding type (for WCF REST service), which has a default limit on the maximum message size allowed in data transfer. Since binary resource streams are often used for transferring large size data, we should also take care of this setting.

Once Named Resource Streams have been exposed from an OData service, we can consume them through the following two means:

 ▶ Using the stream URI pointing to the target resource stream: This works well in case we want to consume the resource stream by using some other components or tools, which accepts an URI string as input (such as the <img> HTML element in web page).

 ▶ Directly fetching the binary data of the target resource stream: This would be preferred if we want to directly handle the raw binary content of the target resource and perform some further manipulation on it. For example, we can programmatically get the image resource stream (of raw bytes) and then perform some graphical transformations over the image data.

See also

 ▶ *Creating a custom WCF Data Service provider recipe in Chapter 1, Building OData Services*

 ▶ *Exploring an OData service through web browser recipe in Chapter 2, Working with OData at Client Side*

 ▶ *Upgrading existing OData service to WCF Data Service 5.0 recipe*

Extending OData service functionalities with Service Actions

As we've discussed in *Chapter 1, Building OData Services*, we can create custom service operations to extend an OData service. However, service operations are always defined within a particular service. Therefore, it is not quite convenient to reuse service operations for multiple services. WCF Data Service 5.0 (OData V3) comes with a new feature called **Service Actions**. A Service Action is a special operation, which can be applied through a provider-based model. Thus, we can separate the Service Actions from the OData service and inject them whenever necessary. Also, Service Actions can be applied not only at service level but also at entity set (or even individual entity objects) level. This makes it quite convenient for developers to create business data specific extension functions.

In this recipe, we will demonstrate how we can use Service Actions to define custom extension functions and apply them to an OData service (built with WCF Data Service 5.0).

Getting ready

Make sure you have installed WCF Data Service 5.0 components and updated your OData service and client projects correspondingly (refer to the *Upgrade existing OData service to WCF Data Service 5.0* recipe).

The source code for this recipe can be found in the `\ch09\ODataServiceActionsSln` directory.

How to do it...

We will still use the Northwind OData service as example and apply two Service Actions (`SayHello` and `GetMoreInfo`) to it. The following are the detailed steps:

1. Create the ASP.NET web application which contains the Northwind OData service (updated to WCF Data Service 5.0).

2. In the `InitializeService` function of the Northwind OData service, enable `All` access rules on the `Categories` entity set and turn on the `Invoke` permission for all Service Actions (see the following code snippet).

```
public class NorthwindOData : DataService<NorthwindEntities>
{
    public static void
        InitializeService(DataServiceConfiguration config)
    {
        config.DataServiceBehavior.MaxProtocolVersion =
            DataServiceProtocolVersion.V3;
        config.SetEntitySetAccessRule("Categories",
            EntitySetRights.All);
        config.SetServiceActionAccessRule("*",
            ServiceActionRights.Invoke);
    }
    . . . . . .
```

3. Create a new class (named `SimpleActionProvider`) that implements the `IDataServiceActionProvider` interface (under the `System.Data.Services.Providers` namespace).

   The following is the declaration of the sample provider class:

```
public class SimpleActionProvider : IDataServiceActionProvider
{
    . . . . . .
}
```

4. Define a helper function (in the `SimpleActionProvider` class) that creates two sample Service Action instances (see the following `GetActionList` function).

```
IEnumerable<ServiceAction> GetActionList(IDataServiceMetadataProvi
der metadata)
{
    // The global SayHello action
    var actionSayHello = new ServiceAction(
        "SayHello",
        ResourceType.GetPrimitiveResourceType(typeof(string)),
        null,
        OperationParameterBindingKind.Never,
        new[]
        {
            new ServiceActionParameter("name",
                ResourceType.GetPrimitiveResourceType
                (typeof(string)))
        }
    );
    actionSayHello.SetReadOnly();

    // The action bound to the Category entity
    var resType = metadata.Types.Where( t => t.Name ==
        "Category").FirstOrDefault();
    var actionGetMoreInfo = new ServiceAction(
        "GetMoreInfo",
        ResourceType.GetPrimitiveResourceType(typeof(string)),
        null,
        OperationParameterBindingKind.Always,
        new []
        {
            new ServiceActionParameter("Category", resType)
        }
    );
    actionGetMoreInfo.SetReadOnly();

    return new []{actionSayHello, actionGetMoreInfo};
}
```

5. Define all functions required by the `IDataServiceActionProvider` interface in the `SimpleActionProvider` class.

The following is the definition of the `AdvertiseServiceAction` function:

```
public bool AdvertiseServiceAction
    (System.Data.Services.DataServiceOperationContext
    operationContext, ServiceAction serviceAction,
    object resourceInstance, bool resourceInstanceInFeed,
    ref Microsoft.Data.OData.ODataAction actionToSerialize)
{
    throw new NotImplementedException();
}
```

The `CreateInvokable` function will return some instances of custom classes (which we will define in the next step) for executing the Service Actions (see the following code snippet).

```
public IDataServiceInvokable CreateInvokable
    (System.Data.Services.DataServiceOperationContext
    operationContext, ServiceAction serviceAction, object[]
    parameterTokens)
{
    if (serviceAction.Name == "SayHello")
    {
        var name = parameterTokens[0] as string;
        return new SayHelloInvokable() { Data = name };
    }
    else if (serviceAction.Name == "GetMoreInfo")
    {
        var objQuery = parameterTokens[0] as
            ObjectQuery<Category>;
        var category = objQuery.FirstOrDefault();

        return new GetMoreInfoInvokable() { Data =
            category.CategoryName };
    }
    else
    {
        return null;
    }
}
```

The remaining three functions (`GetServiceActions`,
`GetServiceActionsByBindingParameterType`, and
`TryResolveServiceAction`) simply find and return the requested Service Actions
based on the `GetActionList` helper function (see the following code snippet).

```
public IEnumerable<ServiceAction> GetServiceActions
    (System.Data.Services.DataServiceOperationContext
    operationContext)
{
    var metadata = operationContext.GetService
        (typeof(IDataServiceMetadataProvider)) as
        IDataServiceMetadataProvider;

    return GetActionList(metadata);
}


public IEnumerable<ServiceAction>
    GetServiceActionsByBindingParameterType
    (System.Data.Services.DataServiceOperationContext
    operationContext, ResourceType bindingParameterType)
{
    var metadata = operationContext.GetService
        (typeof(IDataServiceMetadataProvider)) as
        IDataServiceMetadataProvider;

    var actionList = from a in GetActionList(metadata)
                    where a.Parameters.Count > 0 &&
        a.Parameters[0].ParameterType == bindingParameterType
                    select a;

    return actionList;
}


public bool TryResolveServiceAction
    (System.Data.Services.DataServiceOperationContext
    operationContext, string serviceActionName,
    out ServiceAction serviceAction)
{
    var metadata = operationContext.GetService
    (typeof(IDataServiceMetadataProvider)) as
    IDataServiceMetadataProvider;

    var action = (from a in GetActionList(metadata)
                    where a.Name == serviceActionName
                    select a).First();

    if (action != null)
```

```
    {
        serviceAction = action;
        return true;
    }
    else
    {
        serviceAction = null;
        return false;
    }
}
```

6. Create two classes (for the `SayHello` and `GetMoreInfo` Service Actions), which implement the `IDataServiceInvokable` interface (see the following `SayHelloInvokable` and `GetMoreInfoInvokable` classes).

```
// Class for invoking the SayHello service action
public class SayHelloInvokable : IDataServiceInvokable
{
    public string Data { get; set; }

    public object GetResult()
    {
        return Data;
    }

    public void Invoke()
    {
        Data = "Hello " + Data;
    }
}

// Class for invoking the GetMoreInfo service action
public class GetMoreInfoInvokable : IDataServiceInvokable
{
    public string Data { get; set; }

    public object GetResult()
    {
        return Data;
    }

    public void Invoke()
    {
        Data = "Here is the additional information about " +
            Data;
    }
}
```

7. Implement the `IServiceProvider` interface on the service class of the Northwind OData service.

   In the `GetService` function, we simply return a new instance of the `SimpleActionProvider` class whenever the runtime demands the `IDataServiceActionProvider` object (see the following code snippet).

```
public class NorthwindOData : DataService< NorthwindEntities >,
    IServiceProvider
{
......

    public object GetService(Type serviceType)
    {
        if (serviceType == typeof(IDataServiceActionProvider))
        {
            return new SimpleActionProvider();
        }
        return null;
    }
}
```

8. Create a new Console Application as the OData Client.

9. Use the Visual Studio Add Service Reference wizard to generate the OData proxy against the sample service.

10. Add a function to invoke the Service Actions exposed in the sample service (use the strong-typed OData proxy).

   We can directly invoke the `SayHello` Service Action through its URI string (see the following code snippet).

```
var svcUri = new
    Uri("http://localhost:28424/NorthwindOData.svc/");
var ctx = new ODataSvc.NorthwindEntities(svcUri);

// Invoke the SayHello action
var actionUri = new
    Uri("http://localhost:28424/NorthwindOData.svc/SayHello");

var sayHelloResult = ctx.Execute<string>(
                    actionUri,
                    "POST",
                    true,
                    new BodyOperationParameter("name",
                        "Steven")
                ).First();

Console.WriteLine(sayHelloResult);
```

We do not need to supply any entity object for invoking the `SayHello` Service Action because it is a service level action.

 When invoking Service Actions, we must use the **HTTP POST** method and supply the non-entity (primitive or custom type) parameters through instances of the `BodyOperationParameter` type.

The `GetMoreInfo` Service Action is bound to the `Category` entity type. Therefore, we need to get a `Category` entity first and then invoke the Service Action against the obtained entity instance (see the following code snippet).

```
// Invoke the GetMoreInfo action against the 1st Category
//entity
var category = ctx.Categories.First();

    // Retrieve the action Uri from the specific entity
var entityActionUri = ctx.GetEntityDescriptor(category)
                .OperationDescriptors
                .Where(o => o.Title == "GetMoreInfo")
                .Select(o => o.Target)
                .First();

var getMoreInfoResult = ctx.Execute<string>(
                entityActionUri,
                "POST",
                true
                ).First();

Console.WriteLine(getMoreInfoResult);
```

Since the `GetMoreInfo` Service Action does not take additional parameters, we do not need to supply any `BodyOperationParameter` instances when invoking the service action.

 Instead of manually composing the Service Action URI, we can programmatically extract the URI from the entity descriptor object (of the target entity instance).

How it works...

In the sample Northwind OData service, we have defined two Service Actions. The `SayHello` Service Action is a top-level operation, which is not bound to any entity or entity set. The `GetMoreInfo` Service Action is bound to the `Category` entity type so that it can only be executed against a certain `Category` entity instance.

Most of our work here is focussed on creating the `SimpleActionProvider` class, which acts as the Service Action provider. This class implements the `IDataServiceActionProvider` interface under the `System.Data.Services.Providers` namespace. The following table lists all the member functions of `IDataServiceActionProvider` interface and how we implement them in the sample Service Action provider class:

Name	Description
AdvertiseServiceAction	Determines whether a given *Service Action* should be bound to a certain entity instance. We do not implement this function because we have hardcoded the definitions of our sample service actions (rather than determine them at runtime).
CreateInvokable	Builds up an instance of `IDataServiceInvokable` for executing the actual Service Action code. We simply return the two helper classes, which contain the action execution code logic.
GetServiceActions	Returns all Service Actions in the provider. Here we use a helper function to generate a list of all Service Actions.
GetServiceActionsByBindingParameterType	Gets all Service Actions, which are bound to the certain entity or entity set.
TryResolveServiceAction	Tries to find the *service action* based on the supplied action name.

The `GetActionList` function (in the `SimpleActionProvider` class) helps create two instances of `ServiceAction` class to represent the Service Actions we want to expose in the sample provider. The constructor of `ServiceAction` class demands the following parameters which are necessary for determining the characteristics of a Service Action:

- ▸ name
- ▸ return Type
- ▸ resultSet
- ▸ operationParameterBindingKind
- ▸ parameters

When a Service Action returns an entity or a collection of entities, the `resultSet` parameter should be specified with the `ResourceSet` object representing the target entity set (our sample Service Actions specify `null` for this parameter because they just return simple string values). The `operationParameterBindingKind` parameter is of enumeration type, which indicates whether the Service Action is a top-level (global) action or an entity-specific action. The `SayHello` Service Action specifies `Never` for this parameter since it is a global action; while the `GetMoreInfo` action specifies `Always` here as it is bound to the `Category` entity. For all `ServiceAction` instances we create in the provider, we need to call the `SetReadOnly` method on them (see the following code snippet) so that the WCF Data Service runtime can correctly register them.

```
var actionSayHello = new ServiceAction(
        ......
    );
actionSayHello.SetReadOnly();
```

If we look up the metadata document of the sample OData service, we can find that OData V3 uses `FunctionImport` elements for describing all Service Actions exposed in the service (see the following screenshot). Each `FunctionImport` element contains the complete signature definition of the corresponding Service Action including `Name`, `ReturnType`, `Binding` information and `Parameters`.

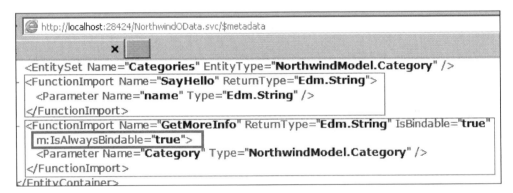

Again, as shown in the previous screenshot, the `GetMoreInfo` Service Action has its `IsBindable` and `IsAlwaysBindable` properties set to `true` because it is bound to the `Category` entity. Also, the only parameter of `GetMoreInfo` Service Action is of the `Category` entity class, which means it can be invoked only in the context of a certain `Category` entity instance.

At the client side, we can use Visual Studio generated OData proxy to invoke the Service Actions exposed in the target OData service. Just like custom-service operations, we can use the Execute<T> generic method (of the DataServiceContext class) to invoke a Service Action by supplying the URI address and necessary parameters. Currently, it is required that we use HTTP POST request to invoke Service Actions of WCF Data Service. And *non-binding* parameters must be supplied in **JSON** format in the request body. The following is the raw HTTP request generated by invoking the SayHello Service Action (captured in Fiddler):

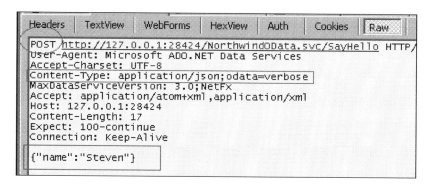

As we can see, the SayHello Service Action request uses HTTP POST verb and it carries the name parameter within its request body as a JSON object.

For the GetMoreInfo Service Action request (see the following screenshot), the request body is empty because the request URI has already embedded the target Category entity instance information.

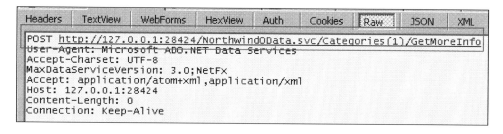

There's more...

For more information about the Service Actions feature of WCF Data Service 5.0 (OData V3), you can refer to the following MSDN reference:

Service Actions (WCF Data Services) available at `http://msdn.microsoft.com/en-us/library/hh859851(v=vs.103).aspx`

See also

- ▸ *Adding custom operations on OData Service* recipe in *Chapter 1, Building OData Services*
- ▸ *Creating a custom WCF Data Service provider* recipe in *Chapter 1, Building OData Services*
- ▸ *Upgrading existing OData service to WCF Data Service 5.0* recipe

Index

Symbols

.NET Framework platform 8, 315
.NET Reflection provider 340
.svc extension
  avoiding 134-136

A

AccessODataService function 265
Activity class 219
addNewCategory function 169-171
AddressItem class 321
Add Service Reference tool 318
ADO.NET Data Service 316
ADO.NET Entity Framework 8
AdvertiseServiceAction function 345, 350
AJAX 161
AJAX style data-driven web pages
  building, with jQuery 161-165
All operator
  about 325
  used, for filtering OData entities 325-327
Android mobile application
  about 187
  WCF Data Service, accessing in 213-219
Any operator
  about 325
  used, for filtering OData entities 325-327
ASP.NET 144, 257
ASP.NET context data
  accessing, in WCF Data Service 36-39
ASP.NET Forms authentication
  used, for securing OData service 262-265
ASP.NET MVC web applications
  about 148
  OData, adopting in 148-156

ASP.NET Page UI, building
  with OData 156-160
  with XSLT 156-160
ASP.NET URL Routing feature
  about 156
  used, for avoiding .svc extension 134-136
ASP.NET Web Form pages
  building, with OData 144-147
Asynchronous Javascript and XML. *See* **AJAX**
asynchronous manner
  OData queries, executing in 75-79
AtomPub 7, 52
Atom XML 137
AuthenticateRequest event 274
authentication 257
authorization
  about 257
  adding, with server-side processing pipeline
    275, 276

B

base URI, of OData entity sets
  resolving, dynamically 331-334
basic access rules
  accessing, on WCF Data Service 131-133
BeginExecute method 79
binary data, on OData entity
  exposing, with Named Resource Stream 334-342
Binary Resource Stream feature 234
Blob storage 235
BodyOperationParameter type 349

C

CategoriesAdapter class 217

ChangeInterceptor 33-35
ChangeInterceptor function 279
Client-side Object Model 234
CLR Objects 8
conceptual schema definition language
    (CSDL) 66
Console application
    WCF Data Service, hosting in 114-116
CreateInvokable function 345, 350
CRUD operations 133, 167
CUD operations 69
custom authorization
    adding, with server-side processing pipeline
        275, 276
custom data objects
    using, as data source of WCF Data Service
        28-31
custom HTTP headers
    injecting, in OData requests 94-96
custom HTTP Module
    OData service authentication, implementing
        with 271-274
CustomODataAuthModule class 272
custom operations
    adding, on OData service 20-23
custom WCF Data Service provider
    creating 40-49

D

data
    deleting, through WCF Data Service client
        library 66-70
    editing, through WCF Data Service client
        library 66-70
database stored procedures
    exposing, in WCF Data Service 23-27
DataBound Controls 144
DataContractJsonSerializer class 200
datajs script library
    about 167
    OData service, consuming with 167-171
DataList control 147
DataServiceContext class 330
DataSource property 147
data source, WCF Data Service
    custom data objects, using as 28-31

DataSvcUtil.exe tool
    about 319
    OData client proxy, generating through 63-66
deleteCategory function 170
Document Library 231
DropDownList control 147, 160
dynamic compression
    enabling, for OData service hosted in IIS 7
        137-141
Dynamics CRM 2011 227

E

eBay.com 248
eBay Inc. 248
eBay online products catalog
    exploring, through OData service 248-252
EditProductEntity function 68
EndExecute method 79
Entity Data Model (EDM) 2.2 340
error information
    WCF Data service, configuring for 124-127
ExecuteOperations function 61
Expand option 83-85
Extensible Stylesheet Language
    Transformation. *See* XSLT

F

Fiddler web debugger
    OData HTTP traffic, inspecting through 299-
        302
Filter option 82
Flash 144
Forms authentication 261

G

Geography and Geometry types 319
geospatial types
    using, in OData service 319-324
GetActionList function 344, 350
GetAuthenticationCookie function 264
getLink method 219
getProperty method 219
GetReadStream method 341
GetReadStreamUri method 341
getRelatedEntities method 219

GetServiceActionsByBindingParameterType function 350
GetServiceActions function 350
GetService function 348
GetStreamContentType method 341
GetStreamETag method 341
GetWriteStream method 341
GridView control 147

H

HTML5
about 144, 205
used, for building native Windows Phone application 205-213
HTTP compression enable
OData service, consuming 97-99
HTTP headers
injecting, in OData requests 94-96
HTTP MERGE request 328
HTTP Module
about 271
OData service authentication, implementing with 271-274
HTTP PATCH requests
OData entities, updating through 328-331
HTTP POST method 349
HTTP PUT request 328
HTTP requests
types 328
HTTPS 266
HTTPS/SSL secure transport 257
HTTPS transport
OData service, securing with 267-270
Hypertext Transfer Protocol (HTTP) 7, 52, 266

I

IDataServiceActionProvider interface 350
IDataServiceActionProvider object 348
IIS server
WCF Data Service, hosting 108-113
IIS web application 257
individual entity set
access, controlling with Interceptors 277-279
InitializeService function 317, 322, 343

Interceptors
about 32
used, for controlling access for individual entity set 277-279
used, for customizing WCF Data Service 32-35
Interface Builder tool 224
iOS application
about 187, 220
WCF Data Service, accessing in 220-226
iOS v4.3 221
IsScriptEnabled property 212

J

jQuery
AJAX style data-driven web pages, building with 161-165
JSON 7, 16, 52
JSON format 137, 352
JSON format, OData service
consuming, without OData WP7 client library 196-200
JSON format response
WCF Data service, configuring for 127-130

L

lazy loading pattern 61
LINQPad
about 286
URL, for downloading 286
URL, for info 289
used, for composing OData query code 286-288
LINQ to Entity methods 61
LINQ to SQL
about 8, 13
OData service, building 13, 15
ListCategories function 59
ListProducts function 60
ListView control 147
loadCategories function 165
LoadProductsAsyncComplete function 79
loadProductsByCategory function 165
Local Data Storage 210, 212

M

Mac OSX 10.7 221
MainActivity class 219
MaxProtocolVersion property 317, 318
Message Inspectors 32
metadata 56
Microsoft Excel PowerPivot component
  OData service, exploring with 296-299
Microsoft Sharepoint 231
MSXML
  used, for consuming OData service in
    unmanaged applications 99-105

N

Named Resource Stream feature
  about 335
  binary data, on OData entity exposing with
    334-342
native Windows Phone application
  building, HTML5 used 205-213
  building, OData used 205-213
Netflix OData online catalog
  about 228
  application, creating 228-230
NSMutableArray object 226
NuGet 244
NuGet packages
  information, tracking through OData feeds
    245-248

O

Object Browser 59
object model, of OData service
  inspecting, OData Visualizer used 303-307
OData
  about 7, 16, 144, 205
  adopting, in ASP.NET MVC web applications
    148-156
  ASP.NET Web Form pages, building with 144-
    147
  entities, updating through 328-331
  Panorama style data-driven Windows Phone
    application, creating with 201-205
  queries, executing in asynchronous manner
    75-79
  used, for building native Windows Phone
    application 205-213
  using, for Windows Azure Table storage access
    235-238
OData4j library 214
OData4ObjC 220, 221
OData client proxy
  generating, via DataSvcUtil.exe tool 63-66
OData endpoint
  exposing, from WCF RIA Service 16-20
  Sharepoint 2010 documents, manipulating
    through 231-234
  StackOverflow forums data, querying with
    240-243
OData entities
  updating, through HTTP PATCH requests 328-
    331
OData entities, filtering
  with All operator 325-327
  with Any operator 325-327
ODataExplorer
  about 289
  OData service, exploring with 289-292
  URL 289
  URL, for source code 292
OData feed
  information, tracking of NuGet packages 245-
    248
  SSRS 2008 R2 report, consuming through
    252-256
OData for Objective-C. *See* OData4ObjC
odatagen utility 222, 226
OData HTTP traffic
  inspecting, through Fiddler web debugger
    299-302
OData queries
  executing, in asynchronous manner 75-79
OData query code
  composing, with LINQPad 286-288
OData query results
  filtering, query options used 80-85
OData requests
  custom HTTP headers, injecting in 94-96
OData service
  about 52
  accessing, via WebRequest class 71

accessing, with OData WP7 client library 188-195

building, via ADO.NET Entity Framework 8-13

building, via WCF Data Service 8-13

building, with LINQ to SQL 13-15

building, with WCF Data Service 13-15

consuming, HTTP compression enabled 97-99

consuming, in Windows 8 Metro style application 308-314

consuming, MSXML used 99-105

consuming, with datajs script library 167-171

custom operations, adding on 20-23

eBay online products catalog, exploring through 248-252

exploring, through web browser 52-57

exploring, with Microsoft Excel PowerPivot component 296-299

exploring, with ODataExplorer 289-292

functionalities, extending with Service Actions 342-352

geospatial types, using in 319-324

role-based security, implementing for 280-284

securing, ASP.NET Forms authentication used 262-265

securing, with HTTPS transport 267-270

upgrading, to WCF Data Service 5.0 316-318

using, in Silverlight data access application 171-179

using, in Windows PowerShell script 293-296

Windows authentication, applying for 258-260

OData service authentication

implementing, with custom HTTP Module 271-274

OData service data

WPF data binding, performing with 89-93

OData service hosted, in IIS 7

dynamic compression, enabling for 137-141

OData V2 318, 334

OData V3 315

OData Visualizer

used, for inspecting object model of OData service 303-307

OData WP7 client library

about 188, 196

OData service, accessing with 188-195

OEntity class 219

onQueryCategories function 278

Open Data Protocol. *See* **OData**

Open Data Protocol Visualizer. *See* **OData Visualizer**

OpenReadAsync method 200

OrderBy option 81, 84

P

Panorama style data-driven, Windows Phone application

creating, with OData 201-205

PhoneApplicationPage_Loaded event 193, 198

PHP pages

WCF Data Service, consuming in 179-184

PostBack events 144

primary key 31

ProcessingRequest event handler 276

Q

QueryInterceptor 33, 35

QueryInterceptor function 278, 279

QueryODataServiceWithAnyOperator function 325, 327

QueryODataWithDynamicUris function 333

query options

OData query results, filtering 80-85

QuerySpatialDataService function 322, 323

Queue storage 235

R

Razor engine 155

ResolveEntitySetUriByName function 332, 333

RoleBasedAuthModule HTTP Module 283

role-based security

implementing, for OData service 280-284

S

SaveChanges method 69, 330

scViewController class 224

security 257

SelectedIndexChanged event 147-160
Select option 83
self-hosting scenario 114
Server-side Object Model 234
server-side paged entity sets
    dealing with 86-88
server-side paging feature 86
server-side processing pipeline
    custom authorization, adding with 275, 276
Service Actions
    about 342
    OData service functionalities, extending with
        342-352
Sharepoint 2010 227
Sharepoint 2010 documents
    manipulating, through OData endpoint 231-
        234
showAllCategories function 169, 171
showProductsOfCategory function 208
Silverlight 144
Silverlight data access application
    OData service, using 171-179
SimpleNamedStreamProvider class 336
SimpleSpatialDataSource class 321
Skip option 82, 84
smartphones 187
SOAP 16
SpatialOperations class 320
SQL Azure Migration Wizard tool 117
SQL Server 2008 R2 319
SQL Server 2008 R2 Reporting Service 227
SQL Server Reporting Services(SSRS) 252
SSL/TLS protocol 266
SSRS 2008 R2 report
    consuming, through OData feed 252-256
StackOverflow 240
StackOverflow forums data
    querying, with OData endpoint 240-243
stored procedures 23
strong-typed OData client proxy
    generating, Visual Studio used 57-62

T

Table storage 235
tablets 187
TableView Control 224

TestSpatialOperations class 320, 323
Top option 81, 84
TryResolveServiceAction function 350

U

UITableViewDataSource interface 226
unmanaged applications
    OData service, consuming with MSXML 99-
        105
UpdateEntityWithPatchOption function 329
UrlDecode method 324
URL Routing feature 134

V

Visual Studio
    used, for generating strong-typed OData client
        proxy 57-62
Visual Studio 2008 SP1 57
Visual Studio 2010 57, 318
Visual Studio Class View 59
Visual Studio IDE 52
Visual Studio Solution Explorer 58

W

WCF Data Service
    about 8
    accessing, in Android mobile application 213-
        219
    accessing, in iOS application 220-226
    ADO.NET Entity Framework, building 8-13
    ASP.NET context data, accessing in 36-39
    basic access rules, accessing on 131-133
    configuring, for error information 124-127
    configuring, for JSON format response 127-
        130
    consuming, in PHP pages 179-184
    customizing, Interceptors used 32-35
    database stored procedures, exposing in 23-
        27
    dealing, with server-side paged entity sets
        86-88
    deploying, on Windows Azure host 117-123
    hosting, in Console application 114-116
    hosting, in IIS server 108-113
    OData service, building 8-15

WCF Data Service 4.0 316, 334
WCF Data Service 5.0
   about 315, 319
   existing OData service, upgrading to 316-318
WCF Data Service client library
   about 52
   data, deleting through 66-70
   data, editing through 66-70
WCF Data Service provider
   creating 40-49
WCF Data Services 5.0 316
WCF RIA Service
   OData endpoints, exposing from 16-20
web applications 143
web browser
   OData service, exploring through 52-57
WebClient class 200
web.config file 262
WebRequest class
   about 52
   OData service, accessing via 70, 71
Web Server Controls 144
where clause 84
Windows 8 Metro style application
   OData service, consuming in 308-314
Windows authentication
   about 258
   applying, for OData service 258-260
Windows Azure 117
Windows Azure host

WCF Data Service, deploying on 117-123
Windows Azure Management Portal 124
Windows Azure Storage service 227
Windows Azure Table storage access
   OData protocol, using for 235-238
Windows Phone 7 187
Windows Phone application
   building, HTML5 used 205-213
   building, OData used 205-213
Windows Phone Emulator 195, 199
Windows Phone SDK 7.1 188
Windows PowerShell 293
Windows PowerShell script
   OData service, using 293-296
WP7 Panorama Control
   URL, for info 205
WPF data binding
   performing, with OData service data 89-93
WPF (Windows Presentation Foundation) 245

X

XCode 224
XCode 4.2 221
XCode IDE 221
XCOPY application 286
XML 7, 52
XmlDataSource control 160
XSLT 156

Thank you for buying
OData Programming Cookbook for
.NET Developers

About Packt Publishing

Packt, pronounced 'packed', published its first book "*Mastering phpMyAdmin for Effective MySQL Management*" in April 2004 and subsequently continued to specialize in publishing highly focused books on specific technologies and solutions.

Our books and publications share the experiences of your fellow IT professionals in adapting and customizing today's systems, applications, and frameworks. Our solution-based books give you the knowledge and power to customize the software and technologies you're using to get the job done. Packt books are more specific and less general than the IT books you have seen in the past. Our unique business model allows us to bring you more focused information, giving you more of what you need to know, and less of what you don't.

Packt is a modern, yet unique publishing company, which focuses on producing quality, cutting-edge books for communities of developers, administrators, and newbies alike. For more information, please visit our website: www.PacktPub.com.

About Packt Enterprise

In 2010, Packt launched two new brands, Packt Enterprise and Packt Open Source, in order to continue its focus on specialization. This book is part of the Packt Enterprise brand, home to books published on enterprise software – software created by major vendors, including (but not limited to) IBM, Microsoft and Oracle, often for use in other corporations. Its titles will offer information relevant to a range of users of this software, including administrators, developers, architects, and end users.

Writing for Packt

We welcome all inquiries from people who are interested in authoring. Book proposals should be sent to author@packtpub.com. If your book idea is still at an early stage and you would like to discuss it first before writing a formal book proposal, contact us; one of our commissioning editors will get in touch with you.

We're not just looking for published authors; if you have strong technical skills but no writing experience, our experienced editors can help you develop a writing career, or simply get some additional reward for your expertise.

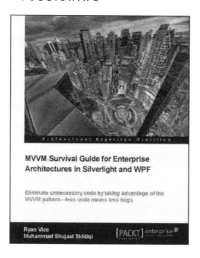

MVVM Survival Guide for Enterprise Architectures in Silverlight and WPF

ISBN: 978-1-849683-42-5   Paperback: 412 pages

Eliminate unnecessary code by taking advantage of the MVVM pattern—less code means less bugs

1. Build an enterprise application using Silverlight and WPF, taking advantage of the powerful MVVM pattern, with this book and e-book

2. Discover the evolution of presentation patterns—by example—and see the benefits of MVVM in the context of the larger picture of presentation patterns

3. Customize the MVVM pattern for your projects' needs by comparing the various implementation styles

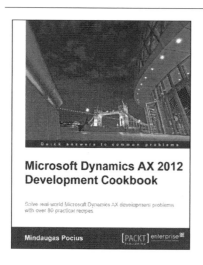

Microsoft Dynamics AX 2012 Development Cookbook

ISBN: 978-1-849684-64-4   Paperback: 372 pages

Solve real-world Microsoft Dynamics AX development problems with over 80 practical recipes

1. Develop powerful, successful Dynamics AX projects with efficient X++ code with this book and eBook

2. Proven recipes that can be reused in numerous successful Dynamics AX projects

3. Covers general ledger, accounts payable, accounts receivable, project modules and general functionality of Dynamics AX

Please check **www.PacktPub.com** for information on our titles

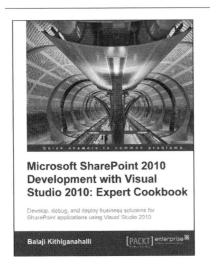

Entity Framework 4.1: Expert's Cookbook

ISBN: 978-1-849684-46-0   Paperback: 352 pages

More than 40 recipes for successfully mixing Test Driven Development, Architecture, and Entity Framework Code First

1. Hands-on solutions with reusable code examples

2. Strategies for enterprise ready usage

3. Examples based on real world experience

4. Detailed and advanced examples of query management

5. Step-by-step recipes that will guide you to success

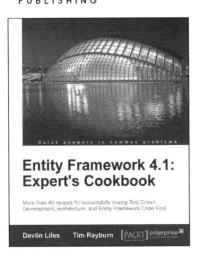

Microsoft SharePoint 2010 Development with Visual Studio 2010 Expert Cookbook

ISBN: 978-1-849684-58-3   Paperback: 296 pages

Develop, debug, and deploy business solutions for SharePoint applications using Visual Studio 2010

1. Create applications using the latest client object model and create custom web services for your SharePoint environment with this book and ebook.

2. Full of illustrations, diagrams and key points for debugging and deploying your solutions securely to the SharePoint environment.

3. Recipes with step-by-step instructions with detailed explanation on how each recipe works and working code examples.

Please check **www.PacktPub.com** for information on our titles

Made in the USA
Lexington, KY
24 September 2013